P9-EDQ-078

Edited and translated by
LARRY SHOULDICE

Contemporary Quebec Criticism

UNIVERSITY OF TORONTO PRESS
Toronto Buffalo London

© University of Toronto Press 1979
Toronto Buffalo London
Printed in Canada

Canadian Cataloguing in Publication Data

Main entry under title:

Contemporary Quebec criticism

(Canadian university paperbooks ; 240)

Bibliography: p.
ISBN 0-8020-2344-4 bd.   ISBN 0-8020-6376-4 pa.

1. Criticism — Quebec (Province) — Addresses, essays,
lectures. 2. Canadian literature (French) — Quebec
(Province) — History and criticism — Addresses,
essays, lectures.* I. Shouldice, Larry, 1945–
II. Series.

PN99.C3C65   801'.95'09714   C79-094639-4
PS9071.4 C613 1979

Contents

Preface

The following collection of essays and articles is intended to present, in English, a representative selection of texts from the field of Quebec literary criticism. It is primarily addressed to the English-speaking reader who, although interested in modern Quebec literature and reasonably well versed in the practices of literary criticism in general, is nevertheless not familiar with the body of commentary that has accompanied the spectacular growth of Quebec writing in the past two decades.

The selection is representative in that it shows a variety of the kinds of critical comment currently written in Quebec. The critics include established literary scholars as well as poets, novelists, and essayists, all of whom tend to view Quebec literature as a primarily national development. The texts reveal a considerable diversity of genres and approaches, ranging from the academic to the journalistic, from thematics to semiotics; taken together, they show many of the concerns and attitudes of Quebec writers and offer the English-speaking reader a view into the intellectual landscape of modern Quebec.

Whatever their representative value, however, the texts presented here cannot be said to reflect the full range or complexity of Quebec criticism. Any anthology is partial by its very nature, and the present collection of ten articles from the late fifties to the mid-seventies is no more than a brief sampling of the field. Several of the most prominent critics of this period, such as Georges-André Vachon, Laurent Mailhot, and Pierre de Grandpré, could not be included here, and restrictions on length have also meant the exclusion of many interesting younger writers like André Brochu and François Charron. The selection is further limited to articles general enough to be accessible to the English-speaking reader. Thus studies that deal with one particular writer – and a great deal of 'practical' criticism falls into this category – have been automatically excluded as being too limited in scope. Conversely, many essays dealing with fields related to literature were rejected as being too general. Any texts previously translated into English were also excluded, as were articles which presumed too great a background knowledge of French literature or of any other national literature. Finally, the selection had to reflect the various methodological approaches of Quebec critics, so that only a limited number of articles were chosen from any particular 'school.' Clearly, any selection of this sort is open to endless discussion. Notwithstanding the anthologist's intention to provide as balanced a collection as possible, the best he can do is to trust his own judgment and his own awareness of the field he is concerned to present.

One criterion not considered in making the selection was the 'translatability' of the articles; obviously, some kinds of discourse lend themselves more readily to translation than others. The practice adopted in the following selections has been to provide an acceptable English version of the essays while maintaining as much as possible of the style and character of the original French. The assistance of the authors has been invaluable in this respect, for in each case they have offered the translator their advice and encouragement. It may be appropriate to remind the reader that, if the results are uneven in quality, this is not necessarily a reflection on the work of the particular writer being translated.

The order in which the articles are presented raises further problems, since any arrangement of such diverse material is ultimately as arbitrary as its selection. The sequence and grouping in the present collection are based primarily on considerations of content. The four articles in the first division, entitled 'Backgrounds,' tend to look to the past and to suggest various perspectives from which Quebec literature can be viewed: historical, cultural, ideological, and national. The second grouping, 'Themes and Genres,' focuses more on the kinds of criticism produced in Quebec during the past two decades and gives an indication of the various critical trends and approaches that prevailed in this period. Although this division may be considered somewhat artificial, it is useful for purposes of organization and it does reveal affinities among the various components that would be less apparent if a strictly chronological order were followed.

The general introduction is intended to provide the English-speaking reader with a broad view of modern Quebec criticism. Since no comprehensive study of the field exists, even in French, it is important to give some idea of its evolution, its frames of reference, its genres, its outstanding

practitioners, and its present directions. In addition to this general introduction, each article is preceded by headnotes which locate it within the
field as a whole. Thus the reader can gain some understanding not only of
the concerns expressed by individual critics but also of the larger contexts
within which their commentary is produced.

Finally, a brief bibliography provides a selection of works[1] considered helpful for the reader who is interested in exploring Quebec criticism
more fully.

NOTE

1 The convention adopted for the capitalization of French titles in the following
pages is to capitalize only the initial letter of the title (and of any proper nouns).

Acknowledgments

Aux critiques dont l'œuvre est présenté dans ces pages j'exprime ma profonde reconnaissance.

I am deeply grateful to many of my friends and acquaintances for their individual help in preparing this collection. In particular I would like to express my thanks to Philip Stratford, C.G. Cappon, Marguerite Fortier, and Ron Schoeffel.

This translation was made possible by a grant from the Canada Council. Publication was assisted by a grant from the Université de Sherbrooke, and by the Canada Council and the Ontario Arts Council under their programs of block grants to publishers.

This book is dedicated, with love, to my parents Jean Campbell Mason and Percy R. Shouldice.

Larry Shouldice
Université de Sherbrooke
February 1979

CONTEMPORARY QUEBEC CRITICISM

Introduction

THE FIELD

It may be well, to begin with, to suggest what is meant by 'contemporary Quebec criticism,' for there is a sense in which each of these terms is problematical. Contemporaneity being a notoriously relative concept, we shall say simply that in this context the adjective refers to writings published in the twenty years from 1958 to 1978.

The use of 'Quebec' as an adjective raises many more important questions – and not only of a grammatical nature. While the political and cultural implications of such questions have generated widespread discussion, the fact remains that in the period covered by this collection the term *Québécois* has come into general usage, largely supplanting *Canadien-français* or the earlier *Canadien* as the word by which the French-speaking people of Quebec refer to themselves. Thus it would seem natural to apply the epithet to writings by and about the same people.

As for the term 'criticism,' it has been used in a literary sense to describe everything from detailed textual explication to far-ranging cultural commentary. In his *Contexts of Canadian Criticism*, Eli Mandel defines his subject as including 'whatever comes into the field of Canadian vision: in brief, all those contexts within which discussions of literature in this country take place.'[1] While this definition – transposed to Quebec – is large enough to facilitate discussion of the field in general, it is rather too generous to be used as a basis for selecting texts. For this purpose, since there is a need to concentrate more on the kinds than on the contexts of the criticism, the term is slightly more circumscribed, being limited for the most part to writings about writings. In a few cases, however, this general rule has been bent to allow the inclusion of essays or articles dealing with areas outside the immediate realm of literature, particularly where the author of the text is also an important novelist or poet.

As Paul Chamberland points out in a later article,[2] even the notion of a literary field is in some ways suspect. In reality, 'contemporary Quebec criticism' is the name given to a vast and ever-changing body of critical writing that emanates from Quebec or that comments in some way upon Quebec literature. The boundaries assigned to it may be useful as guidelines, to help us know what we are talking about, but prolonged attempts at definition usually prove to be a rather inefficient means of description. More is the reason, then, to turn our attention now to other questions, in order to provide some of the background, contexts and dimensions of the field.

THE HISTORICAL CONTEXT

A good example of the difficulty – and arbitrariness – of imposing preliminary definitions is found in the disagreement as to when the first criticism was written in Quebec. Some literary historians attribute the honour of being the first literary critic in French Canada to Abbé Henri-Raymond Casgrain (1831–1904),[3] while others suggest Octave Crémazie (1827–1879)[4] or Louis Dantin (1886–1945).[5] The most frequent choice, however, is that of Camille Roy (1871–1943), who is generally recognized as being the first to write an effective history of French-Canadian literature.[6]

From the point of view of the sheer volume and influence of his work, Mgr Roy can safely be considered the first 'professional' critic; the virtual 'Godfather' of Quebec literature for almost half a century, he greatly expanded Casgrain's attempts to record and encourage the literary production of his compatriots. As Jean Ethier-Blais points out in the first article of this collection, Camille Roy considered literature to be essentially utilitarian and functional, a vehicle for ideology and a tool for propaganda.[7] This attitude is important, for it formed the basis of the kind of criticism that prevailed in Quebec until well into the forties.

As typified by Mgr Roy, the 'official' view of Quebec literature was founded on a number of interconnected beliefs: Catholic morality, fidelity to the French heritage, nationalistic fervour, and an idealized, romantic conception of traditional farm life. These are the convictions which inspired what was clearly the 'mainstream' of Quebec literature for more than a century: works by historians from Garneau through Groulx, by poets from Fréchette through DesRochers, by novelists from Aubert de Gaspé through Ringuet. They can be seen in the 'Ecole littéraire de

Quebec,' in the various incarnations of 'Le Terroir,' and in orators, essay-ists, and journalists too numerous to mention. And yet, despite the rich-ness of the literature they informed, these same convictions produced criticism that was backward looking, prescriptive, dogmatic, impressionis-tic, and uncreative.

Among Mgr Roy's many disciples, none was able to match the originality of the 'Master,' and the best known among them added little of substance to his thinking. Maurice Hébert (1888–1960), 'believing that any enthusiasm was worthy of encouragement,' outdid even Roy in subjecting local authors 'to a uniformly positive criticism, which tended to bathe them all in a hazy glow in which originality became confused with the most awful medioc-rity.'[8] Harry Bernard, as precocious as he was prolific, transformed Roy's penchant for the homestead (le terroir) into an elaborate theory of regional-ism as the basis of all good literature,[9] although his definition of 'regional-ism' was so loose as to render his arguments virtually meaningless.[10] Albert Dandurand, one of a long series of 'priest-critics,' wrote several studies of Quebec literature remarkable for their moralism and their historicism.[11] And as late as 1957, Samuel Baillargeon, perhaps the last of this line, could write in a widely used history of French-Canadian literature that the life of Louis Dantin was a 'lamentable tragedy,' but that 'it would be unhealthy curiosity to go into details.'[12]

So it is that Camille Roy stands as the only effective critic to emerge from the mainstream of traditional Quebec culture, and even his reputa-tion as a critic is now somewhat tarnished. It would be wrong, however, to regard Mgr Roy's hegemony as being total. Throughout the history of Quebec, and particularly after the founding of the 'Institut canadien de Montréal' in 1844, there has always been an undercurrent of free-thinking in some intellectual circles, and the minority, nonconformist view has always been given some degree of expression.

It should also be remembered that there are seldom any hard and fast divisions among currents of thought, so that differences in critical atti-tudes do not always reflect profound oppositions among critics, but may simply result from differing emphases. Albert Pelletier's repeated attacks on Camille Roy,[13] for example, may well stem more from his anti-clericalism than from any deep objection to Mgr Roy's literary doctrines. It can also happen that contrasting impulses exist within the same writer, as is illustrated by the work of Octave Crémazie. Crémazie was extremely popular as a poet precisely because of his retrograde, sentimental patriot-ism in such period pieces as 'The Old Soldier' and 'The Flag of Carillon.' As a critic, however, he showed an altogether different face. Writing from his exile in France, he proves to have been a much more astute critic than one would have guessed, not only expressing informed opinions about literature in general, but also revealing a surprising cynicism about the success of his own verse.[14]

Louis Dantin is also an ambivalent figure, for although his criticism (unlike his life) shows little rebellion against conventional standards, it does differ substantially in kind and in quality from the work of his contemporaries. Dantin, whom Jean Ethier-Blais sees as representing the 'minority opinion' in Quebec criticism, held the view that literature should serve only its own ends. Adopting some of the attitudes of the Art for Art's Sake movement, Dantin based his approach to literature on aesthetic criteria in which the artistic imagination plays a major role. Although Dantin too felt he had to be generous in assessing the writings of his countrymen, his criticism, compared to Roy's, was much more aware of form and less exclusively concerned with content. Writing from his self-imposed exile in Boston, Dantin was able to admit a multiplicity of criteria in matters of art.[15] Considering the conservative, monolithic quality of the Quebec intellectual atmosphere in the first half of the twentieth century, this in itself was a great step forward. Because he was the first to adopt aesthetic and 'literary' criteria in his critical writings, Louis Dantin is often considered the strongest critic of his time.[16]

While none of the 'exotic' critics (as those in the minority group were often called) ever attained the stature of Camille Roy, they did form an undercurrent of opposition to the official view. Henri d'Arles (pseudonym of Henri Beaudé, 1870–1930) was another early critic who emphasized the aesthetic aspects of literature, although he did so in a very traditional manner. Marcel Dugas (1883–1947) was a good deal more adventuresome; in his *Psyché au cinéma*[17] he advocated the techniques of surrealism as a way of bringing Quebec writing more into line with international standards. A small group of avant-garde, francophile writers, including Robert de Roquebrune (b. 1889), published *Le Nigog*, a short-lived literary magazine whose aestheticism was meant to counterbalance the regionalist periodical *Le Terroir*. Meanwhile, a few journalists like Olivar Asselin (1874–1937) and Jules Fournier (1884–1913) were busily attacking what they considered to be the regressive tendencies of ultramontane nationalism in both politics and literature. Another journalist, Victor Barbeau (b. 1896), concentrated on ensuring the survival and improving the quality of the French language in Canada – efforts which culminated in the founding of the Académie canadienne-française in 1944.

A new generation of writers may be said to have come into existence with *La Relève*, a magazine founded in 1934 by a group including the novelist Robert Charbonneau and the poet Saint-Denys-Garneau. Neither regionalists nor 'exotics,' these writers embraced the values of Christian humanism and accepted international standards for their art. Although they caused no sharp break with the past, their influence being too gradual and too restricted to the intellectual élite, the generation of *La Relève* (which in 1941 became *La Nouvelle Relève*) in many ways anticipated the postwar transformation of Quebec from a traditional, agrarian society to an urban, industrial state. In their criticism as in their creative work generally, the writers of this group mark the emergence of Quebec into the modern world.

In the hands of this new generation, criticism changed direction considerably. Whereas the traditionalists, exemplified by Mgr Roy, concentrated almost exclusively on content, and whereas the 'exotic' minority was excessively preoccupied with aesthetics, critics like René Garneau, Roger Duhamel, and Guy Sylvestre were to some extent able to bridge the gap between the two currents. Their criticism was less prescriptive, less didactic, less defensive, and less provincial. Familiar with French literature and often with British and American literature as well, they viewed French-Canadian literature from a 'universal' perspective.

As Gilles Marcotte suggests,[18] most critics from about 1945 on tended to consider literary criticism as a criticism of life and society as well, with human values being as important as – or more important than – aesthetic values. Thus the writings of Jean Le Moyne, literary critic for *Le Canada* and author of *Convergences*,[19] discuss the society and literature of French Canada in broadly cultural terms, seeing them as mutually illuminating. The same attitude accounts for the prominence of psychological and sociological tendencies in the criticism of Jeanne Lapointe, Albert Le Grand, and Pierre de Grandpré, or of Jean-Charles Falardeau in the following collection.

This is not to suggest that aesthetic considerations are completely neglected by these critics, but simply to point out that they are usually incorporated into a general view of literature in which priority is given to identifying and interpreting the particularities of the Quebec experience. It is interesting to note that many of these same critics, like Gilles Marcotte and André Brochu, have shown an increasing interest in questions of style and form in their more recent writings.

In surveying almost one hundred years of Quebec criticism, one sees both continuity and change. The supremacy of content over form as the object of critical concern is a constant. Only in very recent years has anything approaching a balance been achieved, and even now it is fair to say that most critics devote more attention to what the literature says than to how it is said. What has changed radically is the general attitude of the critics themselves. Until about 1945, the dominant view of Quebec literature was monolithic and reactionary. Literature was considered to be an instrument for advancing a particular ideology, and it was judged according to its compliance with the standards implied by this ideology. In the postwar period, Quebec critics have come to agree with Louis Dantin on the need for a multiplicity of criteria, including aesthetic ones, and their emphasis has turned from evaluation to interpretation. These factors have resulted in an unprecedented variety of critical approaches, all of which combine to present a view of Quebec literature in its full diversity.

THE NATIONAL CONTEXT

One of the most pervasive presences in Quebec criticism, as in Quebec culture generally, is nationalism. Throughout the course of this literature, the nationalist component has varied considerably both in kind and in intensity, but it has almost always been an important and distinctive feature of the Quebec intellectual landscape.

Quebec nationalism has its origins in the conquest of 1763, by which French Canada came under British domination. Cut off from their roots in France, and increasingly outnumbered by the English-speaking populations around them, the French-speaking people of this continent faced the real threat of their own disappearance as a viable national group. The progressive assimilation of French-speaking communities in such areas as Manitoba, Nova Scotia, and Louisiana has done nothing to diminish these fears, nor has the constantly growing importance of English as a world language.

Quebec nationalism is thus a defensive posture, based on the will for national survival. Unlike French or American nationalism, it does not usually stem from attitudes of cultural superiority, nor is it often expansionist. As Jack Warwick has shown, in the past two centuries the imaginative frontiers for French-Canadian writers have gradually shrunk to the borders of Quebec;[20] this is part of the reason why, even for a conservative critic like Jean Ethier-Blais, the expression 'littérature québécoise' has become 'a necessary linguistic designation.'[21]

In the traditional, romantic criticism of Camille Roy and his disciples, nationalism played a role second only to religion. French-Canadian literature, wrote Mgr Roy, 'generally draws its inspiration from the abundant springs of the national life...Taken as a whole, the literature is indeed Canadian, and...in it the life of the people is reflected and perpetuated. Many of its works, the best in prose and verse, are the expression—original, sincere and profound – of the Canadian spirit.'[22]

This view, which was a least as prescriptive as it was descriptive, began to change as Quebec society became more urban and its intellectuals more urbane. Critics of the *La Relève* generation, and later those associated with the magazine *Cité libre*, were generally more interested in realism than in regionalism, and more concerned with the French Canadians' role in the world than in simply the French-Canadian world. As Michèle Lalonde points out in her article,[23] the intelligentsia of the late forties and the fifties reacted against the parochialism of the past by looking outward, replacing national preoccupations with international aspirations. Critics like Jean Le Moyne or Guy Sylvestre were proud to be French Canadians, but they by no means felt that their realm of awareness should be limited to the horizons of French Canada.

With what is often called the 'Hexagone' generation of writers (named after one of the most prominent publishing houses in the sixties), nationalism once again became a potent force in Quebec literature. Confronted by an unprecedented outpouring of poetry, novels, essays, and drama, most of which were intimately involved with questions of national identity, critics were forced to seek the meaning of this explosion of creativity and to explore its connections with the burgeoning national consciousness. Not surprisingly, these were the years when the expression 'littérature québécoise' came into general usage.

It seems in retrospect that the sixties produced the most remarkable body of Quebec literature to date, and that it was also responsible for much of the best criticism. Certainly Quebec writers attained a level of concentration and consensus in this period that has not been equalled since; for the first time, critics interested in Quebec literature were able to turn their attention to a sustained volume of high quality Quebec writing.

Investigations of the relationships between geography and the imagination, for instance, or between literature and politics, literary form and social change, national psychology and collective creativity – all proved to be extremely rich terrain for the critics. The results were not uniformly successful, of course. In the hands of the less gifted thinkers, nationalism easily became an obsessive, simplifying influence, reducing everything to questions of collective emancipation and national destiny. One thinks in this regard of such writings as Léandre Bergeron's *Petit manuel de l'histoire du Québec*[24] or Gaétan Dostie's effusions in the literary pages of *Le Jour*, where little if any distinction was made between criticism and propaganda. But with the more talented writers like Hubert Aquin, Paul Chamberland, or Jacques Brault nationalism provided the focus for their examination of the world around them. For these and other prominent writers and critics, nationalism was the creative impulse behind their determination to know themselves and to articulate a collective view of reality. And thus, despite the occasional excesses, there can be little doubt that nationalism in the sixties was largely a positive force, both in terms of the quantity and the quality of the criticism it informed.

The importance of nationalism in literature appears to have been on the wane throughout the seventies. As the 'theme of the land' gradually exhausted itself and as literature became increasingly self-conscious and formalistic, critics began to turn to matters less connected with nationalism – questions of genre, for instance, or of Marxist sociology, structuralism, or semiotics. In the writings of François Charron, Joseph Bonenfant, or Georges-André Vachon – to take three very different examples – nationalism is still an underlying presence, but more as something taken for granted than as a central driving force.

We see then that nationalism, although always present in Quebec literature to some extent, has gone through periods of resurgence and regression. It is clear too that nationalism in criticism has followed these cycles rather closely, keeping pace with the development of the literature as a whole. One might also argue that periods of strong nationalism in literature anticipate corresponding periods of intense political nationalism by several years. Since such considerations are highly speculative, however, we shall have to leave it to some future Quebec critic to explore this connection more fully.

The Quebec conception of *la nation* stems fundamentally from the fact of a shared language, and questions related to this language have long been a central concern for Quebec critics. Although the emphasis on language may seem surprising to English-speaking readers, it should be remembered that, since the French language was codified and standardized much earlier and to a much greater extent than many other languages including English, questions of linguistic purity have traditionally been very important in French literature and criticism. It should also be remembered that the acceptability of American English was a subject for heated debate until well into the present century.

A central fact of life in Quebec is that in the two hundred years since the Conquest, the French spoken by most Québécois has come to differ considerably from the French spoken in Europe. This, of course, has given rise to a great deal of discussion by Quebec critics. In his article in this collection, David M. Hayne provides a full account of the long-standing debate between the advocates of 'international' French and those who favour the use of Quebec French in literature.[25]

It is ironic that just at the time Hayne was reaching the conclusion that a balance had been established between the two tendencies, the whole controversy flared up again. With the upswing of nationalism in the sixties came a strong new impulse to write entirely in *joual*, an anglicized, proletarian kind of French that can perhaps be compared to Cockney or Harlem variants of English. Centred on the *Parti pris* writers but also including more established figures like Jacques Godbout and bright new talents like Michel Tremblay, the *joual* phenomenon soon attracted the support of a number of the younger critics and theorists, like André Brochu and François Charron. The movement may be said to have reached its peak in the early seventies with the publication of Jean Marcel's fiery polemic, *Le joual de Troie*.[26]

Most critics, however, remained dubious as to the merits of *joual* as a literary language, and like so much of the rebelliousness of the sixties, the movement has gradually faded away. Most writers have now returned to the fold of 'standard' French, restricting their use of *joual* to dialogues and certain kinds of theatre. Once again the critics have followed suit, shifting their attention to linguistics as a means of literary investigation. As with nationalism, the role and quality of the French language in Quebec have in recent years become more a matter for political than for literary discussion.

EXTERNAL RELATIONS

The literary criticism of Quebec has always been heavily influenced by the intellectual dominance of France. Even Camille Roy, who tended to mistrust the 'pernicious immorality' of the modern French writers of his day, nevertheless adopted the literary values of the great French classical tradition. The 'regionalists,' too, while vehemently opposed to their 'exotic' compatriots, still looked to the French regionalist writers for support for their own efforts.[27] David M. Hayne has effectively documented the traditional oscillation between xenophobia and francophilia,[28] and while he is correct in suggesting that the situation has now stabilized, the fact remains that the French presence in contemporary Quebec criticism is still very strong.

Virtually every major intellectual development in postwar France has had its repercussions in Quebec. Existentialism, for instance, has left its mark on several of Gilles Marcotte's essays in *Une littérature qui se fait*. The socialism and sociologism of Lukács and Goldmann have clearly influenced the attitudes of many Quebec critics, including Falardeau and de Grandpré. The *Parti pris* writers eagerly subscribed to the anticolonialism of Albert Memmi and Franz Fanon, not to mention Louis Althusser's readings of Marx. Gérard Bessette has adopted the psychoanalytic approach of Mauron, Beaudouin, Marie Bonaparte, *et al.* Bachelard has had a great impact on the thematic critics, Barthes on those inclined towards hermeneutics, and Sartre has influenced just about everyone. The most recent waves of linguistic criticism – formalism, textualism, structuralism, and semiotics – have also been imported largely from France. Clearly, there is no immediate danger of Quebec criticism declaring its intellectual independence.

The extent of French influence on Quebec literature has long been a subject of interest and concern for literary critics and historians. The more francophile critics like Jean Ethier-Blais celebrate this extention of French culture to a Québécois context.[29] Strongly nationalistic commentators like Michèle Lalonde, however, decry the lack of autochthonous intellectual tradition.[30] And most critics seem to share aspects of both attitudes, being proud of their French heritage and at the same time anxious to develop an intellectual infrastructure that will more accurately reflect their condition as Québécois. In any case, the situation is usually seen as hopeful; as Pierre de Grandpré has pointed out, 'it can happen that originality, for a literature as a whole, may be reached through the very process of imitation.'[31]

There are other reasons too for expecting the more autonomous development of Quebec criticism. Higher education has grown dramatically over the past two decades, and a significant number of young scholars are now enrolled in programmes of Quebec studies. Quebec literature has far outpaced French literature as a popular area of academic research and, like André Brochu, many of these young intellectuals are eager to establish their own values and to articulate a vision of reality based on their own experience as Québécois.

It is also important to consider that, while Quebec's intellectual links have always been with France, her imaginative links have often been with America. D.G. Jones has shown how what he calls a 'Whitmanesque' vision of America has long formed a sort of undercurrent in the Quebec imagination, and he traces the impact of this theme on the literature of the fifties and sixties when it emerged as the central and richest vein in Quebec writing.[32] Gilles Marcotte too has documented the importance of this 'theme of the land,'[33] and Paul Chamberland has provided some of the best demonstrations of its informing power in both his poetry and his criticism.[34] It has previously been suggested that the best Quebec literature (and criticism) to date were produced by this meeting of the nationalist imagination with the North American landscape. And yet, of all the developments in contemporary Quebec criticism, this one is the least dependent on French sources. Remaining the one major exception to French intellectual ascendency, the richness of the 'land theme' shows that Quebec criticism, at least occasionally, can achieve great things largely on its own.

Despite the economic and political importance of Quebec's English-speaking neighbours, neither the United States nor the other Canadian provinces have ever had much impact on its criticism. It is true that individual critics like Edmund Wilson, Northrop Frye, and Marshall McLuhan have been given occasional recognition in Quebec, as have other leading intellectuals like Herbert Marcuse and Noam Chomsky. In general, however, these are the exceptions that prove the rule of French predominance. Somehow, although the majority of Quebec intellectuals can read and speak English quite comfortably, the barrier of language remains largely intact.

The case of Quebec's literary relations with the rest of Canada is particularly striking, especially when one considers the relative closeness of their connections in such fields as history, geography, economics, or political science. With very few exceptions, the two literatures have followed their own separate (but sometimes parallel) paths, and critics in each language group have shown little inclination to explore the other's culture. As is made clear by two recent bibliographies – one on the translation[35] and the other on the comparison of Canada and Quebec literature[36] – scholarly interest in these areas is growing but is by no means extensive.

Quebec critics have occasionally commented on neighbouring literatures. Camille Roy, for instance, devoted a few pages to English-Canadian literature in his 1930 publication of *Histoire de la littérature canadienne*.[37] Harry Bernard wrote a study of the regional novel in the United States;[38] and in 1952 Jean-Charles Bonenfant briefly examined the role of criticism in English- and French-Canadian writing.[39] More recent contributors in the field of comparative studies have included Antoine Sirois, Max Dorsinville, and Clément Moisan. Their efforts, however, are far outweighed by the bulk of European-oriented criticism and, perhaps surprisingly, are also outnumbered by English-language criticism in the same areas. It is curious to observe, in fact, that Quebec's English-speaking neighbours have shown a greater interest in Quebec writing than have the Québécois in American and Canadian writing. Whether this is due to Quebec's cultural defensiveness or whether it is simply a question of priorities is open to debate, but in any case Quebec criticism has remained generally immune to the influence of the English-speaking world.

We see then that with regard to literary criticism Quebec still falls clearly within the realm of French intellectual influence, in much the same manner as Belgium, Switzerland or the French-speaking countries of the Third World. Although there are indications of a developing indigenous approach, one cannot yet speak of an established body of distinctively Quebec criticism. There has been a good deal of excellent literary criticism written in Quebec, and much of it has the flavour and colour of the Québécois milieu, but it is still too deeply dependent on French concepts and methods to be considered truly autochthonous. Like the literature as a whole, Quebec criticism has yet to produce a writer of great international stature; the criticism exists, but its level of existence has not yet reached the point where it is likely to have a marked influence on any other national literature.

INTERNAL RELATIONS

In examining the development of Quebec criticism, it is interesting to look briefly at the conditions of its production, for the kinds of criticism produced are obviously determined by the kinds of men and women who have produced it. As Guy Sylvestre has noted, most of the early criticism in Quebec was written either by the clergy or by literary amateurs.[40] The priests, nuns, and brothers of the teaching orders responsible for all French-language education in Quebec quite naturally wrote criticism that was didactic, Catholic, and moral. As for the literati, for whom writing was a hobby, their criticism tended, like their enthusiasms, to be vague and naive, much in the manner of Maurice Hébert.

With the emergence in the thirties and forties of a bourgeois, intellectual élite, critical horizons enlarged to include aesthetic criteria more in tune with the standards of European and American modernism. Relativism, accompanied by what Erich Heller has called 'the discovery and colonization of inwardness,'[41] also became increasingly apparent, as in the writings of Saint-Denys-Garneau or Jean Le Moyne. The transformation of Quebec into a modern industrial society with a rapidly growing urban population is reflected, in criticism as in the literature generally, by a greater concern for the problems of urban existence; thus the previously mentioned emphasis on psychological and sociological considerations.

With the gradual democratization of higher education in the fifties and sixties and the corresponding growth of a literate, urbane reading public, the number of 'professional' critics, especially academics, increased dramatically. Paying closer attention to questions of methodology and scholarship, critics like Jeanne Lapointe, Jean-Charles Falardeau, and Georges-André Vachon contributed to the establishment of Quebec literary studies as a 'respectable' academic discipline.

The growing prominence, particularly during the sixties, of 'committed' writers like Hubert Aquin, Jacques Godbout, and Michèle Lalonde, together with such 'cultural animators' as Gaston Miron, Pierre Vadeboncœur, and Paul Chamberland, resulted in criticism that was increasingly contestatory, ideological, and political in nature.

In the modern period, then, the field of Quebec criticism has grown in breadth and complexity. Journalistic critics abound, writing book reviews and articles for newspapers and magazines, or presenting literary topics on radio and television. Universities and colleges have also become hotbeds of criticism, with academics producing a steady flow of articles, journals, books, critical editions, bibliographies, and dictionaries on a scale that could not have been imagined even twenty years ago. It is worth noting too that in Quebec, unlike the rest of North America, the distinction between journalistic and academic criticism often becomes blurred, since many academics, like Gilles Marcotte or Jean Ethier-Blais, also write regularly for the newspapers. Because so many leading intellectuals practice it, the level of journalistic criticism in Quebec is unusually high.

Although some of the more lucrative aspects of the publishing business in Quebec, such as distribution and educational publishing, are largely controlled by French or American interests, most of the major literary publishers are based in Quebec. Such houses as Fides, HMH, and Leméac have a long tradition of publishing local writers. Other companies, like Les Editions du Jour or Les Editions La Presse, have attempted to strike a balance between books by Quebec authors and the more profitable translations or reprints of commercially successful foreign books.

The role of the university presses is also important, particularly for 'learned' books or scholarly criticism. Both Les Presses de l'Université de Montréal and Les Presses de l'Université Laval are established academic publishers and both have contributed a significant number of important works in literary criticism. Government subsidies have been a major factor in scholarly publishing too, with federal and provincial funding agencies providing support for literary research and publication. And finally, the proliferation of annual literary prizes is enough to ensure that no really talented writer is likely to go unnoticed for long.

In short, Quebec is now equipped with a cultural apparatus designed to favour the production of all forms of literature, including criticism. From this point of view, the situation must be seen as encouraging.

TRENDS

In attempting to form an overall view of Quebec criticism, it is necessary to define some of its constant, recurring characteristics. One of these, as we have seen, is a strong didactic impulse, a sometimes unconscious desire to use literature to inculcate specific values: whether such values are religious, as with the traditional critics, nationalist, as in the case of the Hexagone and later the *Parti pris* generations, or socio-political, as with the current crop of Marxist-Leninists, the didactic intent is still the *raison d'être* of such criticism. Another and related tendency has been to view literature as a reflection of society, and this accounts for the prevalence of sociological and psychological factors in Quebec criticism. A third aspect is derivativeness, the continuing need to import conceptual tools from France; more apparent in criticism than in other genres, this has resulted in a critical approach to Quebec literature based on theories and methods that have not grown out of the literature itself.

The most important constant of all, however, is change, and since the focus of our attention is on contemporary criticism, changes can be just as revealing as constants. Perhaps the central development in Quebec criticism has been its growth, for in the past century the field has become established to the point where it now has the conviction not only of its own existence but also of its own validity. Accompanying this growth in quantity and quality has been a continuing movement towards diversity, towards a plurality of interests, attitudes, and approaches that has never been more apparent than at the present time.

A less dramatic trend has been the slow, steady elaboration of aesthetic or formal criteria, implying a belief in literature as a system unto itself, with its own laws and its own modes of self-organization. To judge from the amount of structural criticism and 'textual' writing now being practised, the idea that literature is essentially 'about' literature is an idea whose time, after a hundred years of fits and starts, has finally come.

Last but not least is a trend whose time has not yet come, although there are signs that it is on the way. This is the movement towards autonomy. In a shrinking world where any sort of independence is largely illusory, the notion of critical autonomy is relative indeed, but perhaps it will be reached when Quebec criticism can stand largely on its own, giving back to the world of literature a part of what it takes from it. That day has not yet dawned, but considering the progress of the past two decades, it may not be far off.

NOTES

1 Eli Mandel *Contexts of Canadian Criticism* (Chicago: University of Chicago Press 1971) 4
2 'Founding the Territory' 122 below
3 Gérard Tougas *Histoire de la littérature canadienne-française* (Paris: Presses universitaires de France 1966) 21; on p. 3 he bestows the same honour upon a Frenchman, Valentin Jautard.
4 Laurent Mailhot, *La littérature québécoise* (Paris: Presses universitaires de France 1974) 37
5 Jean Marcel, 'La critique et l'essai, de 1900 à 1930' in *Histoire de la littérature française du Québec* ed. Pierre de Grandpré (Montreal: Beauchemin 1967) II 181
6 Samuel Baillargeon *Littérature canadienne-française* (Montreal: Fides 1957) 303; Auguste Viatte *Histoire littéraire de l'Amérique française* Québec: Presses universitaires, Laval 1954) 29
7 'Our Pioneers in Criticism' 19 below
8 Tougas 110
9 Harry Bernard 'Du régionalisme littéraire,' *Essais critiques* (Montreal: Librairie d'action canadienne-française 1929)
10 Tougas 244
11 See *La poésie canadienne-française* (Montreal: Albert Lévesque 1933), and *Le roman canadien-français* (Montréal: Albert Lévesque 1937)
12 Baillargeon 305
13 Albert Pelletier *Egrappages* (Montreal: Editions Albert Lévesque 1933) 66–7
14 Octave Crémazie *Œuvres, Prose*, Vol. II (Ottawa: Editions de l'Université d'Ottawa 1976) 93
15 Tougas 111–12
16 Mailhot 46; Marcel 181
17 Marcel Dugas *Psyché au cinéma* (Montreal: Paradis-Vincent 1916)
18 Gilles Marcotte 'La critique littéraire, de 1945 à nos jours' in *Histoire de la littérature française du Québec* ed. Pierre de Grandpré (Montreal: Beauchemin 1967) IV, 345
19 (Montreal: HMH 1961), tr. Philip Stratford, *Convergence: Essays from Quebec* (Toronto: Ryerson 1966)
20 Jack Warwick *The Long Journey: Literary Themes of French Canada* (Toronto: University of Toronto Press 1968) 32
21 Jean Ethier-Blais 'Le roman québécois,' in *Le roman contemporain d'expression française* ed. Antoine Naaman (Sherbrooke: CELEF 1971) 158

18 Contemporary Quebec Criticism

22 Camille Roy 'French-Canadian Literature' in *Bourinot, Marquis, Roy* ed. Clara Thomas (Toronto: University of Toronto Press 1973) 489
23 'The Mitre and the Tuque' 83 below
24 (Montreal: Editions québécoises 1971)
25 'The Major Options of French-Canadian Literature' 37 below
26 Jean Marcel *Le joual de Troie* (Montreal: Editions du jour 1973)
27 See, for example, Harry Bernard *Essais critiques* (Montreal: Librairie d'action canadienne-française 1929).
28 'The Major Options of French-Canadian Literature' 37 below
29 'Our Pioneers in Criticism' 19 below
30 'The Mitre and the Tuque' 83 below
31 Pierre de Grandpré *Histoire* 3, p. 12
32 D.G. Jones 'In Search of America' *Boundary II* 3, No. 1 (1974) 227–46
33 Gilles Marcotte, 'Notes sur le thème du pays,' *Voix et images du pays* 4, 1971
34 'Founding the Territory' 122 below
35 Philip Stratford *Bibliography of Canadian Books in Translation: French to English and English to French* 2nd ed. (Ottawa: HRCC 1977)
36 David M. Hayne and Antoine Sirois 'Preliminary Bibliography of Comparative Canadian Literature (English-Canadian and French-Canadian)' *Canadian Review of Comparative Literature* 3, No. 2 (1976) 124–36; 'First Supplement, 1975–76' 4, No. 2 (1977) 205–9; 'Second Supplement, 1976–77' 5, No. 1 (1978) 114–19
37 Camille Roy *Histoire de la littérature canadienne de langue française* (Québec: L'imprimerie de l'action sociale 1930)
38 Harry Bernard *Le roman régionaliste aux Etats-Unis* (Montreal: Fides 1949)
39 Jean-Charles Bonenfant 'Le rôle comparé de la critique littéraire au Canada anglais et français' *Culture* 13, No. 3 (Sept. 1952)
40 Quoted in de Grandpré *Histoire* 4, p. 340
41 Erich Heller *The Hazard of Modern Poetry* (Pennsylvania: Folcroft Library Editions 1953) 18

BACKGROUNDS

Our Pioneers in Criticism

In many ways, Jean Ethier-Blais is a traditionalist. His literary values such as clarity of thought and expression, are those of the French classical tradition. His style, learned and elevated, has an elegance that verges on preciosity. His enthusiasms are for writers of the past: the great French masters or, in Quebec literature, Aubert de Gaspé, François Hertel, and above all Lionel Groulx. His opinions tend to be radical and conservative, sceptical of contemporary literary fashions. Aware of the past to a degree that is uncommon among Quebec literary critics, Ethier-Blais, like Groulx, is concerned that it not be forgotten, that it be used to temper the present and to inform the future.

Like his three collections of criticism entitled *Signets*, Ethier-Blais's attention is divided between French and Quebec literature, and one senses him not altogether easy within the confines of the latter. Perhaps because he has spent a significant part of his life outside Quebec – born in Ontario, a student in Germany, various diplomatic postings abroad, visiting professor in France – his attitude toward Quebec culture is somewhat reserved and distant. Paradoxically, however, his writings reveal an obsession with questions of national identity. Elitist, francophile, often disdainful of his immediate surroundings, he nevertheless shows a deep patriotism and a profound personal interest in the destiny of his people. A contradictory figure himself, he delights in the contradictions of others.

Jean Ethier-Blais is above all a passionate reader, one for whom the love of literature is a central fact of life. He writes extensively and easily, interspersing his literary insights with anecdotes, biographical digressions, flashes of wit or sarcasm, cultural or social observations, and frequent expressions of personal opinion. The result is a peculiar blend of textual explication and cultural contemplation, with the emphasis tending toward the latter; it is impressionistic criticism in which we see the meeting of an informed, agile, and highly individual intelligence with the past and present writers of Quebec.

Well-known as an outspoken literary critic for *Le Devoir*, Jean Ethier-Blais teaches in the French department of McGill University. The following article, in which he traces the origins of French-Canadian literary criticism was included in the third volume of *Signets* (Montreal: Le Cercle du Livre de France 1973).

OUR PIONEERS IN CRITICISM

It is paradoxical that countries without literature are not necessarily countries without literary criticism. One kind of criticism grows out of the sovereign fact of a literature's existence; an existing body of literature enables the formulations of laws governing its genres, allows for the formation of taste, and provides the language with its showcase. This is not so, however, with French-Canadian literature. Before our literature even existed, the voices of critics could be heard telling it what form it should take and what direction it should evolve in. Thus, on the one hand it had to follow the example of French literature, which is also the example of the classics, and on the other hand it had to yield to the demands of national consciousness, which was still in an embryonic stage. And so it happened that whenever the natural world was being described, French-Canadian writers of the nineteenth century would conceive of the universe in the same manner as Jean-Baptiste Rousseau and Abbé Delille. Such were the examples they followed. And yet it is certain that nature, as it really is in Canada, has nothing to do with the way these two poets pictured it. Nature for us is anything but gallant. Even Chateaubriand's descriptions of it are totally unconnected with any reality (except perhaps for the cosmic development of his style). The roots of French-Canadian writing are elsewhere, and this explains why, even twenty years ago, the novelists and poets of Quebec were still involved in coming to grips with the physical world around them. No doubt they would never find the gentleness of Anjou, which they always tried to evoke in their descriptions; rather they had to face a biting cold, the enveloping snow, and the merciless summer sun.

Historical circumstances meant that early French-Canadian criticism was primarily a school of ideas designed to serve the nationalistic, bourgeois ideology of the late nineteenth century. Left in the hands of priests who were concerned above all with maintaining the Catholic faith and the authority of the Church, criticism was only marginally involved with problems of writing. This tendency to see literature as an adjunct to the Propagation of the Faith is well represented by Abbé Henri-Raymond Casgrain and Mgr Camille Roy. From 1860 to 1935, Louis Dantin and Marcel Dugas were the only writers who attempted to make literary criticism a means of self-expression: Louis Dantin in the studious manner he had retained from his time in the monastery, and Marcel Dugas in the flourishes so liberally scattered throughout his writing. These two conceived of literature as an art. They reacted to the work of their contemporaries, not in terms of an abstract (and outdated) ideology, but rather by basing their standards on art and imagination. They were pioneers, and like most pioneers were quickly forgotten. Today, though, they serve as landmarks and examples, for on the fringes of the official criticism, which represented nothing but itself, these two men were actually dealing with questions of literature. Louise Dantin introduced the poets of his generation to Baudelaire; Marcel Dugas was an ardent and agile defender of both Verlaine and his friends in the 'Action Française.' And so they helped to form public taste – a limited public, perhaps, made up of students and young poets, but one which was to shed its light on the generation that followed.

From 1900 to 1940, therefore, we find two opposing currents. One was centred around the much-honoured Camille Roy, Rector of Laval University and in great demand as a speaker, who went about spreading the good word of faith and moderation. The other was the current first promoted by Louis Dantin, who wrote sparsely from exile in Boston, and then by Marcel Dugas, who refused to leave Paris, and whose voice faded away as it crossed the ocean. Clearly this was a struggle between very uneven opponents, and the result for criticism was a period of benign stagnation. Mgr Roy held the centre-stage, and he suffered no contradiction. Books were writings for the soul. Literature, broadly speaking, was a good deed. Poetry was a song to God and joy. Such were the standards that came to Camille Roy from the late nineteenth century and which, like a new Elisha, he inherited from Abbé Casgrain.

Abbé Henri-Raymond Casgrain was the father of criticism in French Canada. Born into a family of farmers, he grew up peacefully, studying at the Séminaire de Québec in the midst of priests who were much less learned than they thought themselves to be. And so the young Casgrain learned, from childhood on, to blend his love for the native land and for the rural virtues of his forefathers with his passion for fine language – which is to say the romantic, vaporous, and oratorical language that was served up to him in the inner court of the Seminary. A sickly youth and a dreamer, he was advised by his superiors to grow strong in the study of literature and to leave missionary work to others. In this way the young priest visited France and Italy in 1858. Here he completed the formation of his taste, listened to the harmonious language his teachers had spoken of, and returned to Quebec haloed with the mysteries of his voyage to the Eleusis of literature. It is hard to imagine what these trips to Paris meant in the middle of the nineteenth century. Few intellectuals were able to live in France, to rediscover a part of their French soul. The return was difficult: seeking forgiveness for having left, learning to toe the line again, and repeating a few of the ideas that had been picked up over there. From his stay in Paris Abbé Casgrain retained the influence of Charles Nodier, the use of folk tales in a literary context, and the need for writers to group together. In Quebec City, he soon became known as a forerunner and an organizer. Like all the writers of his time, Abbé Casgrain had been profoundly marked by the *Histoire du Canada** written by François-Xavier Garneau (1809–1865), a work which had revived French Canadians' sense of their historic nobility. Even more important, while reinforcing their language and the sense of their civil rights, Garneau's *Histoire* offered them the magnificent adventure of a French mission in America. Garneau himself, impelled by a desire to give French-Canadian patriotism back its wings, had emphasized in his work the discovery, exploration, and final abandonment of the French Empire in America. Out of this geographic immensity, unconsciously at first and later in order to provide ideological support for the social and political transformation of French-Canadian society, his readers conceived the mysterious and moving theories of *messianism* and agriculturalism. Abbé Casgrain was the herald of this development.

According to messianic belief, the French Canadians, descended from the France of *le grand siècle*, had come to America in order to spread the reign of God. At first it was not a question of colonization but rather of evangelization, with the arable land being exploited only in order to ensure the logistics, or the intendancy, of the evangelizers. This French mission extended to all of America – not only to the Indian lands but also (and perhaps even more strongly) to the lands settled by foreigners of Anglo-Saxon, Protestant origin, who were to be led back into the fold of the Catholic religion. For the chosen people, there was never any thought of possible self-interest or wealth. There could be only one goal, and this was to colonize in order to evangelize, in order to set an example. The fact that

*Translated by Andrew Bell as *History of Canada, from the Time of its Discovery till the Union Year, 1840–1* (Montreal: J. Lovell 1860, 3 vols.) (ed.)

the Empire that had been theirs had fallen apart in 1763 was of relatively little importance. It all boiled down to a question of civilization, and the French, Catholic civilization of the North would win out because it was the only true one. Mgr Camille Roy, who was to take Abbé Casgrain's place in Quebec City, was later to say that Quebec was the Athens of America. This amazing declaration is a perfect expression of the state of mind that animated the French Canadians' civilizing and religious messianism in the nineteenth century. Messianism may well have evolved as a compensation for the defeat of 1763, but this does not explain why the same state of mind is found in almost every French-language book published in Canada, from the poetry of Octave Crémazie (1827–1879) right up to the great lyric novels of Félix-Antoine Savard (1896–). Foreigners were considered evil. Crémazie's old soldier of Carillon mourned the passing of a world that had been sacred, while Savard's Menaud, a man of the forest, went mad because the owners of his lands were English. This messianism, doomed in advance by history and geography, was essentially tragic. It could be saved only by the bucolic virtues of agriculturalism. The missionary nation *par excellence* would have to return to the land. Mechanical civilization was harmful, destructive of both life and faith. People had to flee it and seek refuge in the forests or on the land itself. The *habitants* were the only full participants, with the priests, in the mission to save the French-Canadian nation. This is why the French Canadians, gathering around Church and priest, prayed and waited. The great vision glimpsed by Maria Chapdelaine at the fateful hour, so admirably described by Louis Hémon, was precisely the vision of this choice: the land of the forefathers had to win out, not only because it was stronger and healthier, but also because it assured our survival. It was not until 1938, with the publication of Ringuet's *Trente Arpents*,* that the myth of agriculturalism started to crumble. Ringuet showed the French-Canadian farmer grappling with the real land, the land that killed him, that forced him for lack of bread to flee to the United States, where he ended up as a night watchman in a garage. The land of Quebec was producing a proletariat – hardly the priests of a new civilization.

Nevertheless, this was another myth that lasted for almost a century, its vigour and longevity being largely due to Abbé Casgrain. A great founder of magazines (*Les soirées canadiennes, Le foyer canadien*), he used them to publish the first novels of messianic and agricultural propaganda; thus the settler (1862) and economist (1864) Jean Rivard,† by Antoine Gérin-Lajoie

*Translated by Dorothea and Felix Walter as *Thirty Acres* (New York: Macmillan 1940; rpt. Toronto: McClelland and Stewart, NCL, 1960) (ed.)
†Translated by Vida Bruce as *Jean Rivard* (Toronto: McClelland and Stewart, NCL, 1977) (ed.)

(1824–1882), was published in the *Soirées canadiennes*. There can be no doubt that the love of literature attracted numerous admirers to Abbé Henri-Raymond Casgrain; his coterie took form gradually and included such diverse personalities as Crémazie, Joseph Taché, Gérin-Lajoie, and Philippe Aubert de Gaspé (1786–1871). Here we see an admirable attempt to gather together the literary energies of a small nation, energies that these writers used to serve the people. Abbé Casgrain was right, at the end of his life, when he ventured that his work had not been completely useless. He had no aesthetic theory: his only pleasure and his only criteria were fine language, harmonious turns of phrase, select images, and scenes that were tender, sentimental, and religious. In his own time and place, however, a love for such things came close to being a provocation, almost an excess of aestheticism. Abbé Casgrain never let himself be won over by the vulgarity of his era; with his fundamental naiveté, he believed in the pre-eminence of spiritual values. Around him a new French-Canadian ruling class was on the rise, and it knew how to use such noble, abstract, grand themes as messianism in order to be elected to parliament and to grow rich in the service of English and American capitalism. Casgrain's work, which was dynamic at a literary level since it forced French-Canadian writers to group together and to question their motives for writing, was static from the point of view of history; his writings and those of his disciples had the effect of putting the French-Canadian nation to sleep, creating a feeling that nothing would ever prevail against it, keeping it in a state of blessed cultural ignorance. In the final analysis, from deep within the Petit Séminaire de Québec, Abbé Casgrain above all served (as Camille Roy would later serve) the interests of the French-Canadian priesthood, this caste which itself was intimately linked with the emerging French-Canadian bourgeoisie and the great foreign interests. A race of drawers of water (*Maria Chapdelaine*) and crazed backwoodsmen (*Menaud, maître-draveur*)* was counterbalanced by a race of unconscious exploiters who, using their dictionaries and their categories of romanticism to serve a great mythic ideal, gradually receded, like Abbé Casgrain, into the shadows. The future was to retain nothing from the school of Abbé Casgrain, except a few verses by Octave Crémazie and *Les anciens Canadiens*† (1863) by Philippe Aubert de Gaspé – a novel written by a descendant of the seigneurs to the glory of French-Canadian assimilation by the conquering English. By a

---

*Translated by Richard Howard as *Master of the River* (Montreal: Harvest House 1976) (ed.)
†Translated by Charles G.D. Roberts as *The Canadians of Old* (New York: Appleton 1890); rpt. as *Canadians of Old* (Toronto: McClelland and Stewart, NCL, 1974) (ed.)

strange reversal, however, the sister of the anglophile hero became the symbol of French-Canadian resistance. Blanche d'Haberville is the prototype of the French-Canadian heroine: pure, generous, and completely centred on the notion of the motherland. An incarnation of the nation, she refuses to die. It is thanks to Blanche d'Haberville and her stubbornness that *Les anciens Canadiens* has survived; she is the forerunner of the many wives, mothers, and sisters who fill the pages of French-Canadian novels and who symbolize the will to keep on living. But is this enough to form a literature? This woman can be found, in different guises, in almost every French-Canadian novel. She has become an archetype, a sort of Colette Baudoche* with superhuman strength.

Apart from his grand themes, here then is the true legacy of Abbé Casgrain: the image of a sad, courageous woman who haunts our literature like the spectre of defeat. The works by Casgrain's disciples extolled the virtues of strength, a sense of grandeur and fidelity, and a reversed conquest by means of faith. But only this woman has survived – because she is a literary image, because she exists deep within the wounded heart, because she corresponds to what we are. Abbé Casgrain thought in brilliant formulas thanks to which literature gently melted into politics. In his old age, Philippe Aubert de Gaspé created a living, human character who, through her actions, speaks for us all. None of Casgrain's critical works has survived except, by proxy, this Blanche d'Haberville, who in spite of her inflexibility, breathes with a rhythm that became for a half-century the heartbeat of French-Canadian literature.

This woman is particularly present in the poems of Emile Nelligan (1879–1941), a poet who became insane at nineteen and who left some of the most beautiful verses in French-Canadian literature. His is a tragic vision in which the mother becomes one with the fiancée, in which sin stalks through the cruel universe of the French-Canadian soul. Emile Nelligan was discovered by a priest, Louis Dantin (1865–1945), and it was Dantin who encouraged his gift of self-expression. Dantin was a contemporary of Camille Roy, who was the most influential critic of his time. Never were two men less alike, although both were priests. Camille Roy turned his talent to the service of what he thought were useful ideas; Dantin lived for the love of literature. His major work was the 'Preface' he wrote for the first edition of the works of Emile Nelligan in 1903. His ideas were new for his time and his milieu. Dantin did not believe that beauty

*Heroine in Maurice Barrès's novel of the same name, who symbolized the virtues of fidelity to the land and its traditions (ed.)

was one and the same as idea. Rather than the moralizing thoughts of Abbé
Casgrain, he assigned to art a place that was far removed from morality.
Religion might give rise to art, as often it did, but art was able to exist
without religion. The same was true for nationalist ideas. The writer did
not, and should not serve a cause; rather he served himself, and his gifts.
The defence of the nation would in some way come of its own, since its
greatness was implicit in the perfection of language and in the genius of the
writers it produced. Only aesthetic questions were important, since they
alone determined the success or failure of a work. All criteria were valid, so
long as they produced a book that was well thought out and well written.
The critic, wrote Louis Dantin,

> must force himself to understand all that is comprehensible and to admire anything
> that produces even a flash of beauty. He must be prepared, if need be, to let his
> doctrines give way to the facts – and the fact is often that beauty strikes you in
> guises that go against the rules, or in forms that are different from the ones you
> expect.

Although he advocated literary freedom, Dantin was not opposed to the
classics. As a poet, he wrote purely classical verse; as an editor, he removed
some parts of Nelligan's work which he though corresponded in a negative
way to what he expected of his genius. The perfection of talent, for Dantin,
was still to be found in Racine, and it was Racine whom, no doubt unconsciously, he wanted others to imitate. In this he is similar to Mgr Camille
Roy, who was also an absolute defender of Boileau's precepts. Actually,
Louis Dantin was a traditionalist, but he was also open to whatever was
new in poetry (and writing), provided that it was not excessive. In his time
he represented the tastes of the most enlightened of the French-Canadian
intelligentsia, whereas Camille Roy, who was just as firmly anchored in
tradition, accepted virtually nothing outside this tradition unless he did so
out of generosity, pity, or occasionally boredom.

Like his rival, Louis Dantin wrote in a precise, intentionally classical
language. His talent was cramped by the critical material that French-
Canadian literature had to offer him. It is always amazing to notice the
silence critics like Dantin and Roy observed on the subject of French
literature, for they never spoke of it except to praise the classical antecedents and to use them as examples. Yet they said nothing about Baudelaire
(whom Louis Dantin liked), Verlaine, or any of the great writers of the
early twentieth century. This must be seen as the sign of a timid mind that
considers its judgments valid only inasmuch as they remain within our

borders. Like Camille Roy, Louis Dantin suffered from never having medi-
tated, pen in hand, on great and powerful works of literature.

Camille Roy (1870–1943) was thirty years old in 1900. Without delving
into the political struggles which, by and large, never seemed very important to him, let us look at his milieu, the French-Canadian world he was
part of. It is important to note first of all that, in the one hundred thirty
years since the trauma of the Conquest had shaken French Canada
through and through, this society had been geared to only marginal development. Descended from poor people, maintained in its poverty, indifferent to power and fearful of intelligence, it was a society that had produced
great minds only for the political parties. In 1937, Mgr Camille Roy would
echo the attitudes that had characterized the situation in 1900. 'We French
Canadians,' he wrote,

have no aversion to building industries and making a fortune. But we truly believe
that the foundations of our French-Canadian influence in America are not to be
found in either gold or factories.

This is a basic fact for the intellectuals and the social theoreticians of this
era: the almost systematic rejection of everything that was not of the spirit.

Opposing currents, meanwhile, were gaining strength. At the very time
Camille Roy was embarking on his literary career, an important new class
was beginning to make its appearance in the national life of French Canadians. This class was anxious to acquire material goods, but it also wanted, to
some extent, the spiritual goods of science, arts, and letters. The emergence of the middle class was accompanied by a search for balance and
continuity. When he reproached French-Canadian fathers for not surviving in their sons, Mgr Roy was recording the past rather than predicting a
trend. With hindsight, it now seems quite the opposite, that the very goal
of this new class which appeared early in the century was, from the very
beginning, to consolidate their foundations and assure continued growth.
If one were to analyse the French-Canadian people in general terms, one
would find that this strengthening of the bases of the French-Canadian
bourgeoisie took three particular forms: (a) the emergence of a new wave
of nationalism; (b) the positive acceptance of our national identity as being
French; and (c) the appearance and organization of forms of social liberties.
The first two of these breakthroughs by the French-Canadian bourgeoisie
received Mgr Roy's full support – which is to say his full but nuanced
support, for he was a past master at intangible statements. And nowhere in
his life was this pursuit of the nuance affirmed with more sensitivity than

in his support of French-Canadian nationalism and the French fact in America.

He could not conceive of one without the other. The French fact in Canada and our presence on this continent, he felt, would necessarily have to condition our behaviour as a group. This is to say that the deliberate acceptance by the French-Canadian people of its French and Catholic character would lead it, at a particular moment in its social history, to affirm itself as it was. In addition, considering the play of opposing forces and our past history (the Conquest, the progressive impoverishment of the nation, the political clashes), our evolution would almost inevitably express itself in terms of a struggle. In temperament, in taste, and in his readings, Mgr Roy was not and could not be a friend to violence. His nationalism was not grounded in revolt; rather it stemmed from a profound knowledge of and enduring love for French civilization. It was not that the Herculean labours of the historian Lionel Groulx did not matter to him; in fact, it was quite the contrary. With his thoroughly classical soul, however, he tended to view Groulx's work in a highly intellectual context, and thus from a perspective that had little to do with the struggles of French civilization. The result was that, while he deplored what he could only view as an excess, in historical terms he nevertheless agreed to the struggle and even, in his own fashion, took part in it. For him, this struggle was more a symptom of the vitality of the French spirit on American soil than a means of attaining political goals. In a word, contrary to many of the nationalists of his time, the nationalist thinking of Mgr Camille Roy was focused much more on the universal French fact and on his conviction that French Canadians were an integral part of French civilization than on any development of a French-Canadian civilization rooted in – but different from – the civilization of France. Perhaps I am drawing Mgr Camille Roy too much in the direction of my own ideas in saying that, for him, the history of French Canada was simply the history of a civilizing nation named France, bridging the gulf of the ocean and continuing on *chez nous*. It was thus that he referred to 'our long history.'

Yet another incitement to Mgr Roy's total acceptance of the French intellectual tradition was the priesthood, through which he felt doubly bound to the past. Speaking one day about education in Canada, he quite understandably took pride in praising all the priests who had made it possible for French Canadians to preserve their French spirit, and thus their religion. He would have abhorred nothing more than the separation of these two living forces which, in his mind, were inextricably linked together. Both his work and his life proclaimed the indissolubility of the French language and the Catholic religion in the French-Canadian context.

Thus, in terms of rising national consciousness and its nationalistic overtones, it is fair to consider Mgr Camille Roy as a man of the golden mean, in the strict, creative sense. As such he represented a profound tendency in French-Canadian intellectuals, and it was a tendency to which he gave active encouragement. He placed national considerations above and beyond the concerns of his own time, concerns which stemmed from a revolt against injustice (and thus a quest for liberty), and which almost automatically tended towards violence – or at the very least towards verbal violence. In this he bears witness to one of our long intellectual traditions, a current of thought in which nationalistic stimuli are not rejected but rather are tentatively rechannelled towards a fully French development. There is a pride in being French Canadian, but much of the direction of one's national conscience depends on which of the two terms in this single designation is emphasized: 'French' or 'Canadian.' In Mgr Camille Roy's thoughts on the national question, the accent always fell on the word 'French.' Mgr Roy's ideas did not simply hark back to the French regime with its intendants and its *chasse-galeries;** instead, they represented a return to our veritable sources, to our authentic national heritage, which made us part of an unbroken line. These premises, however, are valid only if the spirit is given precedence over historical facts. Mgr Roy believed in his precedence, and his thinking, without his having deliberately wanted it to, thus reaches right through to us: healthy, peaceable, and creative.

Educated in Canada and later in Paris, Mgr Camille Roy was a product of the classical disciplines. His literary doctrine, which he applied to himself, was based on a slightly naïve enthusiasm for writing, on an openness of mind, on the primacy of reasonable literary forms, and on purity of style. His masters had been Lanson and Faguet, and he remained faithful to them. In studying literature, the analysis of inner motives and considerations of creative impulses did not strike him as being absolutely necessary. For him, the primordial criterion was whether the style and the thought adhered to the subject.

When he published his first literary studies in Quebec City (1902), the young Abbé Roy found himself, in the field of literature, faced with a

---

*Legend in which lumberjacks from the north country, in league with or against the devil, travel south to see their families in the holidays by paddling precariously through the skies in a canoe (ed.)

situation that was similar in many respects to the one previously described. The romanticism of Crémazie and Fréchette (1839–1908) was on its last legs. A new generation was taking over.

What did romanticism mean in French Canada? To begin with, it meant the first cries our people had uttered in the realm of literature. Very soon afterwards it became the image of our protest. For the first time, again in a literary sense, our tragic destiny had taken shape. Abbé Groulx said that we were a tragic people because, in our very condition, we were constantly vacillating between being and nothingness. The French-Canadian Romantics anticipated this tragic formula. However, they did not adopt it only in a literary sense. For them, the tragedy also stemmed from an inner combat: the struggle for faith, at first, and then the struggle for expression. For poets like Crémazie and Fréchette, French Canada, held for historical reasons to forms of thinking which left no room for liberal-mindedness, represented a force of inertia even in religious matters. For them, French Canada was a force hostile to the development of poetic thought. And so it is important that these writers be judged from within their tragic conception of the world and of themselves. Their cries are the cries of an ignorant, poor people; they are also a cry against the very structure of our civilization.

With the establishment of a wealthy bourgeoisie, poetry began to reflect a different *état d'âme*. It became escapist; it again wanted to protest – only this time the protest was not against intellectual conformism but against the reign of Mammon. On another front, language had become firmer. Lacking a verbally musical vocabulary, didactic poetry gave way to more pleasurable and subtle renderings of the soul.

From the beginning, Camille Roy was deeply involved in this debate. He could only applaud the novelty of the poetic conceptions of the Ecole littéraire de Montréal, only commend attempts at verbal virtuosity. He was taken with anything that tended to move French-Canadian literature closer to its ideal (which was an ideal of perfection). It should also be noted that in our literature, post-romanticism and symbolism represented something more than a formal adherence to literary fashion. Although they imitated the French of France, they also have a deeper sense as a sign of the transformation and disintegration of the specifically religious thinking of our people. Romanticism had outlined this tendency, and the poets of Mgr Roy's era confirmed it. Linguistic freedom was no longer the only question; religious freedom was also in the air. The most typical poets and novelists of the new wave were influential, to be sure; but they were also influenced. Thus they were not, and could not be, simply the spontaneous emergence of a religious revolt that dared not – and still dares not – reveal its true identity. They were a reflection of the rising class to which they belonged; they expressed its feelings, and they were making ready to cast off the traditional restraints.

Perhaps unwittingly, but none the less vigorously, Mgr Camille Roy countered this unconscious literary and religious revolt with the veto of his creed. He never condemned for the pleasure of condemning. Indeed, it is possible in his case to speak of evangelistic criticism. Nevertheless, he understood – and this is the deepest significance of his work as a critic – that this was only a case of growing pains, that even the inclination to revolt was based on elements of faith. Camille Roy's approach can be summed up in a single expression: his taste was never tainted by his faith. Whether dealing with Paul Morin (1889–1963), Nelligan (1879–1941), or Jean-Charles Harvey (1891–1967), he was always able to recognize that their cries of revolt could have a meaning in the French-Canadian context. Sometimes he showed a lack of persistence, an unwillingness to follow the writers' ideas to the end, but he never indulged in what is called a 'put-down.' Perhaps this explains why he was often criticized for being over-benevolent, for being too 'soft' as a critic.

From a literary point of view, then, Mgr Camille Roy exemplified two impulses: for truth through gentleness, and for art through a great demand for perfection. He himself gave the example of a pure and personal language – and he demanded it of others. His most frequent reproach had to do with imprecise language. He believed that ideas that were not carefully expressed were not ideas at all.

This is the essential Camille Roy. He understood the word 'fidelity,' and he lived it. He was the first, or at least one of the few to take our literature seriously, as representing, within narrow boundaries, a pillar of French civilization. He had a feeling for the mission of the writer and the writer's role in our society, and he devoted a large part of his life, thoughtfully and ardently, to giving this role its full meaning.

The work of this famous (and seldom read) man may be said to contain several of the most accurate thoughts ever expressed about our national destiny, and about literary piety. In the end, it is of little consequence that these ideas never had the creative impact that they might have had. It matters little to us, and Mgr Roy, who hated grandiloquence, would have been pleased to be admired only by the 'happy few.' The academic world had given him its official sanction. His ideas and doctrine, precisely because of their subtlety, could appeal only to minds that were out of the ordinary. And yet their positive effects are still being felt. In some degree thanks to him, the civilization of our forefathers has played a role in the emergence and formation of our national awareness. In our literature he propagated ideas of sound beauty, the necessity of work, and a certain confidence in the use of language; surely this counts for something.

The times needed a Malherbe, and he played this purifying role with affability. The high priest of our literature, he devoted his life to the most rational side of beauty. In this too he represents us; he gave to our conformity, so to speak, the wings of a chastened language and a subtle mind. His time would never have allowed him to go any farther, and his tastes would never have attracted him to the bizarre. But his pure mind was adept at nuance, and his sympathy for Nelligan, the black angel whose sickly wings were so soon stilled, is a sign of the universality and charity of his spirit.

Unlike Camille Roy, Marcel Dugas (1883–1947), critic, poet, and essayist, never spoke of anything but himself. Still, in his dreams and opinions, although they were often hasty and sometimes strident, we see the outline of an era. When he was still quite young, Marcel Dugas left Canada and took refuge in France; there, in the deceptive guise of an archivist, this clear-minded funambulist found his calling. Dugas's heart was constantly wavering between Montreal and Paris. His most important work, *Louis Fréchette, un romantique canadien* (1934), was intended to be both literary and historical; Marcel Dugas was not a Sainte-Beuve, however, and as soon as his dreams or raptures started to fade, a slight boredom began to rear its head. For Marcel Dugas, criticism could never be anything but a means of exalting the ego through the delirium of confession. He was always talking about Olympus, divine perfumes, supernatural sounds, Elysian inspirations. It seems as though the poet or novelist in question was always, on every page, the object of the Muses' attentions. This kind of criticism causes some initial surprise, and then provokes a few smiles. However, it would be unjust towards Marcel Dugas to emphasize only the lyrical aspects of his writing, for his judgments, though sometimes clothed in astonishing terms, were excellent. This man knew French literature, and when he was addressing a French-Canadian public, he never forgot the French models. And thus he never settled for easy praise. His writings were less concerned with critical judgments than with the formation of taste. Marcel Dugas was the first French-language critic in Canada who was also a creative artist, who was concerned with problems of harmonious language, and who chose to go beyond the great rural themes without ever a backward glance. An expatriate critic, he was just what was needed in Montreal after the First World War. Obviously the critical production of Marcel Dugas did not have the scope of the work of Mgr Camille Roy, who represented good taste at its healthy, universal best. But Marcel Dugas added a poetic dimension to French-Canadian criticism, and that set him apart in this modest company. He was not afraid to use the language of praise or, more courageously, the language of regretful disagreement in order to express himself as he was, with his excessive kindness, his fright-fully tender emotions, and the myriad nuances of a mind too delicate to be perfectly sound. All in all, the critical essays of Marcel Dugas depend as much on poetry as on criticism. His books were widely read and he himself, in Paris during times of peace and in Montreal during the wars, was a very likeable character. Dugas has bequeathed to us a body of writing in the pointillist manner, containing a few dense pages on poetry and many beautiful outbursts.

Dugas's spasmodic cries from Paris, however, did nothing to change the general literary atmosphere of French Canada. Despite the railings of men like Victor Barbeau or Paul Morin against the rampant conformity, the foundations of intellectual immobility held solid. Everything conspired to maintain the somnolence: the traditional political parties battling in a vacuum, youth's pressing need to make money, the atrophy in the courses of study at the classical colleges, and so on. It is fair to say that between the two world wars (1919–40), French-Canadian society quite deliberately went into a state of suspended animation. Nothing could have been less auspicious for encouraging great literary talents, and criticism responded to this inertia by bestowing benedictions upon it. Camille Roy was the apologist for this sort of nothingness. He made it almost likeable. It was a time when lady poets flourished, from Jeanne l'Archevêque-Duguay to Jovette Bernier, tirelessly repeating the song of the cradle or the anguish of unrequited love. The only reason for believing that French-Canadian litera-ture still existed was historiography, thanks to the inventive genius of Abbé Lionel Groulx. The prevailing conformity and impotence quite natu-rally looked to Greek and Latin models in order to justify their quiet possession of the truth. Modern writers or those on the Index were rigorously banished, all novelty was reproached, and any attempt at escape was severely punished. The natural indolence of French Canadians came to the rescue of the intellectual hierarchy, with the result that all that remains from this era are a few poems and the work of Abbé Lionel Groulx. Literature had become utilitarian and functional. And this accounts for the sheer volume of the works of Mgr Camille Roy and his epigones Maurice Hébert (1888–1960) and Emile Chartier (1876–1951): the fewer books that were published, the more they wrote, for their role was not to encourage writers but to make it look as though there were a lot of them, and a lot of very good ones. Camille Roy and his disciples constantly went around bestowing their blessings hither and yon. It was a game, however, for which literature paid the price.

This is what explains the violence of the reactions of French-Canadian writers after the Second World War. They could count on the support of only a few young critics like Guy Sylvestre, Roger Duhamel, and René Garneau. It was they who gave birth to the new school of criticism in French Canada, they who encouraged literary sentiments where literature was concerned, and they who rejected the traditional, anti-intellectual ideology in favour of critical conceptions based on the work of Sainte-Beuve, Albert Thibaudet, or Charles du Bos. The great masters of criticism were to serve as examples, and critics were to serve literature. This is what their illustrious predecessors, Abbés Casgrain and Roy, had never understood.

DAVID M. HAYNE

The Major Options of French-Canadian Literature

In 1969 Les presses de l'Université de Montréal published *Conférences J.A. de Sève*, a collection of ten essays originally presented in an annual series of lectures by authorities on Quebec literature. While the inclusion of David M. Hayne in such a distinguished gathering shows the respect with which his work is regarded in Quebec, it also serves as a reminder that not all Quebec criticism is written by the Québécois themselves. Like Mason Wade, an American whose *The French Canadians* has long been considered a classic, or Auguste Viatte, a Frenchman whose *Histoire littéraire de l'Amérique française* and *Anthologie littéraire de l'Amerique francophone* both received widespread distribution and attention in Quebec, David M. Hayne is an 'outsider' whose knowledge of and opinions on Quebec make him a respected figure.

Professor of French at the University of Toronto, Hayne is an exemplary practitioner of what might be called academic criticism: minutely researched and documented, measured yet engaging in style, carefully structured and clearly developed. His discussion, which moves between literary history and thematic synthesis, results in a blend of scholarship and critical insight that is thorough, instructive, and enlightening.

As in the following article, written in 1964, Hayne frequently adopts the methods and perspectives of comparative literature in order both to gain a larger view of Quebec literature and at the same time to demonstrate its uniqueness. Perhaps this view from 'outside' also accounts for the seeming objectivity and serenity of Hayne's criticism, for he approaches the field with the perceptions of an informed but detached observer.

David M. Hayne's contributions to literary studies in Quebec include such original and painstaking research as his joint authorship of a bibliography of the French-Canadian novel from 1837 to 1900. More recently he has collaborated with Antoine Sirois in the compilation of an annual bibliography of comparative Canadian / Quebec criticism. Since the relationships between Canadian and Quebec literatures have recently become a subject of widespread scholarly interest, Hayne has emerged as an authority in this area as well, providing much of the academic 'groundwork' for its development.

THE MAJOR OPTIONS OF FRENCH-CANADIAN LITERATURE

In judging a body of literature one loves, it is not easy to remain objective. The Canadian scholar doing research on Japanese or Arabic literature can approach his subject with a freedom of mind and lack of bias never possible for one studying the intellectual life of his own country. Canadians interested in Canadian letters are always liable to two contrary temptations; either to be uncritically chauvinistic or determinedly but perhaps excessively objective.

In order to gain the necessary perspective, let us assume for a moment the stance of a comparatist who becomes aware of Canadian literature in French for the first time. He observes that it is a relatively small literature which has emerged only recently and is written in French, that is, written in a major language with its own literary tradition. A provisional classification of this French-Canadian literature places it in the category of minor literatures in a major language, a category that it shares with Australian literature or English-Canadian literature written in English, the various Latin American literatures written in Spanish, and Brazilian literature written in Portuguese.

This seems an appropriate classification because the groups that we have just distinguished offer several similarities:

1 / It may be first noted that these are all *minor* literatures. The volume of their literary production is relatively low, amounting to perhaps a few hundred titles per year; the number of copies printed is rather small in comparison with printings in the great world literatures; their international circulation through foreign editions or translations is only beginning; and finally their influence on other literatures is minimal.

2 / They are, moreover, *modern* literatures, usually dating back only about a century. True, in almost all cases a colonial literature preceded the emergence of the tiny national literature. But this colonial literature was more a collection of writings than the expression of a people; made up of accounts

of voyages or explorers' narratives, administrators' correspondence and memoirs, religious annals, or histories of the colony, it was the work of mariners, civil servants, distinguished visitors or missionaries. Although they actually dealt with the past and future of the colony, these writings were really part of the literature of a mother country, France, England, Spain, or Portugal.

At some point in the history of the young nation, we notice the decline of colonial literature and the birth of an indigenous literature. This renaissance occurs most often in the first third of the nineteenth century, and it is interesting in this regard to compare dates: the first Spanish-American novel[1] is dated 1816, while the first English-Canadian,[2] Australian,[3] and French-Canadian[4] novels appeared in 1824, 1830, and 1837 respectively. The first volume of poems written by an Australian[5] was published in 1823; in Canada the corresponding dates are 1825[6] for English Canada and 1830[7] for French Canada. One of the first literary magazines to be published in Australia goes back to 1821;[8] it might be compared to the *Nova Scotian* which Joseph Howe bought in 1828 or Michel Bibaud's *Bibliothèque canadienne* founded in 1825.

3 / It should be stressed that this convergence of dates is not purely fortuitous; in fact, each of these young literatures was born in a time of political emancipation or national independence. At the end of a more or less extended colonial period, and after more or less violent struggles, each nation began to become aware of its own existence and to want to express this awareness in writing. Thus it is only natural that the first literary works should be strongly impregnated with patriotic fervour. In Latin America an almost uninterrupted series of revolutions between 1810 and 1824 is reflected in the patriotic odes of José Joaquin Olmedo; these can be equated with the patriotic poetry Octave Crémazie composed after the troubled period of 1837–8.

There is obviously a break in the literary history of the colony when the young indigenous literature is left to itself after the liberation or emancipation of the country. As a result, the writings of the colonial period are rarely taken as models; rather they are neglected and sometimes even held in contempt, as in Latin America. In any case, the literary break is likely to be a sharp one, and the young literature finds itself deprived of any native intellectual tradition.

4 / It may be noticed lastly that each of these small literatures utilizes as its means of literary expression a 'cultivated language,' the language of a great civilization which has through the centuries developed a rich, abundant, and world-famous literature. This inescapable presence hovering over the painful beginnings of the young literature has the effect of considerably

prolonging in literature the period of dependency which the young nation is trying to terminate in politics. Having barely emerged from the colonial era of their history, the young nations want to rush headlong through the whole process of maturation and attain the level of the older countries as soon as possible. Since they are totally lacking in intellectual and artistic resources, however, each is forced to nurture its literary tradition on that of the mother country. But in doing so the infant literature runs the risk of being only the pale reflection of another literature whose central preoccupations and profound needs are out of touch with its own. Or the small literature may end up being absorbed by the large one, thus completely losing its autonomy.

This brings us to the crux of the problem for any minor literature in a major language. Corresponding to the geographical division 'homeland/motherland' we find a deeply imbedded dualism in the mental constitution of the young nation, evident in many aspects of the life of the collectivity; it is this phenomenon which Jean Le Moyne has so nicely expressed in a single sentence from his article on Henry James: 'It has always been a question,' he says, 'of the new world and the old.'[9] In literature this dualism is felt as a double tension which acts secretly on the evolution of the national literature and, with a few exceptions, gives rise to the principal initiatives of its writers.

I shall thus attempt to demonstrate that the whole history of French-Canadian literature is dominated by this double tension and that the principal options of this minor literature in a major language stem to some extent from its necessarily bipolar character.

It must first be shown to what degree all options of this literature, both large and small, stem from this duality; later I shall choose three major options among those available and examine them more closely; finally I shall show how the bipolarity I refer to is linked to the alternation of literary generations in French Canada.

Let us attempt to survey the variety of options open to the author, publisher, retailer, and reader of a French-Canadian book.

As soon as he decides to write, the French-Canadian author must ask himself, consciously or unconsciously, a series of questions which reveal an unavoidable dualism.

1 / What is the French-Canadian writer's goal in writing? Should he be doing it only for the pleasure of creating, for the enrichment of Canadian literature in French, or for the world development of the French culture and heritage?

2 / Precisely what readers is he aiming at: his fellow French Canadians who are apt to share his tastes, or a larger but also more demanding audience, the reading public in all French-speaking countries?

3 / What themes and what subjects will he write about? Where will he seek the setting for his novel or the images for his poetry?

4 / Once all these questions have been decided, what literary techniques and what style will he use? To what degree should he follow the practices of one or of several French writers, and to what degree should he try to be original? Should he eliminate Canadianisms from his diction or should he consciously attempt to write in the language that French Canadians speak?

5 / When the author has finally laid down his pen, what publisher should he send his manuscript to? Will he mail it to a publishing house in Montreal or be bold enough to ship it off to Paris? In the first case, how is the local editor likely to respond when faced with a choice between the risk of publishing a home-grown work and the surer profits from publishing school texts or re-editions of continental French authors? Perhaps it is better not even to mention the delicate situation of the French publisher considering the advantages of publishing a manuscript from distant Canada.

6 / Finally, are French-Canadian books likely to be the first choice of booksellers, critics, readers, and book lovers, or will they rate only second place?

That it is possible to ask all these questions and to reply with two series of answers that are diametrically opposed shows that the dilemma between a *French-Canadian outlook* and a *French outlook* is apparent at all levels of literary activity: writing, publishing, distribution, reading, and criticism. The attention of our writers has always vacillated between their own small country and what lies overseas, and in each generation they have defined and situated themselves in relation to this double attraction.

In the light of this basic assumption I shall examine three of our major problems: literary language, subjects and themes, and literary relations with France.

It is with deliberate intent that I approach the language problem first. As the basic characteristic of any national group, language is the necessary starting point of any literary expression. This explains why a theory of language is the cornerstone of all great literary theories. The Pléiade took great pride in its *Deffence et illustration de la langue françoyse*, just as French classicism is inconceivable without Vaugelas's *Remarques sur la langue française* or the *Entretiens d'Artiste et d'Eugène* of Bouhours. Likewise Victor Hugo was justly proud of his efforts to bring the old dictionary down to the level of the people, for this was a necessary step in literary reform. Similarly, the cultivation of rare words by the Parnassian poets and the Surrealists' distrust of logical syntax were in no way mere caprices, for these linguistic elements are an integral part of their literary doctrine.

Writers in French Canada realized at a very early date the primordial importance of this question of language. In a letter addressed to Abbé Casgrain in January 1867, Crémazie reflected upon the problem of minor literatures in major languages:

What we lack in Canada is a language of our own. If we spoke Iroquois or Huron our literature would survive. Unfortunately we write and speak, albeit in pitiful fashion, the language of Bossuet and Racine...I repeat, if we spoke Huron or Iroquois the work of our writers would attract attention in Europe...A novel or poem translated from the Iroquois would have them all aflutter, whereas they don't even bother reading a book written in French by a settler in Québec or Montreal.[10]

The feeling of linguistic inferiority with regard to France was soon to become one of the constants of the French-Canadian national conscience. About 1880 this feeling was expressed in a great number of magazine articles, brochures, and even books, in which Arthur Buies, Oscar Dunn, Jules-Paul Tardivel, and somewhat later Louis Fréchette denounced their compatriots' barbarisms and anglicisms. Twenty years later the Société du bon parler français continued the well-intentioned but amateur crusade of the 1880s in a more methodical and competent manner. Up to this time people were concerned almost exclusively with the spoken language, but the new Société intended not only to study and defend the language but also to encourage the writing of literary works 'suited to transform French speech in Quebec into a language that would respect both tradition and the natural progress of the idiom.'[11]

For, states Camille Roy about this time,

...our written language is usually quite poor and lacking in many of the words we should have to convey clearly all the nuances of thought...[12]

This is precisely what Joachim du Bellay complained about. Thus the founding of the Société du bon parler français may be said to constitute our *Deffence et illustration de la langue françoyse*.

The Société continued its work in promoting literature by soliciting original articles on Canadian customs for its *Bulletin du parler français* and by organizing in 1911 its first literary contest, to which twenty-five contestants submitted manuscripts. The tremendous success the following year of the Premier Congrès de la langue française, held in Quebec, closely followed by the publication in 1914 of Adjutor Rivard's *Etudes sur les parlers de France au Canada*, seemed evidence of the new movement's success.

It was about this time that the theory of a French-Canadian literary language was called into question. Jules Fournier, who had maintained since 1906 that there was no French-Canadian literature,[13] protested that a programme to purify the French-Canadian language would not compensate for the lack of intellectual development in his compatriots.[14] The same tune was to be heard from the *Nigog* group and especially from Marcel Dugas: 'A French language exists; a Canadian language does not.'[15] Later, a few individuals like Jean-Charles Harvey stated that 'the French language is one and indivisible.'[16]

Meanwhile, the advocates of an autonomous French-Canadian language were formulating an opposing theory which they spared no pains in promoting. In 1929 Harry Bernard declared that 'the French language of the rest of the world...is not the language of French Canadians,'[17] an opinion shared by Albert Pelletier, who wrote, 'Parisian French is not our language.'[18] He went on to explain, a bit maliciously:

And if our 'patois' becomes too difficult for the academicians, well, so much the better: that way we will have our own language... The French, if they want to read us, can translate us, just as they translate Provençal literature; and you can be sure that they will do a much better job than we could because they know their language much better than we can ever possibly hope to.[19]

However, in spite of the mock aggressiveness, he merely asked that 'Canadian writers...make sensible, tasteful and artful use of our Canadian vocabulary.'[20]

About 1933 Claude-Henri Grignon joined the fray and immediately outdid all the others:

If we continue to write in the language commonly spoken by French writers, we shall never be able to produce better books than theirs, and no nation on earth will read our works, whether they deal with regional themes or not.[21]

And he added:

We do not write the French of French men of letters. That would be impossible. We are taught two languages at school. We speak two languages fluently. We can never know either of them perfectly ...[22]

This false modesty, however, gives way to a sort of lexicographer's pride when the same writer protests that in *Menaud, maître-draveur** the Canadian-isms were printed in italics:

The ultimate blasphemy! Why did the novelist have all these touches of local flavour printed in italics? Was he afraid of committing some awful sin? ... It is both inexplicable and unpardonable.23

There is no need to look for italics in the postwar novels. The group of novelists one might call the 'generation of 1945,' a group which included Gabrielle Roy, Roger Lemelin, Germaine Guèvremont, Yves Thériault and others, freely used Canadian expressions and even anglicisms in their dialogues – for instance the 'neveurmagne't in *Le survenant.‡*

Subsequently, since about 1950, there has been an ever-increasing campaign to make the French-Canadian language more French. One of the original founders of this movement, Rex Desmarchais,25 is still deeply involved in it, as shown by a recent article in *Le Devoir* in which he sums up his point of view:

Our writers do not have two or ten different varieties of French to choose from, but only one: international French, Parisian French, that pitiless filter and living hearth of the language. The French our writers write must be understood in Paris and throughout the world. Our books should need neither translations nor glossaries.10

The final sentence in this passage refers to the glossaries several Parisian editors had included in the back of French editions of Canadian novels.

At the current stage of this back-to-French movement, we find a number of university linguists leading the fight, including Roch Valin who emphatically attacks the concept of a French-Canadian language:

Attempting to set Franco-Canadian speech up against the French of France, as people are unthinkingly and chauvinistically doing now, is not only childishly presumptuous but suicidal as well.10

René de Chantal, in his *Chroniques de français*, shares the same views but makes a useful distinction where creative writing is concerned.

---

*Translated by Alan Sullivan as *Boss of the River* (Toronto: Ryerson 1947) (ed.)
†A phonetic transcription of the English 'never mind' (ed.)
‡Translated by Eric Sutton as *The Outlander* (Toronto: McGraw-Hill 1950) (ed.)

Our local and regional novels may pulse with the speech of French Canada, but works of international scope, which we will one day produce, will be written in French.[28]

And this is apparently what is shown by a careful reading of the young novelists who have emerged over the past four or five years.

From a linguistic point of view, then, it seems that the two 'magnetic poles' are Canadian French and international French. This at least is the opinion given by Jean-Marie Laurence in a speech to the Troisième Congrès de la langue française au Canada:

Our inferiority complex with regard to France creates problems in the development of our national character and causes us to react in two opposite ways, which are particularly clear in the field of linguistics: identification and opposition.

The extreme Francophiles choose identification, maintaining that our language (phonetics, vocabulary, and syntax) should be completely identified with Parisian French. Those who advocate complete independence, on the other hand, hold that we should invent an original French based on the popular language spoken here, without regard for, if not in opposition to, Parisian usage.

And he concludes that outside 'these two extremes reactions (identification and opposition), the choice of free imitation would seem most normal...'[29]

No doubt we must make a distinction here: spoken language, being more flexible and racy than literary language, can accommodate local archaisms and neologisms for a longer period. Literary language, on the other hand, being more finished and precise, will draw imperceptibly closer to international French as authors come to reserve their Canadian vocabulary for descriptions and dialogues. But here we have started to leave the linguistic field for the literary one, where we shall see that the bipolar character of the linguistic options is equally apparent in the choice of themes and subjects.

Between 1840 and 1860, in the period when French-Canadian literature was taking its first painful steps, the eyes of all young French-Canadian writers were glued on the great French masters. Newspapers and magazines of the time frequently printed poems by Lamartine and Victor Hugo, or featured novels by Balzac or Dumas in serial instalments. The poet Lenoir-Rolland was an avid reader of Lamartine's *Graziella*, P.J.O. Chauveau's *Charles Guérin* was modelled on Balzac's novels, and Georges Boucher de Boucherville wrote a serial novel in the style of Eugène Sue.[30] French influence was so prevalent that the young Abbé Casgrain felt compelled to protest, in the preface to his *Légendes*, against the invasion of 'modern writings, even the most dangerous,' and undertook to 'give Canadian letters a healthier direction.'[31] As early as 1866 he declared himself in favour of Canadian themes and against the French school of realism. The path of our literature, he wrote, is laid out before us:

It will be the faithful mirror of our small nation's different phases of existence, with its ardent faith, its noble aspirations, its bursts of enthusiasm, its heroic character, and its generous, passionate devotion. It will be free of the stamp of modern realism which reflects both impious thought and materialism; and it will thus gain in life, spontaneity, originality and action.[32]

This narrow conception of the nature and function of Canadian literature governed the writings of the 1860 movement and was reaffirmed in identical form by Pamphile Le May in a speech given in 1880.[33] The unanimity of French-Canadian writers in this period explains not only the dismal uniformity of the era's literary production but also the total absence of a realistic or Parnassian movement in nineteenth-century French Canada. The systematic exclusion of French writers as evidenced in this period, for reasons most often unconnected with literature, is a phenomenon that has no parallel in other minor literatures at this time. In distant Brazil, for instance, Théophile Gautier was admired as early as 1870 and a French-style Parnassian movement came into being about a dozen years later.[34] In French Canada, on the other hand, writers like Pamphile Le May were busy composing their sonnets without ever having read Heredia;[35] according to Fréchette, the first time anyone in Canada heard the name of Leconte de Lisle was about 1875.[36] As for the novelists, Flaubert, Zola, Maupassant, and the Goncourt brothers were banned, while Balzac, George Sand, and Stendhal were little known. It is not surprising, then, that French-Canadian fiction took so long to produce any realistic novels. The fact is that for a whole generation French-Canadian literature marked time, a victim of the fear its intellectual leaders had of the French realists, naturalists, and even the Parnassians.

About 1890 the intellectual blockade was lifted and Verlaine and the 'decadents' were read. Poetry entered a period of renewed vitality with the Ecole littéraire de Montréal, and Emile Nelligan dared to write poems that were not specifically Canadian. The novel continued to doze, although Rodolphe Girard committed the sin of writing a realistic novel which the authorities quickly condemned for immorality. In the month of June, 1904, Ferdinand Paradis published a belligerent article in La Nouvelle-France entitled 'The Emancipation of Our Literature.' After condemning Chapman for having had one of his books published in Paris, he went on:

The French were of no use to our ancestors in their struggle to transplant our family heritage intact, and we can do just as nicely without them now that it is a question of our creating a literature and of our intellectual progress.[37]

Several months later, Abbé Camille Roy, then at the beginning of his career, made a more discriminating plea for 'the nationalization of our literature' at the annual public meeting of the Société du parler français au Canada. This authoritative lecture marks an important date in French-Canadian literature. While acknowledging the need for French-Canadian writers to look occasionally to French sources, he warned his audience:

We must recognize that a system of free trade, if too widely adopted, could in this way compromise the independence of Canadian letters...[38]

In fact, he goes on, 'from this point of view...our greatest enemy is contemporary French literature.'[39] Contexts and attitudes are so different in France that Canadian literature must be distinct and independent. The preoccupations of this literature are those of the nation:

Thus we must keep constantly returning to the study of our history and traditions, and must base our aesthetics on the combined virtues, merits, and aspirations which distinguish our race. We must consider literature not as a superficial and frivolous matter of mere form but as the expression of all that is most intimate, serious, and profound in life. We must infuse it with all the thoughts, sentiments, and emotions which best reveal the Canadian consciousness. And we must fill it to overflowing with all the things which make up the very fabric of our history and our national life.
Let us build here a literature which is both of ourselves and for ourselves.[40]

This view was broad enough that, several years later, Abbé Roy could approve of the exoticism in Paul Morin's poetry:

Although it is good to nationalize one's literature, this must not be to the extent of narrowing the visual field of the Canadian mind to the precise limit of our own horizons. Canadians too can be interested in all that is human...[41]

With other literary theorists, however, this broad and intelligent concept actually narrowed to the point where the doctrine of a national literature was transformed into a theory of regionalism. Much of the impetus for this change came from the literary magazine Le Terroir and the first works of the literary school of the same name. Thus we see the emergence about 1918 of two opposing factions: the regionalists on one side, and on the other, the 'exotics' or advocates of a universal literature. The battle between regionalists and exotics broke out two years later,[42] and although Canadian literary historians continue to ignore it, it marked a decisive turning point in the evolution of this literature. Olivar Asselin, Victor Barbeau, and Marcel Dugas were the chief spokesmen for the universalists, but in the end it was the regionalists who won out. A dozen years later Harry Bernard would coin the catchword for the whole movement:

Catholic and French in essence, our literature will be Canadian in its achievements. This means that our books, written by Canadians, will strive to show the souls of our people, to paint and interpret the place in which they live and the landscape that surrounds them. This they shall do with such precision and authority that from the first glance there shall be no possible doubt as to their author's nationality... We wish to *write Canadian*.[43]

And between the wars, this is what they did, creating a French-Canadian regional literature that was national and utilitarian, but which lacked the frankly political character of French regionalism. And just as French region- alism was very much out of favour at the time of the Liberation,[44] the Canadian movement died out quietly as the province of Quebec became more industrialized. Mgr Félix-Antoine Savard put an end to the long controversy in 1953:

For heaven's sake, let us reach the point where people can fill their buckets wherever they want.[45]

Actually, Canadian authors had already widened their range of writing since the Second World War. Following the poetic revolution initiated by Saint-Denys-Garneau, poetry had redirected itself toward the universal. The novel had broken with rural regionalism; like Gabrielle Roy, its practi- tioners followed the example of Georges Duhamel, or like Robert Charbon- neau, the model of François Mauriac. Only the theatre, where dialogue is all important, had remained faithful to local concerns, waiting for Jacques Languirand to make his appearance.

With regard to themes and subjects, then, it is clear that the positions taken by Canadian writers reveal the same dichotomy as we previously saw concerning language. The third major option, that of the literary affilia- tions of French-Canadian authors, must now be considered briefly. From the very beginnings of Canadian literature it had been fashionable to speak of Canada as a literary province of France. Abbé Casgrain had identified it as 'an intellectual colony'[46] of the mother country, while Faucher de Saint-Maurice envisioned a Canadian literature which would be to French literature 'what Brittany is to the rest of France.'[47] Jean-Charles Harvey affirmed that in literature 'Quebec is a province of France,'[48] and Jules Léger stated that 'only one history of French literature exists, and it includes all works written in French by writers living in every latitude.'[49] Also, feelings of inferiority and dependence with regard to France were frequently found in writings by French Canadians. Nevertheless, I propose this time to abandon my historical analysis and to deal with only one stage of this third evolution: the controversy carried on in 1945 between Robert Charbonneau and several French writers.[50]

When the Comité national des écrivains, presided over by Jean Cassou, opposed the reprinting of works by French writers charged with being collaborators, Robert Charbonneau, in his capacity as publisher of the Editions de l'Arbre in Montreal, maintained that he had the right to publish the prewar books of such writers as Maurras, Bainville, and Massis. 'The fact that Maurras and the others were collaborators,' he wrote in April 1946, 'changes nothing in works published before 1940.'[51] This attitude was violently denounced by Jean Cassou and Louis Aragon in *Les Lettres françaises*.[52] Meanwhile, the quarrel had widened. Georges Duhamel, on his return from Canada, had compared the Canadian literary world to a branch on a French tree:

...a healthy branch which now seems separated from the original trunk by a thick wall, but a branch none the less, and one which does honour both to the tree and its vitality.[53]

Etienne Gilson, however, knew Canada better. 'If we are the tree,' he said, 'there has never been a tree that took less care of its branch ... It is no longer a branch ... but a tree in its own right ... Canadian culture owes its survival and fruition only to Canadians ...'[54]

It was on this question of French Canada's cultural autonomy that the quarrel was to continue during the winter of 1946-7. In his articles in *La Nouvelle Relève* and *Le Canada*, Robert Charbonneau held firm against the combined forces of Stanislas Fumet, André Billy, Jérôme and Jean Tharaud, and even René Garneau, in affirming that Canadian letters had no need to copy French models:

Our writers have only to continue as they began. They need only be Canadian and look for their techniques not in a single country, nor even throughout a single country, but everywhere. This is what will enable them to maintain their place in world literature.[55]

This was seconded by Professor Gilson:

...if people really think that French-Canadian literature takes its life-blood from French sources, I shall continually oppose them, because it seems to me to be simply untrue.[56]

In the summer of 1947 the debate grew more bitter following the banning in Quebec of the film *Les enfants du paradis*. This was seen as proof of a concerted offensive against French culture, and François Mauriac maliciously suggested 'sending massive doses of the works of Delly* to our dear Canadian friends.'[57]

This kind of bickering can easily blind us to the importance of such a minor controversy. Its meaning is clear, however: for the first time in a hundred years of book publishing in French Canada, a Canadian was arguing a literary question on equal footing with Frenchmen. If we recall that it is about this same time that Parisian editors started publishing and distributing French-Canadian books in France, that Canadian works began to win literary prizes in France, and that Canadian books began to be translated into other languages, we can begin to appreciate the real significance of this transatlantic quarrel. In fact it marks the end of the intellectual tutelage of French-Canadian literature to the mother country. French literary influence in Canada remains as important as before, but intellectual relations with France have now entered a new phase, paralleled in the administration field by the establishment of *La maison du Québec* in Paris.

We have thus far been examining the three major options (language, orientation, and affiliation) as though each had its own existence independent of the others, and while this perspective lends itself to the analysis of tendencies, it must now be abandoned at the end of this article. Fustel de Coulanges asserted that a life of analysis was necessary for each hour of synthesis; thus it is perhaps permissible to sum up these dozen or so pages of analysis with one page of synthesis.

---

*Delly, pseudonym of Marie Petitjean de la Rosière and her brother Frédéric, was the author of a great number of sentimental and melodramatic novels which were extremely popular in France. (ed.)

If the three currents of thought previously outlined are superimposed upon one another, we discover that as a general rule the periods of identification with French literature alternate with those of opposition to this literature: each period of literary dependence is followed by a period of consolidation during which there is an attempt to adapt the new lessons to the needs of the community. The young francophile Romanticism of 1840 is followed by the patriotic Romantic movement of 1860; the eclectic Ecole littéraire de Montréal gives way to the nationalistic regionalism of the rural 'terroir' school. The rhythm of these alternations generally parallels that of successive generations. It is a well-known fact that we often react against the tastes of the previous generation in favour of those of our grandparents.

From these observations we see that the bipolar movement of French-Canadian literature in the course of its historic evolution resembles the oscillations of a pendulum, or a series of waves which follow the rhythm of literary generations. These oscillations, which were very wide in the beginning, have become progressively more restrained, so that in our own time the contrasts are much less pronounced: the pendulum has been slowing down. As French-Canadian literature becomes increasingly mature, its internal divisions become less important.

We have stated that French-Canadian literature is a minor literature in a major language. Like other literatures in the same category, it has had to contend with the problems stemming from the overpowering presence of a great international literature in the same language, in this case the literature of France. This presence has given rise within French-Canadian literature to opposing tendencies which have always acted upon its evolution, provoking certain attitudes with regard to the literary language, the orientation of the literature, and the affiliations of its writers, all of which have varied more or less regularly as generations of writers have opted for 'the new world' or 'the old.' In our own time the movement of the pendulum seems on the point of stopping altogether; French-Canadian literature has at last reached its equilibrium.

NOTES

1 José Joaquin Fernández de Lizardi *Periquillo Sarniento*
2 Julia Beckwith *St. Ursula's Convent*
3 H. Savery *Quintus Servinton*
4 Ph. Aubert de Gaspé, Jr *L'influence d'un livre*
5 W.C. Wentworth *Australasia*

6 O. Goldsmith *The Rising Village*

7 M. Bibaud *Epîtres, satires, chansons, épigrammes et autres pièces de vers*

8 *The Australian Magazine*

9 Jean Le Moyne *Convergences* (Montreal: Editions HMH 1962) [tr. Philip Stratford, *Convergences: Essays from Québec* (Toronto: Ryerson 1966) 17]

10 O.Crémazie *Œuvres complètes* (Montreal: Beauchemin et Valois 1882) 40-1

11 *Bulletin du parler français au Canada* I (1902) 3

12 C. Roy *Essais sur la littérature canadienne* (Quebec: Garneau 1907) 351. The text dates from 1904.

13 'Comme préface,' *La Revue canadienne* LI (1906) 23-33, especially p. 25 and 'Réplique à M. ab der Halden,' LII (1907) 128-36. These two pieces are reproduced in *Mon encrier* (Montreal: Mme Jules Fournier 1922) II, 5-34.

14 *Mon encrier* II, 162-209

15 M. Dugas *Littérature canadienne. Aperçus* (Paris: Firmin-Didot 1929) 123

16 J.C. Harvey *Pages de critique* (Quebec: Le Soleil 1926) 48

17 H. Bernard *Essais critiques* (Montreal: Librairie d'Action canadienne-française 1929) 85

18 A. Pelletier *Carquois* (Montreal: Librairie d'Action canadienne-française 1931) 29

19 Pelletier 26

20 Pelletier 28

21 C.-H. Grignon *Ombres et clameurs* (Montreal: Lévesque 1933) 189

22 Grignon 191

23 C.-H. Grignon *Les pamphlets de Valdombre* I (1937) 393

24 cf. J.S. Tassie *The Noun, Adjective, Pronoun and Verb of Popular Speech in French Canada. An Examination of the Morphology and Syntax of the Spoken Word in the French-Canadian Novel* Diss. University of Toronto 1957.

25 R. Desmarchais 'Langue et culture' *Amérique française* I (1948) 1-4

26 R. Desmarchais 'Oui ou non?' *Le Devoir* 30 November 1963

27 R. Valin 'Quelques aspects linguistiques de l'enseignement du français' *La Nouvelle Revue canadienne* III (1953) 340

28 R. de Chantal *Chroniques de français* (Ottawa: Editions de l'Université d'Ottawa 1956) xv

29 J.-M. Laurence 'Littérature et patriotisme' *Mémoires du Troisième Congrès de la langue française au Canada* (Québec: Ferland 1953) 263

30 We have examined this question at length in two articles included in volumes I and III of the *Archives des lettres canadiennes*.

31 H.-R. Casgrain *Œuvres complètes* (Montreal: Beauchemin et Fils 1885) I, 11. The preface dates from 1861.

32 Casgrain, I, 368. First published in *Le Foyer canadien*, IV (January 1866)

33 H.-J.-J.-B. Chouinard *La fête nationale des Canadiens français célébrée à Québec en 1880* (Quebec: A. Côté 1881) 382

34 G. le Gentil *La littérature portuguaise* 2nd ed. rev. and augm. (Paris: A. Colin 1951) 189

35 Letter of 1 September 1905, quoted by Mgr C. Roy *A l'ombre des érables* (Quebec: L'Action sociale 1924) 31, note

36 M. Sauvalle *Le lauréat manqué* (Montreal: 1894) 62

37 *La Nouvelle-France* III (1904) 291

38 Roy *Essais* 352. Lecture delivered on 5 December, 1904

39 Roy *Essais* 354

40 Roy *Essais* 365–6

41 C. Roy *Nouveaux essais de littérature canadienne* (Quebec: L'Action sociale 1914) 290

42 cf. A Lozeau 'Le Régionalisme littéraire. Opinions et théories' *Mémoires de la Société Royale du Canada* 3rd series, XIV (1920) section 1 pp. 83–95; F. Robert 'Littérature nationale et littérature régionale' *Le Canada français* IV (1920) 235–40, 336–49

43 H. Bernard *Essais critiques* 44

44 cf. G. Roger *Situation du roman régionaliste français* (Paris: Jouve 1951)

45 F.-A. Savard 'L'Ecrivain canadien-français et la langue française' in *Mémoires du Troisième Congrès de la langue française au Canada* 272

46 H.-R. Casgrain *Œuvres complètes*, I, 361

47 N.-H.-E. Faucher de Saint-Maurice *Choses et autres* (Montreal: Duvernay et Dansereau 1874) 32

48 J.-C. Harvey *Pages de critique* 48

49 J. Léger *Le Canada français et son expression littéraire* (Paris: Nizet et Bastard 1938) 6

50 The principal documents of this controversy are reproduced in R. Charbonneau *La France et nous* (Montreal: L'Arbre 1947).

51 *La Nouvelle Relève* IV, No. 10 (April 1946) 848

52 Issues of 21 June 1946 and 17 January 1947. Quoted in part in *La France et nous* 27, 28 and 39–41

53 *Le Figaro* 4 January 1946. Quoted in *La France et nous* 27

54 *Le Monde* 6 January 1946. Quoted in *La France et nous* 27

55 *La France et nous* 47

56 *Une semaine dans le monde* 2nd yr. No. 50, 26 April 1947, p. 11. Quoted in *La France et nous* 62

57 *Combat* 25 April 1947. Quoted in *La France et nous* 67

HUBERT AQUIN

The Cultural Fatigue of French Canada

Hubert Aquin's fame as a novelist tends to obscure the fact that he has also produced a considerable body of non-fiction, much of which has been published in *Point de fuite* (1971) and *Blocs erratiques* (1977). Like his novels, Aquin's essays and articles show a wide variety of subject and approach; writing about everything from religion to miniskirts, his manner ranges from the scholarly to the scabrous, from cool logic to passionate polemic. Whatever the topic, Aquin's treatment of it is likely to be radically original, for his intelligence is probing, eccentric, and extreme. Occasionally his delight in paradox and enigma brings some of his texts to the brink of incomprehensibility; others, however, are models of reasoned analysis.

Because Aquin's non-fiction does not often deal directly with literature, its status as 'criticism' is somewhat uncertain. Several essays are concerned with the act of writing (and of reading), but it is more typical of Aquin to explore cultural questions of a larger nature. His early articles in particular reflect the philosophical bases of his classical education, just as they reveal a penchant for abstraction that marks his entire literary output. During his association with the magazine *Liberté* in the early sixties, his attention turns from religious topics to increasingly nationalistic considerations. Then, after a period of intense preoccupation with the question of revolution, his interests widen to include the most controversial issues in Quebec society and culture: history, language, politics, and the quality of life.

The following essay was written in 1962 as a response to one of Pierre Elliott Trudeau's famous attacks on Quebec nationalism. Revealing Aquin's broad cultural background and his talent for reasoned, intelligent debate, it also displays his formidable, abstract intellect. Although his discourse becomes more emotional towards the end, one senses the author's efforts to remain as objective and logical as possible, and the measure of his success in this regard can be gauged by a comparison with Trudeau's article: here it is Aquin, and not the future prime minister, who may well be the master of 'reason over passion.' The pertinence of Aquin's arguments to the 'national debate' some seventeen years later is a tribute both to the author's prescience and to his grasp of the issues at stake.

As erratic and energetic as his writing, Aquin's career including broadcasting, film-making, politics, teaching, and publishing. He was often in the public eye, whether for his outspoken opinions, his celebrated resignations, or for the prestigious literary prizes awarded him. Remembered as one of the most brilliant writers Quebec has produced, Hubert Aquin died in Montreal, 15 March 1977.

THE CULTURAL FATIGUE OF FRENCH CANADA

A total earth requires nations that are fully aware.[1]
Teilhard de Chardin

The minds of French-Canadian 'thinkers' are infused with unconscious relativism. Except for a prudent minority who manage to maintain an independent or neutral stance, any intellectual who attempts to understand the French-Canadian problem is subjected to mental vivisection by those who try to determine which side of the fence he is really on. And as soon as his brain has been surgically classified, his ability to know anything is immediately challenged and it is assumed that his particular conditioning is known once and for all. Our scholars have encouraged this sort of relativism themselves, and it inevitably turns against them; thus it becomes useless to give any credence at all to a writer like Michel Brunet, an historian of the 'nationalist' school or, from a different angle, Jean-Charles Falardeau, a sociologist of the so-called 'Father Lévesque' school and an avowed federalist. Labels, although they are not always quite so blatant or undeserved, are exclusive things, and I know very few journalists or academics who have not in this way come to be identified with a specific, closed, ideological group. Ideas tend to be automatically considered as being strongly representative, and as a result they become connected with a particular bias or school of thought and lose their dialectical effectiveness. By considering their rivals simply as products of a narrow conditioning, intellectuals in French Canada have come to resemble deaf people shouting at one another; at the same time they have destroyed any hope one might have had in their own powers of intellection.

For my part, I refuse to accept the idea that any one person can dogmatically speak of reality as though his special way of presenting it were completely objective; on the other hand, I do not want to get involved in ideological skirmishes and start accusing others of presenting only a partial view of a reality they are trying to make me understand in its entirety. That tactic is too easy. Besides, I hold that the act of thinking has a definite power of elucidation that no conditioning can account for. In other words, the real dialectic is in dialogue, and not in two parallel monologues. It is still possible to think, and it is such an important act that even if it is done by a social or political 'adversary,' it should not be thought of as a hymn that only members of one's own congregation can sing. An adversary may discover just as much truth and may understand just as much about reality as the person on 'my' side or one who shares 'my' views.

Situations of this sort must be defined from within the dialectical tension between different viewpoints and situations – not from the outside, or from above. The dialectical process generates lucidity and logic but under no circumstances should it ever stoop to the level of opposition between two political parties which, as we know, by their very nature refuse any attempt at comprehension. Political partisanship is a means of action, not a mode of thinking: at best, parties think of themselves as 'ideological,' locked into a preconceived system of society whose perfect self-image should reveal how precarious or idealistic it is.

If I make these precautionary remarks, it is because I want to stress clearly that the study I am undertaking, based on an article by Pierre Elliott Trudeau called 'La nouvelle trahison des clercs,'[2] is not completely gratuitous; nor is it an underhanded attempt to prove that Trudeau's ideas are only the relatively brilliant reflection of a different option from one used to define me! His article is clearly an attempt at rational argumentation, and I would hate to see it construed to be simply the 'conditioned reflex' of a political activist or an anti-separatist.

NATIONALISM AND WAR

Pierre Elliott Trudeau's opinions and thoughts first struck me as forming a fairly coherent logical structure, nicely articulated in a vigorous style. And since he himself adopted a rational approach to his subject, I shall try to debate with him on the same level.

I agree with him that nationalism has often been a detestable, even unspeakable thing: the crimes committed in its name are perhaps even worse than the atrocities perpetrated in the name of liberty. In the nineteenth century, the resurgence of nationalistic feeling was marked by wars which gravely tarnished every possible form of nationalism and any system of thought stemming from it:

the nation-state idea has caused wars to become more and more total over the last two centuries; and that is the idea I take issue with so vehemently ... And there will be no end to wars between nations ... until the nation ceases to be the basis of the state. As for interstate wars, they will end only if the states give up that obsession whose very essence makes them exclusive and intolerant: sovereignty.[3]

The connection made between war and nationalism ('the nation-state idea') seems a bit doubtful.[4] The convergence of these two phenomena, even several times in succession, does not in itself establish a real causal relationship. The resurgence of wars poses a philosophical problem that is too easily restricted to its coincidence with nationalistic movements or outbursts of religious or ideological 'statism.'

War is a collective – or world-wide – extension of the notion of conflict, and I tend to believe that if war were studied scientifically (which strikes me as being as urgently necessary as the desire for peace), perhaps we would begin to discover basic explanations related to the entire human phenomenon. Until now, thinkers have either opposed war or else devised plans for peace, like those of Abbé de Saint-Pierre in 1713, and Jeremy Bentham in 1789; curiously, however, few have used their minds to study the phenomenon of war. A kind of social or individual repression causes men of learning to bury their heads where war is concerned. It took many centuries and one lucid man to separate the earth from the cosmos, and several centuries more before a certain Viennese doctor made the subconscious and its sexual fountain-head a subject for study; in the same way, war has produced a variety of convictions, emotions and mental blocks in men of learning, but it has never generated much lucidity. Such reactions are so prevalent that war, one of the most destructive phenomena in the history of man,[5] finds itself subjected, so to speak, to all sorts of hasty and partial explanations: wars are caused by God, Jews, economic conflicts, assassinations of princes, royal families, munitions manufacturers, nationalism, and so on, depending on the ideology of whoever is using war as an argument. Thus, in Trudeau's article, war is seen as resulting from nationalism, although the author never makes clear what correlation there is between this micro-phenomenon (the emergence of the nation-state) and its gigantic corollary which has steeped humanity in blood from the beginning. If reflection is to go beyond mere appearance in its search for a profound and comprehensive system of explanations for undeniable though perhaps still circumstantial coincidences, it had better not depend on dubious causality.

The causal connection between wars and nationalism is fragile, and it minimizes the importance of the phenomenon of war. How can these minor historical crises be the cause of such a terrible and mysterious phenomenon, particularly since war was part of man's experience long before the emergence of nations, and since by its own extension it has also overtaken the modern super-nations?[6]

The condemnation of war, however well justified, can never be a substitute for its rational comprehension by the human mind; the same was true of sex for a long time ... War is a destructive and dangerous occurrence that has often been denounced; responses to it, however, have always taken the form of combat attitudes (rejection, pacifism, condemnation) rather than scientific attitudes. Total war poses a philosophical problem for mankind; preoccupied in the past by a 'totality' that was never questioned, man must now study war in the same way he attempts to understand death; and, for the same reason, he must stop viewing war as a pure and undifferentiated evil. Instead of being a subject for scandal and peace conferences, war must become a field of humanistic study; it should no longer be used for instant arguments whose inherent maliciousness, too often unchallenged, acts like a bludgeon upon thought.

THE 'SUBCONSCIOUS' OF PEACE

War is a philosophical mystery which should be elucidated. Intimately connected with the particularity of man, war is one of his characteristic functions, and this fact should, in the minds of our thinkers, help rehabilitate what is considered to be an especially 'shameful' function. If war is considered as a function, it becomes instantly associated with all the contradictory, ambivalent characteristics of other human functions. In any case, it would be difficult to consider peace without recognizing the importance of its shady 'subconscious.'

Who knows whether our future historians may not include in the notion of war such things as conferences on disarmament, like the ones in Geneva, for example? Such conferences are obviously an expression of conflicts whose goal is the end of all armed conflict. They are, so to speak, variants of war, and when put together with all the other variants in which history abounds, they may help us understand war as a general phenomenon resulting from communication between any two groups of whatever size. If such were the case, Geneva diplomacy and verbal clashes at the UN would come to be considered as much a part of the full definition of war as military battles; thus war would have to be considered no longer solely as a catastrophe but as a confrontation in which the less heated issues might form

the basis for dialogue.⁷ In so-called 'primitive' societies, where great emphasis was put on unanimity, dissension was exorcized through a prescribed
ritual of confrontation and combat. ('In other words, there must be no
minority,' wrote Claude Lévi-Strauss, and I hope no one will accuse me
here of stealing his ideas!).

On the whole, these societies are egalitarian, mechanical in type, and governed by
the law of unanimity... The civilized peoples, on the other hand, produce a great
deal of order... but they also produce a great deal of entropy... in the form of social
conflicts and political struggles... things that primitive people guard against... The
great problem of civilization has, therefore, been to maintain differentials... They
work on the basis of a difference in potential, which finds concrete expression in
different forms of social hierarchy... We have seen these ensured by means of
slavery, then serfdom, and lastly with the creation of a proletariat. But as the
working-class struggle tends, to some extent, to iron out the differences, our
society has had to look for fresh ways of establishing differentials – colonialism and
the so-called imperialist policies, for instance – that is, it has had constantly to try,
either within the society itself or by subjecting conquered peoples, to create a
differential between a ruling section and a section that is ruled; but such a differential is always provisional...⁸

According to this view, the individual 'differentials' that are quickly
eliminated through ritual in primitive societies are reduced in great modern
societies by collective struggles and, to an increasing extent, at the price of
human lives. These differentials among classes, states, groups of states, or
cultures contain the seeds of all future struggles, whatever form these
struggles may take, whether military, parliamentary, or ideological. 'Differentials' breed struggle; by their constant, formless, protean metamorphoses, they also form a dialectic by continually recreating two
differentiated poles which will logically tend to move towards a balance
between the two. This basic inequality of all civilizations can be eliminated
only by relegating the inequality to a third consideration: nature. All in all,
power would no longer be based on the lesser power of another group, but
should be shared with it on the basis of power over inertia. This means that
the problem of disarmament cannot be formulated without a total revolution of all societies; once they have purged their tension against the superior term of opposition and gone beyond it, thus being somewhat equalized
in every sense, they could begin to identify themselves in relation to a new
dialectic term: nature, or the cosmos. States or groups so conceived cannot
be disarmed so long as there are other groups which, through differentials,
force them to define themselves as *opposites*. In order to change these groups'

inclination towards contradiction and struggle, it is first necessary to eliminate the original differentials between the groups.

It is misguided to expect groups divided into unequal, inferior, or differentiated divisions to bypass a stage in the dialectical process that regulates
even international gatherings. There is no possible short cut for moving
from a position of inferiority, of which the collectivity is painfully aware, to
a position of co-operation among equals, unless perhaps this short cut
simply involves the complete suppression of the minority group in question. 'At the same time as we are invited to build a universal civilization, we
are asked to renounce our own culture ...' said Léopold Senghor, reminding
us that the 'universal' can exist only through the free and active participation of all the particular elements which have chosen to create it. If the
particularities are really extravagant or merely strange whims, they will
not long withstand the 'excommunications' directed against them.

If we had the example of a country which had unilaterally renounced its national
culture and its past in order to become more progressive, more universal, then we
could follow its example. But this has not happened yet ... We are concerned to
fashion a national culture which will quite simply be a protective rampart for us
until the security of our whole planet can be realized.[9]

NATIONALISM VERSUS INTERNATIONALISM

War, you may say, is leading us away from the main point. Not at all. If I
first examined the second section of Pierre Elliott Trudeau's article, in
which he establishes a causal relationship between nationalism and war, it
is because this first dialectical weakness struck me, paradoxically, as the
most difficult one to expose. In point of fact, the argument that nationalism
causes war is very persuasive, and precisely because of the historical 'evidence,' it is very difficult to challenge. It is an argument which shuts people
up and which, apparently based on facts (which, of course, are not open to
question), is slow to reveal its dialectical vulnerability. It triggers an emotional reaction in the person hearing it, and thus masks the emotionalism of
the person using it. Emotionalism about the subject of war has something
noble, grand, and excusable about it, and better still, forms the basis for
pacifism and humanitarianism. None the less, it is emotionalism that I
think I recognize in Pierre Elliott Trudeau's thinking: that is, a personal
attitude that is unequivocal and unyielding on a particular subject. This
emotionalism is apparent in the second section, entitled 'The Historical
Approach,' and it seems to be made up of two major components: first,

faulty reasoning (that is, causality suggested between two entities that are really not comparable: nationalism and war),[10] and an overemphasis of what, at this level of explanation, can only be a coincidence in which the actual degree of 'interaction' is real but rather limited; and, secondly, an attitude based on a refusal to think about war and a desire to think only about peace. This 'structural' scheme involves some obvious corollaries; for example, with war now threatening to become 'international,' peace should become 'internationalistic.' A second corollary is that the overemphasis of organizing peace and avoiding war implies an underestimation of any particularity which, from this point of view, can only be conceived as a hindrance to the process of world-wide pacification and thus becomes a negative or at least 'retrograde' factor. From this it is only a small step to say that evil (war) comes from internationalization; since nationalism and war are paired off at the beginning of the article, this step has already been taken in advance. The internationalism advocated by the author logically demands the rejection of its principal opposite, nationalism, which is seen as a narrowing rather than a broadening movement.

In this framework, then, it is logical to link nationalism with regressive and almost malefic associations. The only extenuating consideration in this verdict is found in the notion of transition as applied to the nation-phenomenon: 'Nations belong to a transitory period in world history.'[11] If such is the case then nationalism can no longer be considered the cause of future wars. Logically, these two terms should be separated; it is even possible to consider certain forms of nationalism, particularly the most isolationist or insular ones, as political symptoms of a desire to escape from the interplay of force and power which degenerates into wars. And if there is transition, it must be in a direction which diminishes the nation because it is transitory, which implies that there is an existential 'bonus' in the fact of not being transitory. Now, in relation to what are the realities of nation-hood or statehood transitory? What is the basis for comparison, and how is one reality superior to another? If it is a question of God, then that closes the discussion. But if this superior basis is the world or even the cosmos, who can say that these realities are not also transitory?

TRANSCENDENTAL PEACE

In this context, pacifist thinking gives us an everyday example of the 'inter-nationalizing' dialectic:

It is a commitment transcending any other commitments to one's native land, economic system or religion; countries, economic systems and religions are meaningful only if mankind is preserved... Thus pacifists are not subject to shallow emotions or juvenile idealism: they submit to the most rigorous logic and attack the only problem whose solution must come before all others.[12]

If the world is in a state of emergency, as the pacifists see it, any activity not aimed at abating this fear is considered unimportant and, to go to extremes, laughable. This reasoning has often been explained: it consists in emphasizing the dangers of nuclear destruction and declaring any other vital investigation to be invalid. 'Pacifist' anguish takes precedence over any other form of questioning.

In the name of a positive peace, any activity not geared to working for peace is finally ignored, which is tantamount to a premonitory annihilation of any problematic not connected with this state of emergency. Thus pacifism implicitly decides that any other problematic is unimportant; it annihilates all other philosophies *a priori*. In the name of a peace plan whose failure would be fatal for the world, we are incited to fear such a failure, the philosophic opposite of which is a detachment from everyday reality. This fear of atomic nothingness exclusively preoccupies those who sense it and counters all other commitments to reality, which, in view of the expected annihilation, become mere self-deception or, at best, a stay of execution.

Philosophical anguish feeds on everything. It is a mental attitude which consumes a great many symbols and justifications. It would be an error to see nothing but strictly political attitudes in the contemporary pacifist movements. For every man on earth, the 'total' bomb poses the question of 'the existence or annihilation of the world,' extending to the whole cosmos the ancient doubts which in the past concerned only individual lives and which implicitly invested the rest of the world with unshakeable reality.

I too want peace, but I refuse in the name of the present political climate to dismiss everything that is not central to this concern. Pacifism means fear of the bomb, and however effective this fear may be politically, it contains a philisophical ambiguity.[13]

Now let us come back to nationalism.

NATIONS AS CONCEPTS

Should people stop making revolutions because they know that revolutions always pass, as they always – or almost always – have done? Must we, in the name of vast federal or imperial political entities, which too will eventually be engulfed in the depths of time, must we dismiss movements or revolutions which will, in the end, end? If nationalism in any group – be it Senegalese or French-Canadian – is regressive, I still believe that it is for reasons other than the immortality of the 'French Community' or the inherent superiority of a large grouping like Confederation over a small grouping like the state of Quebec. Is it perhaps because nationalism causes war? I think the fragility of the correlation between nationalism and war has already been proven. Is it then because nationalism tends irrevocably toward the socio-political right? This presumes a future orientation based on political adventures of the past, and nothing can make me believe that tomorrow's reality will be like yesterday's or the day before yesterday's (although I admit that this is unfortunate). I no more believe in the predetermined characteristics of a people than I do in those of an individual person; in politics, a doctrine of predestination can lead only to immobility. Nations and peoples have no essence. During a specific period of observation, they may display particular attitudes or institutions, but this is not their essence. National groups are ontologically indeterminate, and this indetermination is the very foundation of their freedom. The future history of a human group is not fixed; it is unforeseeable. 'A man is defined by his plans,' said Jean-Paul Sartre. The same is true for a people.

Should nationalism be condemned because it implies a movement towards smaller communities at a time when the forces of History are moving irreversibly towards internationalization? To that I would answer that the human race has supplied historians with a fine collection of fallen empires: Alexander the Great, Genghis Khan, Solomon, Mohammed, Franz Joseph, Hadrian, Caesar, and Victoria all proclaimed the perpetuity of multiethnic and multicultural empires which in every case have fallen into decline. If history with a capital 'H' has a meaning, we may well learn that there is as much irrefutable evidence that this meaning is to be found in fragmentation as in planetary and world-wide integration. Nevertheless, I am still trying to discover why Trudeau considers nationalism, and more particularly its present separatist form in French Canada, as a seedbed for historical, social, human, and logical regression.

Is the nation-state a despicable trap into which the best elements of the left are stupidly lured by their emotions? Does the concept of the nation-state have a sort of malevolent and intrinsically negative essence that we should banish from our minds for ever and ever as one of the 'transitory phases' of humanity which, like cannibalism, must be superseded? It is to this question that Pierre Elliott Trudeau proposes a brilliant reply that is rhetorically convincing, yet that seems to me to be a false question, or rather, a dialectical trap.

Let me explain. By postulating the premise that separatism assumes the establishment of a nation-state, it is relatively easy and even amusing to refute the aspirations of the French-Canadian people to becoming a nation-state. In point of fact, the concept of the nation-state is clearly outdated, corresponding neither to reality nor to the most recent scientific findings. The nation is not, as Trudeau suggests, an ethnic reality. Ethnic homogeneity no longer exists, or at least is very rare. Shifting population, immigration, assimilation (which Jacques Henripin quite rightly refers to as 'linguistic transfers') have produced an intermingling of ethnic groups which has undeniably led, in French Canada for example, to regroupings that are no longer based on ethnic origin (or race, as it was still called twenty-five years ago) but rather on belonging to a homogeneous *cultural group*[14] whose only real common denominator is a linguistic one. One has simply to look around among one's personal acquaintances to count the number of true-blue French Canadians who are not 'real' French Canadians: Mackay, Johnson, Elliott, Aquin, Molinari, O'Harley, Spénart, Esposito, Globenski, etc....This says a lot about the French-Canadian ethnic-nation. The 'linguistic transfers' referred to by Henripin have worked both for and against us, and the core of immigrant settlers that assured our survival has been long since mixed, ethnically speaking, with all the additions that immigration or flukes of love have brought to our national ethnic purity. In fact, the French-Canadian people has been replaced by a cultural-linguistic group whose common denominator is language. The same thing will happen to the Wolofs, Seres, and Fulani in Senegal who, if nothing interrupts the process of education and the resulting eventual formation of a cultural linguistic group of varied ethnic origin, will one day become Senegalese.

French Canada is polyethnic. And it would be pure folly, I agree, to dream of a nation-state for French Canada precisely at the time when the French-Canadian people has been succeeded by a culture that is total, coherent, and differentiated by language. If this new conglomerate is to be called a nation, fine, but from then on there can be no question of the nation being a source of racism and all its abominable derivatives.

What distinguishes Canada from French Canada is not that the former is polyethnic and the latter monoethnic, but that the one is bicultural and the other culturally homogeneous (which, thank God, does not exclude pluralism in all its forms!).

The pairing of nation and state, against which Pierre Elliott Trudeau fulminates, no longer corresponds to reality; this fact in itself means that any minority which actually set this as its goal would never see its dreams fulfilled. It would be more precise to speak of a monocultural state. The few old fogeys who still dream of a pure French-Canadian race may simply be written off as intellectual delinquents! However, it seems to me unfair to argue against contemporary separatism by accusing it of racism and ethnic intolerance. It would be more appropriately studied as an expression of the culture of French Canadians seeking greater homogeneity.

From this perspective, and limiting ourselves strictly to the study of this phenomenon, nationalism *a priori* is a force neither for good nor for evil: it acts as a sort of collective voice that one is free to hear or ignore. It may be opposed for reasons of political ideology, but not in the name of lucidity or knowledge. Besides, separatism may be seen as a particular form of *national presence*, but it is far from being the only one. Nationalism can be said to be the political expression of a culture; in the case of French Canada it is quite clearly the expression of political aspirations. Because of this, non-French Canadians see it as a constituent element of the French-speaking cultural group in Canada. In reality, proof of the existence of this cultural group can be seen in a variety of other forms: literature, the arts, the generalizing methodology of our researchers in the humanities, and surely also in our linguistic dynamism, demography, social struggles, religious peculiarities, and so on.

THE CULTURE OF CULTURE

We are thus looking at a culture which we will call 'national' and whose existence, however fragile, can be verified by a certain number of factors. French-Canadian separatism is only one of these factors, but it has a greater striking force than other forms of cultural existence because it contains the embryo of a revolution than could pose a threat to the present constitutional order in Canada. English Canadians have been quick to notice this and have hastened to isolate nationalism from all the other forms of cultural expression in French Canada. They have, for example, been generous and efficient in promoting the artistic peculiarity of French Canadians because this heightens the ambiguity of a connection which the separatists forcefully maintain is one-sided and 'degrading.' Patterning their behaviour on a number of well-known models in other parts of the world, English Canadians have invested a great deal of money and genuine interest in the 'entertaining' aspects of French-Canadian culture. This has been accomplished so efficiently and so speedily that it has caused the beneficiaries to be mentally torn between their allegiance to a generous federal government and a not very profitable attachment to their own soil.

The pettiness, intolerance, and political partisanship of the Duplessis regime caused this split to reach distressing proportions; many artists and intellectuals were thrown into the arms of the federal government, which meant that they were sentenced either to sterile anxiety or to becoming rootless spokesmen for a culture that had once appealed only to those who feared its full repercussions. One of the many consequences of this state of affairs was its influence on the Canadian use of the word *culture*.

Culture, in fact, has been restricted to the limited horizons of the arts and humanities; the word *culture* has contracted to the point where it now signifies only the artistic and cognitive characteristics of a group, whereas for anthropologists and many foreign intellectuals it describes the full range of behaviour patterns and symbols of a particular group and thus refers to a society that is sovereign and organic but not closed. The state of federal-provincial politics here has led us to depoliticize the word *culture* or, more precisely, to reject arbitrarily the comprehensive meaning conferred upon it by contemporary semantics. The Massey Report, with great precision, codified this reduction of French-Canadian culture to elements of cognition and artistic expression; coming at a time when great works of anthropology have established opposite connotations for the same word, it reveals a rejection of French-Canadian culture in its totality. It must be added that French-Canadian intellectuals immediately accepted this variant, and enthusiastically set about shaping their attitudes to conform with those of English Canada by urging upon French Canadians the merits and specialized practice of formalism, as if this would neutralize the propensity for exhibiting a total culture. Thus the problem is not to know whether we would be better poets in an independent state once the people are cleansed of the effects of a degrading political and emotional atmosphere, but to know whether the existence of French-Canadian *culture* is truly accepted or whether only a limited fragment of it is acknowledged, so that it can be included in a political conglomerate whose existence is considered a sort of priority.

A *complete* French-Canadian culture in no way presupposes any real homogeneity. No matter how dynamic a culture is, it is composed of a residue of indigenous and borrowed elements, the latter being at first heterogeneous and then gradually more or less assimilated and homogenized, until finally they are integrated into a total culture as much as the original elements. This is true of French-Canadian culture, which has already been moulded by at least three spheres of cultural heterogeneity: French, British, and American.

Because culture is not merely a juxtaposition of cultural traits, there can be no such thing as a half-breed culture ... And for the same reason, one of the characteristics of culture is its style, a distinguishing mark that is peculiar to a people or period and which is evident in all areas of this people's activities at a given time ... One objection to this theory is that all cultures are a mixture of terribly heterogeneous elements. The case of Greek culture may be cited in this instance, being composed not only of Greek but also of Cretan, Egyptian, and Asiatic elements ... Heterogeneity is certainly the rule here. But beware: this heterogeneity is not experienced as such ... It is rather heterogeneity experienced from within as homogeneity. Heterogeneity may be quite apparent when the culture is analysed, but however heterogeneous the elements may in fact be, they are experienced in the community consciousness as being just as much *theirs* as the most typically indigenous elements. What has taken place is a process of naturalization, which stems from the dialectic of *possession*.[15]

To be or not to be a separatist is a question of political choice and I can well imagine that French Canadians who see themselves as part of a total culture might still prefer to see their *culture* remain as part of Confederation rather than any other political regime. Besides, no one is forced into politics or even into political opinions; no one is compelled to commit himself to a political system that is conceived as a function of the totality of his culture. In theory, however, a rejection of the entirety of French-Canadian culture is implied by conceiving of it as part of a larger whole; from this point of view, separatism is no longer connected, relatively speaking, with the totality of French-Canadian culture, but has become only one aspect of it, opposed to Confederation, which makes it easy to suggest its narrowness as compared to the federal approach.

French-Canadian nationalism is the normal, if not predictable, expression of a culture whose comprehensiveness was being very subtly called into question at the same time as money was being provided for supposed compensations. Even before any value judgment is made about our sins, deficiencies, mistakes, or achievements, French Canada must be examined in the cold light of a culture which, whatever its shortcomings, is none the less total. On a rational level, this is much more important than worrying about whether separatism has died down in the past six months. One doesn't have to be a prophet to know that if French-Canadian culture exists, it will always have a tendency to reveal itself in its entirety and to break out of the limitations and 'specializations' within which it has been 'encapsulated.' In a culture so oriented towards totality and homogeneity, this is an expression of a collective determination to survive.

Otherwise, French Canada is rejected as such and allowed to exist only in an *unchangeable* Confederation; this attitude may be likened to *'negative radicalism'* which assumes the impossibility of tolerating the slightest change in the regime.'[16] Some mention must be made here of those who tell French-Canadian nationalists that all the 'changes' they want are legal and possible within the framework of the constitution; this is a way of saying that it is possible to change everything except the political system:

By the terms of the existing Canadian constitution, that of 1867, French Canadians have all the powers they need to make Quebec a political society affording due respect for nationalist aspirations and at the same time giving unprecedented scope for human potential in the broadest sense.[17]

OUR 'EXCEPTIONAL' SUCCESSES

Only the abolition of a total French-Canadian culture can enable Confederation to function smoothly and allow it to develop 'normally' as a central power that reigns, not over two total cultures, but rather over ten administrative provinces. This abolition could come about in a variety of ways that would not prevent certain French-Canadian cultural stereotypes from surviving. By ceasing to be total, the culture of French Canada would enrich several spheres of Canadian life without any danger and without any political implications. We ourselves, just like our English-speaking partners, place a certain value on the survival of the folklore of the American Indians. We have even cultivated a kind of snobbishness about the supposed drop of native blood in our veins, elegantly acknowledging our wild, instinctive, more remote origins! In our role as colonizers and conquerors, we naturally promote Eskimo art, Huron pottery, and the war chants of peoples whose culture has ceased to be total, no longer expressing a collective instinct for survival. As the attentions of the conquering majority become more and more sharply focused and full of concern, it becomes increasingly clear that they no longer fear the total expression of the minority culture.

In this respect, it must be recognized that English Canada has come very close to definitively mastering the situation, and may well still get the better of our *cultural fatigue*, which is very great. Each surge of nationalism catches English Canadians off guard, for they had thought, in good faith, that the problem was solved; then, after a period of hesitation and uncertainty, they take stock and decide that, after all, the minority's 'nationalistic' outburst was well founded and that they must once again pay the price of harmony by making yet another concession. Or else (and this is an attitude that is common with certain French Canadians who follow the general trend of the fragmentation of French-Canadian culture), they take heart, saying that nationalism is like yellow fever and flares up periodically, in cycles.

The particularity of the majority position can be seen both in the sincerity and guilty conscience of the former attitude and in the theoretical exorcism of the eternally recurring nationalist 'menstrual cycle' that characterizes the latter attitude. Domination is never unequivocal, except in detective films or westerns. The act of dominating (which is equivalent to having greater numbers or greater strength) eventually embarrasses those who dominate and pressures them into multiplying the ambiguities of the situation, which means that, because they have very guilty consciences, they do all in their power to camouflage their dominating position. Sometimes the majority loses patience and ends up accusing the minority of counter-domination through foot-dragging and obstructionism that finally actually do occur. The minority, accused of being dead weights, assume this role of villain more and more painfully. Actually, they *are* the villains, they are an obstacle, a ball and chain, an inert force whose demands and sensitivity constantly impede the progress of the dynamic majority; and they know it.[18]

Is it necessary, in this context, to catalogue all the psychological implications caused by the awareness of this minority position: self-punishment, masochism, a sense of unworthiness, 'depression,' the lack of enthusiasm and vigour – all the underlying reactions to dispossession that anthropologists refer to as 'cultural fatigue'? French Canada is in a state of cultural fatigue and, because it is invariably tired, it becomes tiresome. Here we have a vicious circle. It would no doubt be much more relaxing to cease to exist as a *specific culture* and to sell our soul to English Canada once and for all for a Canada Council fellowship or a peaceful reservation protected by the RCMP. This cultural hypothesis, however, is no doubt impossible because of our numbers and also because of the unpredictable will to survive which we find sporadically and unevenly surging within each one of us.

A depoliticized French Canadian behaves like the member of a group that seems negligible in comparison to the infinite scope of the challenges facing it: God, world disarmament, hell and the atomic bomb, Confederation. This sublime unimportance is a path to mysticism and it creates an 'order' which, like a sacrament, casts a pall of disrespectability on anyone who is not 'set apart' by it. Nationalism, a profane impulse and practically considered a form of juvenile sacrilege, thus becomes a sin that more or less stigmatizes anyone who advocates it even temporarily. It is a form of adolescent impulsiveness that can be forgiven when those who have succumbed to it later reconsider in the serenity or repentance of maturity. This impulsive and 'verbal' expression of nationalism is tolerated and is seldom loudly condemned, which explains how in French Canada it has become a kind of cathartic melodrama. Its very toleration is an effective form of subordination whereby nationalism is made into a kind of sinful excess built into the system it is incoherently trying to overthrow, but which it never really disturbs. It is all right to be a nationalist – for a while, as in the thankless years of one's adolescence...so long as you eventually get back to more serious matters, back to reality.

At first, nationalism comes as a surprise, like a teen-age son's first acts of rebellion; later it starts to be viewed with concern, not only by the Federalists but by French Canadians exhausted from thinking of the effort it would take to live outside the system of acceptance and grandeur proposed by their leaders, those disciples of understanding, unity, and vast entities, spokesmen for the great urgent problems facing the world, and for religion. This system (has it occurred to anyone that it might not be more coherent than any other!) has worked well for a long time and in no way threatens the existence of the French fact in Canada; it means simply that this French fact must be domesticated at all levels and in every conscience. Just how effective this attitude is can be seen by its pervasiveness in French Canada, where we find its greatest advocates. Speaking in French, their voices packed with emotion, they easily convince their fellow citizens that remaining French Canadian is the only way, repeating the old adage that 'it's up to us to make ourselves felt, for only by being better can we show English Canada how dynamic French-Canadian culture is.'

If Quebec became such a shining example, if to live there were to partake of freedom and progress, if culture enjoyed a place of honour there, if the universities commanded respect and renown from afar, if the administration of public affairs were the best in the land (and none of this presupposes any declaration of independence), French Canadians would no longer need to do battle for bilingualism; the ability to speak French would become a status symbol, even an open sesame in business and public life. Even in Ottawa superior competence on the part of our politicians and civil servants would bring spectacular changes.[19]

The logic of the system seems unwittingly subservient to its own ends. It is hardly necessary to point out here the no doubt unconscious attempt to 'dis-effect' French Canada in its totality. Anyone who wants to get ahead must reject the cultural impetus given him by French Canada and start from a position of cultural fatigue; this is like having a devil inside him, which he himself must kill just to prove that, through him, French Canada has a right to exist! But we forget that this can happen only in exceptional cases, and that therefore only the individual is important, for the culture he represents is, by implication, diminished by the 'exceptional' nature of his success. 'Specific personal successes tend to be considered as increasingly significant for oneself to the degree that collective successes seem more doubtful or distant.'[20]

TOTAL 'FUNCTIONARIZATION'

Why should French Canadians have to be better? Why should they have to 'get ahead' to justify their existence? This exhortation to *individual* superiority is presented as a challenge that must absolutely be answered. We should not forget, however, that a cult of challenges depends on an initial obstacle or handicap and that it finally boils down to a test of strength to which each individual is subjected. Only the achievement counts, and strictly according to this criterion, we would have to concede that Maurice Richard was more successful than our federal politicians. We have a sportsman's attitude to national affairs, and by dreaming of creating heroes rather than a state, we force ourselves as individuals to win struggles that are really collective.

If the individual challenge that every French Canadian tries in vain to take up depends on the position of the French-Canadian group as a whole, why should this collective challenge be taken as if it were an individual one? Would it not be more logical to respond collectively to collective challenges and to cope totally with the total threats that are built into French Canada's position vis-à-vis her English-speaking federalist partners in Confederation?

'If Canada as a state has had so little room for French Canadians,' writes Trudeau, 'it is above all because we have failed to make ourselves indispensable to its future.'[21] Making ourselves indispensable for the destiny of others! Here we see the theme of cultural exorbitation expressed with rare precision. It consists in creating in the majority group a need for the minority, an 'indispensability' which immediately confers upon us the right to the dignity of a minority; thus, in the scheme proposed by Pierre Elliott Trudeau (and which is familiar to all consumers of federalist French-Canadian thinking), the minority group would fully and dynamically occupy the 'little bit of space' it now has, or would play a much larger role if it earned it. In other words, the existence of the French-Canadian group can only be justified if it remains grafted onto an English-speaking majority which can no longer get along without it. At the end of this brave new world, French Canada would have a better place in the federal state, but it would always be only one place; that is, it would play a larger or more fitting 'role.' But this role, however large or small, will always be only one role: its political trajectory would be shaped from the start by the consenting majority, and it would remain part of an entity into which it would have to fit harmoniously. In this scenario, French Canada would play a role, sometimes even a starring role, in a story it could never write itself.[22]

This glorious and heroic future, however, is strangely reminiscent of our past. As long as it has been held within the confines of a structure it never invented, French Canada has played a 'role' in federal affairs, courageously, brilliantly, or wearily filling in a space for which it was never really fitted. It could have done better, of course, but a civil servant is not a cabinet minister: he is less involved in the business, tires quickly, is not so keen, is a bit wary, and can often be found thinking about his retirement. Now, if I may be excused for making a scholastic analogy, French Canada on the whole is like a collective civil servant; it finds itself on the payroll of great employers who are resolute and just – the federal government and the Catholic Church. In choosing 'publicservantism' rather than totalization the French Canadian enjoys all the benefits that come with the function (salary, status, security, promotion) and has no other responsibilities or inconveniences except those inherent in the subordination of all functions to the organism. Faithful to the terms of the contract, and grateful for all the comforts of paternalism, French Canada is collectively a functional employee who never causes any 'trouble' and never resents his bosses. A functionary is neither an entrepreneur nor a politician. And it seems to me that there is a link between our lack of entrepreneurs, which in the past was considered a racial deficiency, and our total, continuous conscription by large employers: the federal government which protects us from ourselves (read 'Duplessis') and the Church, which for a long time acted as a substitute government for us, to such an extent that French Canada has an abundance of religious institutions and a numerous clergy who work efficiently, but who, conversely, do not offer a good example of either faith or holiness.

French Canada as such is a good public servant and its behaviour in this sense abounds in signs that are far more convincing than any analogies can suggest: identification with the bosses, desire for promotion, very noticeable social conformity (calling it low profile is an understatement!), marked talent for being agreeable, general desire to raise its standard of living, and to end my comparison on a cruel note, full integration into the system of which it is only a function. In this way our representatives in Ottawa are elected as 'MPs' but become functionaries as soon as they reach good old Parliament Hill. And here they are in a perfect conundrum: they are the people's elected representatives but, with rare exceptions, can conceive of themselves only as functionaries because they represent a functionarized people!

ECCENTRICITY

Traditionally, the key to success for French Canada has been to look outward, toward a heterogeneous culture. Our MPs in Ottawa and our writers in France, by seeking their mission and fulfilment elsewhere, have thus saddled themselves with such an enormous handicap that they are condemned to a single form of action and success: apotheosis. In both cases their valiant exiles have also meant demoralizing reversals. The break-through in Ottawa and recognition in Paris have led to sacrifices that are fruitless, if not downright overwhelming. The loss of one's roots – an endless source of cultural fatigue – or exile, renunciation, and removal from one's own element, can never completely free the individual from his original identity, yet at the same time they prevent him from fully identifying with his new surroundings. He is a double expatriate, cut off from both cultural sources and twice deprived of a homeland. This voluntary and eventually fatal orphanhood, even if not reflected in consular irregularities, eats away at him like a tapeworm. Setting down roots, on the other hand, is to take constant, secret, and ultimately fulfilling nourishment from the original soil.

Tell me that Joyce wrote *Ulysses* because of his exile and I will answer that, precisely, Joyce only found a meaning to his exile by poetically 'going home.' For him, Trieste, Paris, and Zurich were simply nostalgic spring-boards which he used, in a mental process that eventually ended in delirium, to effect a daily, hour-by-hour return to his dreary Ireland. That he was buried outside his isle in a Swiss cemetary strikes one as an accident, especially considering that his entire work is a brilliant resurrection of the Ireland he never saw again, and which, with his dimmed eyes, he could never have seen again even if he had returned. He brought his native land to life in books that are as extravagant as his obsessions. One might even wonder whether the almost incomprehensible English in which *Finnegans Wake* was composed during his 'blindness' was not a final revolutionary act by this exiled writer who, from the time of his youth in Dublin, was already exiled by the language that had become the 'mother tongue' there: English, historically a 'foreign' language.

Perhaps it was not so much his own country that he fled so rapidly, but rather his own language, which he was disowning by speaking it. He fled the English language through those 'foreign' languages that he taught for Berlitz, thus clinging to anything 'foreign' (non-British) in the English tongue. Condemned to speak a foreign language, he took his mysterious revenge by making it foreign unto itself. After conquering it completely and investing it with universal semantic overtones, he set about disarticulating it to the point of incoherence; he expressed it so thoroughly that finally, in an exploded language bordering on the incommunicable, he was able to describe a painful and passionate experience of setting down roots. The deliberate use of Gaelic, which he thought a ridiculous project, could impress him only as chauvinism – the very proof that his own culture had been reduced to folklore. Taking a language that was both foreign and his 'mother' tongue, he chose rather to exhaust it by wildly inflating its meanings, contradictions, origins, and derivations, so that out of this magical, irresistible torrent of 'uprooted' words there emerges his native Ireland, thoroughly contaminated by the cross-breeding of words, tragic, laughable, unsure, loved, hated, and defunct: a motherland regained, yet still somehow unattainable.

Besides – and here I am trying to refute the claims that Joyce's experience was exceptional – Faulkner, Balzac, Flaubert, Baudelaire, Mallarmé, and Goethe all produced works that are universal because they are so rooted in the countries in which they were written. As one's self-identification becomes clearer, one becomes better at communicating it, for expression comes from deep within the self. Understanding does not result from an initial, deliberate depersonalization of the speaker; on the contrary, dialogue is enriched to the extent that both participants are profoundly and particularly themselves.

In this regard, French-Canadian literature is distressingly poor. In far too many cases our authors have opted to leave their own 'native element' and have systematized this rejection, hoping thus to attain universality. Other 'regional' authors have opted for 'folkloric authenticity,' and because they have managed to flog some mileage out of the local scene, or simply because of their mediocrity, they think of themselves as being more French Canadian. An author can't come to terms with his origins simply by adding a few bits of local colour that would be more obvious to reporters from the Parisian magazine *Marie-Claire* than they are to us. Some authors think that just because they spice up a familiar sentence with a few curses they have given a literary existence to their birthplace. This is sad, because in their thirst for the exotic they end up seeing themselves through the eyes of foreigners who come to spend a couple of weeks in Quebec. That which is typical is profound and should not be confused with either superficial stereotypes or regionalism, which to my mind is rooted only in its localism. The problem is not to write stories that take place in Canada, but to assume all the difficulties of one's identity fully and painfully. French Canada, like Fontenelle on his deathbed, feels 'a certain difficulty in being.'

Our federal politicians, having taken the first step towards becoming part of a great 'whole,' are in a continual state of emotional exile which, incidentally, prevents them from being aware of the strains of their situation. They are procrastinators by profession, always telling us about a Confederation which in fact does not exist. It is a conditioned reflex: how could they sincerely root themselves in French Canada when, politically, by their very presence in the federal government, they have shown themselves ready to sacrifice it to appease the stronger? Traitors? No! Our federalists are sincere, and thus their ambiguity.

The French Canadian is both literally and figuratively a double agent. He wallows in 'eccentricity,' and in his fatigue longs to reach political nirvana through self-dissolution. The French Canadian rejects his centre of gravity, desperately searching for a centre elsewhere and wandering through any labyrinth he comes across. He is neither preyed upon nor persecuted, yet he always leaves his country behind in a continual search for exoticism that never satisfies him. Homesickness is both the need for and rejection of a cultural matrix. All these transcendental impulses towards great political, religious, or cosmological entities can never replace the need to put down roots; as complementary processes, they could have an enriching influence, but by themselves these impulses turn French Canadians into 'displaced persons.'

I myself am one of these 'typical' men, lost, unsettled, tired of my atavistic identity and yet condemned to it. How many times have I rejected the immediate reality of my own culture? I wanted total expatriation without suffering, I wanted to be a stranger to myself, I used to reject all the very surroundings I have finally come to affirm. Today I tend to think that our cultural existence can be something other than a perpetual challenge, and that the fatigue can come to an end. This cultural fatigue is a fact, a disquieting, painful reality, but it may also be the path to immanence. One day we will emerge from the struggle, victorious or vanquished. One thing is certain: the inner struggle goes on, like a personal civil war, and it is impossible to be either indifferent or serene about it. The struggle, though not its outcome, is deadly.

Culturally fatigued and weary, French Canada for a long time now has been going through an endless winter; every time the sun breaks through the ceiling of cloud that has obliterated the heavens, in spite of our weakness, our sickness and disillusionment, we start hoping for spring again. French-Canadian culture has long been dying; it makes frequent recoveries, followed by new relapses, and thus leads a precarious existence of fits, starts, and collapses.

What will finally become of French Canada? To tell the truth, no one really knows, especially not French Canadians, whose ambivalence on this subject is typical: they want simultaneously to give in to cultural fatigue and to overcome it, calling for renunciation and determination in the same breath. If anyone needs to be convinced of this, he need only read the articles our great nationalists have written – profoundly ambiguous speeches in which one can scarcely distinguish exhortations to revolt from appeals for constitutionality, revolutionary ardour from willed obedience. French-Canadian culture shows all the symptoms of extreme fatigue, wanting both rest and strength at the same time, desiring both existential intensity and suicide, seeking both independence and dependency.

Independence can only be considered as a social and political expedient in a relatively homogeneous culture. It is not historically necessary, any more than the culture that calls for it is. It should not be seen as a superior, preferential form of existence for a cultural community. One thing is sure, however: independence is just as valid a form of cultural existence as dependence. From an intellectual point of view, the forms of existence for any given cultural group are equally interesting. Knowledge is concerned with realities, not values.

DIALECTIC FATIGUE

The struggle is for intelligibility.
Jean-Paul Sartre[23]

If the presence of tension is inherent to dialectics, and if dialectics opposes two opposite extremities which are progressively revealed to one another, then it would be a dialectical error to deny the fact that Canada is a well-defined dialectical case in which two cultures confront one another. If one wishes to reach an understanding of the Canadian situation, it is more logical to consider it in the framework of a critical opposition of two cultures than to dismantle, by over-valuing the superior term of reference, the historical dialectic of which French Canada is a part. A logical disman-tling of the dialectic amounts to saying 'French Canada is very small compared to reality X ... and its totality becomes simply a particularity in this new scale of size.' For example, French Canada can be crushed dialectically by making the point of comparison either the huge, invading bulk of America, or the threat of world-wide atomic war, or the urgent need for universal disarmament, or the universality of the Catholic religion, or world socialism, etc. ... Our ideologists frequently make overwhelming comparisons between our culture and remote, ideal considerations; in practical terms, this reveals a desire to see French-Canadian culture as a 'diminished' entity. The great considerations advanced by our intellectuals are not without importance or significance, but they are distinguished, in the French-Canadian context, by a lesser degree of dialectical action upon its culture. The presence of these great considerations acts against the interests of French Canada; caught in a crushing comparison, French Canada must feel tremendous guilt simply for existing while these enormous problems remain to be faced.

Another means of diminishing French Canada is to accept it only in its administrative interpretation as a province. 'Quebec is a province like the others' boils down to accepting the reality of French-Canadian culture only in the legalistic terms of Confederation, thus regionalizing and provincializing the culture. This reasoning is the inverse of the other in terms of the size of the opposing term of reference, but structurally it is similar in that it circumvents the French Canada / English Canada axis, which is the most significant (historically and politically), but which of course does not exclude French Canada's multidimensional relations with both the world and history.

On the whole, our intellectuals have repeatedly rejected the historical dialectic by which we are defined and have turned to another dialectic which, in widening the confrontation or narrowing it excessively, shows a refusal to consider French Canada as a total culture. This repudiation has formed the ideological basis for several systems of thought in Canada. Our intellectuals have deployed a vast logical arsenal to escape from the French-Canadian dialectic, a situation which even today is exhausting, depressing, and degrading for French Canada. 'How to get out of it' has been the basic problem for our intellectuals, and their dialectical escapes only give tragic expression to the morbid taste for exile that has been prevalent in our literature since the time of Crémazie. What they have been fleeing, whether by writing ideological rubbish or by travelling, is an intolerable position of subordination, disgust with themselves and their people, bitterness, unrelenting fatigue, and a firm intent not to undertake anything else. French Canadians are often represented by their most prominent spokesmen as a jaded people who believe neither in themselves nor in anything else. Self-devaluation has done its work for a long time now, and if only one proof were to be given, I would mention the delirious exaggeration indulged in by French-Canadian separatists. Although they do puff themselves up, it must be said in their defence that if they did not do so, conditioned as they are to collapse and defeat, they would probably have to take themselves for absolute idiots, an idea which is constantly being reinforced by the society around them.

French Canada, a dying, tired culture, is at square one in politics. Those who have been most successful politically are 'a-nationalists.' They are the ones who have best 'represented' this unrealized, parcelled, and dispossessed people. Success for our federal politicians has depended on their cultural 'dis-integration.' Their 'inexistence' has reflected the constrained culture they represent and which they have almost all been eager to 'fatigue' even more by turning it into folklore so successfully that the federal government, by its very existence, proclaims that there is no longer any dialectical tension between the French- and English-Canadian cultures. The federal government is not the focus of a basic, elemental struggle; in fact it has never been so, or very rarely. The federal superstructure, in sanctifying the political appeasement of French Canada, does not stem from the historical dialectic of the two Canadas, but from a desire to suppress this dialectic, so that Ottawa, a capital between two provinces, rules over ten of them. The political portrait of Ottawa masks the real *confrontation* between two cultures and glosses over this confrontation in a disguised monolithic regime which legalistically considers French Canada to be one province in ten. The dialectical struggle between the two Canadas does not take place in Ottawa; it is 'depoliticized,' at least in the sense that there are no 'institutions' either resulting from it or containing it. The dialectical struggle is in fact taking place elsewhere, almost everywhere, and deep within our consciousness as well. It is not for us to say how it will end, but it is important to know that it is going on and becoming more and more unavoidable. Fatigue, however great, is still not death.

UNIVERSALISM

I will have been misunderstood if in the course of this article I have been taken to be disparaging *universalism* in my attempt to re-establish the reality of 'transitory' phases of History and to underline the importance of one's own culture and the 'national fact.'[24]

Universalism should in no way evoke supremacies of ancient empires, and must never be built on the corpses of 'national' cultures any more than of

men. I sincerely believe that humanity is involved in a process of convergence and unification. But this project of *unanimization*, as described by
Senghor after Teilhard de Chardin, must, in order to be successful, resemble a project of love and not one of bitter fusion in a forced and sterile
hegemony. The dialectic of opposition must become a dialectic of love.
Universal harmony must not be achieved at the cost of ignoring either the
person or the *'human branches.'*

May I be permitted here to quote Teilhard de Chardin, whose thinking I
feel adequately expresses this ultimate reconciliation of the general and the
particular, the 'indigenous' and the 'universal':

Love has always been carefully eliminated from realist and positivist concepts of the
world; but sooner or later we shall have to acknowledge that it is the fundamental
impulse of Life, or, if you prefer, the one natural medium in which the rising course
of evolution can proceed ... It links those who love in bonds that unite but do not
confound, causing them to discover in their mutual contact an exultation incompar-
ably more capable than any arrogance of solitude of arousing in the heart of their
being all they possess of uniqueness and creative power ... Union differentiates, as I
have said; the first result being that it endows a convergent Universe with the
power to extend the individual fibres that compose it without their being lost in the
whole ... In a convergent Universe, each element achieves completeness, not
directly in a separate consummation, but by incorporation into a higher pole of
consciousness in which alone it can enter into contact with all the others. By a sort
of inward turn towards the Other its growth culminates in an act of giving and in
excentration.[25]

Union, if you wish, but between entities which accord each other mutual
recognition. The planetary union to which Teilhard de Chardin refers can
mean neither the constitutional rule of more powerful elements over a
group which has virtually *ceased to exist*, nor domination by an external legal
body over its constituent parts. To return to Teilhard de Chardin: 'A total
earth requires nations that are fully aware.' This formula seems to me
more a basic prerequisite for convergence than an expression of fervent
universalism seeking to prove itself even at the expense of all the lives it
intends to transform, but not of the individual *super-being* without which a
desire for unity would be futile.

Continued and irreversible progress is perhaps real, but it is so vast in
scope and in such huge measures of human time that no one revolution can
dogmatically decree that others which do not seem to be continuing it are
superfluous or superseded. Who could claim to have advanced humanity so

much that initiatives unforeseen by him would necessarily be steps back-wards? No one has a sure monopoly on revolution, and consequently no one has the right to condemn divergent revolutions or those on a different path. 'Ideally,' writes Roland Barthes, 'revolution being an essence that is at home everywhere, it is logical and necessary at any point in the unfolding of time.'[26]

NOTES

1 Pierre Teilhard de Chardin, *Œuvres* 5, p. 74
2 Pierre Elliott Trudeau 'La nouvelle trahison des clercs' *Cité Libre* No. 46 (April 1962) [tr. Patricia Claxton, 'New Treason of the Intellectuals,' *Federalism and the French Canadians* (Toronto: Macmillan, 1968)]
3 Trudeau [tr. Claxton 157–8]
4 The 'nationalistic' wars of the nineteenth century are sometimes attributed, by going back through the series of 'causes,' to the Congress of Vienna in 1815, the first 'summit meeting' for peace: 'At Vienna, the map of Europe was remade, but freedom, national spirit and the rights of national groups were all ignored in this restructuration. In the final act of Vienna were sown the seeds of wars which would bathe the second half of the nineteenth century in blood. The repression of various national groups accentuated the strife between governments and peoples.' Félix Ponteil, *L'éveil des nationalités et le mouvement libéral* (Paris: PUF 1960) 4
5 'Professor Wright notes that between 1579 and 1941, that is between the Treaty of Arras, which sanctioned Louis XV's victories and in effect marked the end of feudalism, and the United States' entry into the Second World War, it is possible to count 278 wars and 700 million casualties.' General Gallois, quoted by Louis Armand in *Plaidoyer pour l'avenir* (Calman-Lévy 1961) 146
6 Pierre Elliott Trudeau also mentions modern technology as an external cause of war. On this point he makes a causal inversion. The correlation between war and technology seems to me to work in the opposite direction: surely it is warfare which has created its tools, and not the other way around. Conversely, however, tools of war must have had an effect on perfecting or extending methods of destruction; but it would be difficult to put all the blame on technological progress, which on a functional level can be useful as well as destructive. The same, after all, is true of fire.
7 I found the following phrase in Teilhard de Chardin: 'true peace ... betokens neither the ending nor the reverse of warfare, but war in a naturally sublimated form.' Teilhard de Chardin [tr. Norman Denny, *The Future of Man* (London: Collins 1964) 153]

8 Claude Lévi-Strauss *Entretiens avec Claude Lévi-Strauss* (Paris: Julliard 1961) 41–5 [tr. John and Doreen Weightman (London: Jonathan Cape 1969) 33–42]
9 Sheik Anto Diop *Présence Africaine* No. 24–5 (1959) 376
10 'The concept of nations ... is a concept that spoils everything.' Trudeau [tr. Claxton 167]
11 Trudeau [tr. Claxton 177]
12 André Langevin 'Einstein and Peace' *Le Nouveau Journal* (Montreal: April 1962)
13 'This terror of inevitable war, which sees no cure for warfare except in even greater terror, is responsible for poisoning the air we breathe.' Teilhard de Chardin [tr. Denny 149]
14 The notion of culture, according to E.B. Tylor, is 'That complex whole which includes knowledge, belief, art, morals, laws, custom, and any other capabilities and habits acquired by man as a member of society.' *Primitive Culture* (London: 1871) I, 1. A more recent source, Claude Lévi-Strauss, specifies: 'Language is at once the prototype of the cultural phenomenon ... and the phenomenon whereby all the forms of social life are established and perpetuated.' *Anthropologie structurelle* (Paris: 1958) 392 [tr. Claire Jacobson and B.G. Schoepf, *Structural Anthropology* (New York: Basic Books 1963) 358–9]
15 Aimé Césaire 'Culture et colonisation,' lecture delivered at the Sorbonne (September, 1956)
16 Jean-Paul Sartre *Critique de la raison dialectique* (Paris: Gallimard, 1960) 715
17 Trudeau [tr. Claxton 180]
18 'The image a people forms of itself is no less stereotyped than the image it forms of others, for it emerges in the same irrational, arbitrary and irresponsible manner.' Jean Stoctzel *Jeunesse sans chrysanthème ni sabre* (Paris: 1953) 15
19 Trudeau [tr. Claxton 180]
20 Sartre 572
21 Trudeau [tr. Claxton 166]
22 Lord Durham was right, in this sense, when he wrote that French Canadians were a people without history! (History obviously belonged to English Canadians, and all we could do was to take it as one takes a train.) If we agree to play a role, however noble, it has to be in a history written by others. It is impossible to be both a function and the organism controlling it, a 'role-playing' cultural entity and an historic totality. I am using the word 'history' here in an Hegelian sense, which is also the way the *Montreal Star* uses it ('History in the making'). As for historical science, that's something else. We have a history, but it interests no one but us, unfortunately.
23 Sartre 753
24 'Marx minimized the national fact. The nationalism of new, coloured states proved him wrong. But where nationalists want only to see racial, religious,

political or social phenomena, Teilhard de Chardin distinguishes an 'ethnico-politico-cultural' synthesis. He concludes: 'The subdivision or natural unit of humanity is thus not merely the anthropologists' race nor merely the sociologists' nations or cultures; it is a certain amalgam of the two, which, for lack of anything better, I would call the *human branch*.' Teilhard de Chardin, 3, p. 284. 'And for which I would give the example of France.' Léopold Sédar Senghor, *Pierre Teilhard de Chardin et la politique africaine* (Paris: Seuil 1962) **49**

25 Teilhard de Chardin [tr. Denny 54–5]
26 Roland Barthes *Michelet par lui-même* (Paris: Seuil 1954) 55

MICHÈLE LALONDE

The Mitre and the Tuque

It might be argued that Michèle Lalonde's prominence owes as much to her gifts as a performer as to her considerable poetic talent. Her symphonic poem 'Terre des hommes,' for instance, received widespread attention in the year of Expo '67, for which it was written and set to music. Later, participating in such highly publicized shows as 'La nuit de poésie' and the 'Poèmes et chants de la résistance,' her spectacular recital of 'Speak White' or 'Outrages au tribunal' amplified the already forceful content of her poetry of protest.

Firmly established as a left-wing, anti-establishment intellectual, Michèle Lalonde has published several essays and articles, and more recently a play. Although they take a variety of forms, the common elements in virtually all her writing are anti-colonialism and nationalism, a concern with the destiny of her people that places Lalonde in a long and respectable tradition in Quebec letters.

Lalonde sees writing as a profoundly social act; in an article entitled 'Writers and the Revolution' (originally published in *Liberté* and translated in *Open Letter* 2nd series, No. 2), she argues that communication with the people is the only hope a writer has of playing a meaningful role in the community. An earlier essay dealing with the image of the father in Quebec literature (*Interprétation* 3, Nos. 1 and 2) explains her conviction that writers, whether they are aware of it or not, are always articulating the collective unconscious, a process through which social reality, literary expression, and myth are all related to the national problem.

Like her nationalism, Lalonde's criticism has many dimensions: social, historical, political, and literary. The tone of her discussions is personal, authoritative, and frequently ironic, while the style is compact, intense, and carefully nuanced. These qualities are readily apparent in the following article, first published in 1974 in a special issue of the magazine *Maintenant* devoted to a survey of the significant events in the evolution of the Quebec intelligentsia.

THE MITRE AND THE TUQUE

The Quebec 'intelligentsia' has come a long way in the past twenty years. The road may have been somewhat rocky at times, but it has always been quite clearly directed towards what I would summarily define as a process of secularization and systematic decolonization of the French-Canadian mind and society. Although this process is still incomplete (and sadly static at the present time), it has been marked by a series of milestones: following the loud cry of Borduas's *Refus global*, the magazines *Cité libre, Liberté, Parti pris*, and perhaps more recently, albeit still in a diffuse and precarious manner, *Maintenant*. I have no wish to minimize the importance of other publications or to overlook the impact of such famous works as *Les insolences du Frère Untel,** *Nègres blancs d'Amérique*,† and so on. Nevertheless, I feel that the successive careers of the above-mentioned periodicals, together with their relevance and their relatively long-lasting influence, reveals more about the evolution of the Quebec intelligentsia than any single isolated phenomenon or piece of writing. These magazines strike me as having followed one another in a remarkably logical sequence. Each in its own time has acted as a powerful centre of attraction and has responded to a certain need for theorization. In the same twenty-year period, the corresponding need for action was centred on the union movement, the RIN (Rassemblement pour l'indépendance nationale) and finally the Parti québécois, which has acted as a conciliator for (but also, in a way, as a moderating and inhibiting influence upon) the currents of thought among the Quebec 'left.'

'To hell with mitres and tuques!' shouted Borduas and the fifteen signatories of the Automatist manifesto: 'A new collective hope shall be born.' Kindled in the deep shadows of the Duplessis era, the fiery lyricism of *Refus global* proclaimed the profound misery of the tiny French-Canadian nation 'clasped tight in the skirts of the priests and shielded against the universal

---

*By Jean-Paul Desbiens. Translated by Miriam Chapin as *The Impertinences of Brother Anonymous* (Montreal: Harvest House 1962) (ed.)
†By Pierre Vallières. Translated by Joan Pinkham as *The White Niggers of America* (New York: Monthly Review Press 1971) (ed.)

evolution of thought.' In the same breath, however, it declared the bankruptcy of the entire Christian, rationalistic civilization of the Western world, as shown in the barbarity of the Second World War. The 'total revolution' prophesied by the rebels of 1948 was in essence a process of personal emancipation and explosive creative activity. It drew its energy from a particular conception of universal man (who would be transfigured by his absolute freedom of expression) as well as from a spontaneous act of faith in the still youthful creativity of North American man. (In two letters written to Claude Gauvreau in 1958 and 1959, Borduas, after a reminder that he had always been 'apolitical,' affirmed that he 'had a horror of all forms of nationalism,' and that he considered himself more North American than Canadian and, strictly speaking, more Canadian than French-Canadian. He also said that there was 'no future for French anywhere in the world. As far as I am concerned, the dies are cast.') All this to say that, at the same time as they were calling out the need for Quebec society to emerge from the long night of the Duplessis era, the tenants of the *Refus global* were not at all interested in making a minute analysis of the economic and historical stranglehold in which we found ourselves, let alone in formulating a revolutionary conception of the problem in terms of a federal-provincial fight to the finish, and so on. Their sole concern was to overthrow Our Master the Past, with never a backward glance. They maintained that here, as elsewhere in the world, destitution resulted from the decay and hypocrisy of societies 'caught in the deep rut of Christianity,' in which sooner or later all the political revolutions, whether French, Russian, or Spanish, had fouled themselves. With *Refus global*, then, we heard a cry of anger against the clergy and the Duplessis regime, but also, by extension, a categorical affirmation of atheism, apoliticism, internationalism, and anti-nationalism. All of these were intellectual positions that made a spectacular break with traditional Quebec thought (even though the apoliticism may at the time have been no more than a sophisticated version of the disgust ordinary people feel for the 'dirtiness' of party politics ...). In short, seeing themselves as a fringe group in Quebec and as emigrants to 'the whole world,' the majority of the protesters of 1948 went into geographical or moral exile in pursuit of fiercely personal destinies, sometimes finding prestige (like the painter Riopelle, *et al*) and sometimes tragedy (like Gauvreau, who later committed suicide). Black stars shine alone.

Cité libre sprang from exactly the same premises (the urgent need to conjure away the Great Darkness, to open windows on the world, etc.), but it took up the protest at a slightly lower level, thus without losing sight of the local socio-political context and most of all without cutting itself off from the religious foundations which had characterized the collective identity. Although there was no rejection of faith as such, there was a repudiation of governmental and clerical hypocrisy, attacked precisely in the name of a virile Christian faith committed to social justice, ecumenism, and so on. (To provide a theoretical foundation for this revolutionary, leftist Catholicism, these writers looked to Maritain and the so-called 'personalist' philosophy of Mounier, importing, along with the Spirit of *Esprit*, specifically European models for interpreting world problems. The former militants of the JEC,* now at *Cité libre*, fell into line with their French anti-fascist intellectual masters just as today the Marxists of *Stratégie* take their inspiration from foreign intellectual circles ...) Thus we find a recognition of the backwardness of Quebec society, which they considered a direct result of collusion between an obscurantist clergy and an obtuse provincial authority; thus their anti-clericalism, anti-Duplessisism, and, by extension, as in *Refus global*, their anti-nationalism. However, all these concerns were to be given form in a new struggle for liberation, but one which was less lyrical and more down-to-earth than its predecessor. Borduas's political and poetical globalism could be replaced by a ready-made and electorally profitable internationalism: Canadian federalism, which was promoted as an eminently feasible way of opening up to the world and as a powerful antidote to current attitudes of folksy provincial nationalism and narrow-minded Catholicism. In short, the collusion between Duplessis and his Church was perceived at *Cité libre* as constituting a cause, a system unto itself, perpetuated by the passivity, incompetence, and credulous ignorance of the Québécois. This attitude derived from a circular diagnosis that was later considered suspect by the intellectuals grouped around *Liberté*. Nevertheless, the specific contribution of *Cité libre* was to introduce the idea that liberation could be collective and political (mobilization of the unions, electoral campaigns), and based upon our cultural heritage (which in this case was strictly identified with Christian values).

At the time it was founded in about 1958, the magazine *Liberté* (whose subsidized longevity has left it open to some harsh criticism) gathered around it a group made up principally of literary people concerned with socio-political problems. The more Marxist members of the original team almost immediately dissociated themselves from the magazine, thus leav-

---

*La Jeunesse étudiante catholique, branch of the Action Catholique, a Quebec movement to increase the power of the laity within the Church and to promote Christian values among young people (ed.)

ing it to pursue a course of critical thought less ideologically defined yet still quite far removed from the Catholicism of *Cité libre*. *Liberté* differed from its predecessor in its decidedly secular and specifically cultural approach, and especially in its systematic examination of such problems as expression, language, creative originality, and so on. This growing sensitization led in turn to a deeper analysis of French-Canadian impotence, guilty conscience, submissiveness, and intellectual backwardness. Asking a series of *whys*, such writers concluded that the dictatorial collusion between Church and State (in this instance the Province) was only a system within a system, that the obscurantism of these two indigenous powers was – and historically always had been – at the service of a third force of domination. This blew a hole in the vicious circle of explanations advanced by *Cité libre*. The *Liberté* group also recalled that anti-clericalism was nothing new to Quebec, and that a long tradition of secularism and free-thinking – associated, as if by chance, with the anti-colonialist struggles and republicanism of 1837 – had been totally suppressed. In short, a closer examination revealed that the syndrome of moral, economic, and cultural backwardness in the 'little people clasped tight in the skirts of the priests' seemed strangely similar to the portraits Fanon and Memmi were drawing of colonized nations. At *Liberté*, the phenomenological analysis of our national problems culminated in a famous article by Hubert Aquin entitled 'La fatigue culturelle du Canada français,' and later in Fernand Ouellette's essay on the language struggle. Thus, by the end of the period between 1959 and 1964 (the era, incidentally, of the Quiet Revolution and the founding of the Mouvement laïc de langue française and the RIN), *Liberté* was engaged in demystifying the federalist thesis and advocating instead a secular and socialistic new nationalism. (The internationalist preoccupation remained, but with a rejection of abstract internationalism and an insistence upon the necessity of national cultures). However, *Liberté*'s efforts at political theorizing did not remain systematic for long, largely because the editors' intellectual background made them wary of adopting dogmatic positions; in spite of their resolutely negative attitude towards the Church, they still remained sensitive to the Christian humanism of the Western world. In 1963 *Parti pris* arrived on the scene. Using Marxist models of interpretation as its primary tool and publishing issue after issue of the most insistent and coherent analysis of the stagnant situation in Quebec, it called for 'the creation of an active and genuinely revolutionary party.' In the meantime, however, the appearance of the first FLQ (Front de libération du Québec) had brutally altered the state of public awareness of these problems.

With the benefit of hindsight, a rereading of *Parti pris* reveals its content as being so astonishingly lucid and relevant that it deserves a more generous analysis. Here I can simply note that in all areas of collective life *Parti pris* promoted a struggle for decolonization that was intended to anticipate and historically to precede a proletarian revolution. 'Independence is only one aspect of Quebec liberation... We are fighting for a free, secular and socialist State... The revolution can only be nationalistic; in its national form, it will be socialistic only if it aims at destroying the powers of oppression which alienate the majority of the people: American, English-Canadian and even French-Canadian capitalism...' This position was not only one of declamation; it was documented by detailed studies of the Quebec reality – the agricultural situation, the cinema, and so on. Also, it underlined the ambiguity of the Quiet Revolution. With *Parti pris*, the fairly loose concept of the Quebec 'left,' which had been applied to a great variety of critical or merely progressive attitudes, reverted to something closer to the classical European sense of the word: either leftists are Marxists or they are not leftists. This logical position, however, was conveyed in a tone that in retrospect seems grossly intransigent for the times. Relying upon tactics of persuasion all too popular with anyone in Quebec who is fighting for a cause, this amounts to cudgelling the non-converted or ridiculing them for stupidity or bad faith, rather than trying to approach them in some pedagogical manner. (There is a certain terrorism of 'in' thinking which is often a misguided attempt at consciousness-raising.) In spite of this, *Parti pris* had strong and widespread repercussions; no magazine since has had such a great impact, and none has played such a systematic role of analysis and animation. By the time its activities had come to a close, the movement towards secularization and decolonization had become quite obvious. *Parti pris* followed immediately on the heels of *Liberté* and outdistanced it, so to speak, on the left. Moreover, although all evidence points to an absolute incompatibility between *Parti pris* and *Cité libre*, there was, in a sense, no historical discontinuity between the two; the working-class preoccupations of 1950 were fully taken up again, but they were now associated with the need for class struggle and a preliminary campaign against colonialism. The atheism of *Refus global* also gained in philosophical expression through its exposure to the Feuerbachian criticism contained in Marx, which leads to political action.

I should again refer to an historical circumstance which in my opinion has influenced the development of the intellectual community or has at least conditioned it psychologically. I am referring to the intervention of the first FLQ. It is disconcerting that violence should have appeared on the scene before the intelligentsia, which had barely given up its belief in Federalism, had had time enough to articulate effectively the terms of the master-slave dialectic implicit in any struggle for decolonization. In order to have the fact of the bombs sink into our national conscience (which had hardly emerged from the confessional), it was necessary to precipitate the process of politicization and exculpation that at that point had barely begun; for the same reason, it was necessary to administer large doses of theoretical justifications in an effort to exorcize the moral anguish (actually more moral in Quebec than truly political) engendered by the 'problem' of terrorist violence. In their hurry to find explanations, intellectuals improperly cited Algerian and Cuban models which, although eminently useful as references, did not completely mirror the local situation. Seeking intellectual security, they sometimes also turned feverishly to Marx and the Marxist ideologists rather than examining the psychology and history of Quebec. In spite of its usefulness, this instrumental recourse to the Marxist-Leninist doctrine imported by *Parti pris* was not without secondary effects that in the long term proved paralysing: childish dogmatism, ideological mimicry, unproductive populism, and so on. Actually, because of this obsession with terrorist-style violence and its Marxistic or Maoistic rationalization, little attempt was made to envisage other means, outside the political arena, of unequivocally rejecting the colonizer and resolving our alienation. This paralleled a considerable loss of contact with the popular mentality. Actually the fantastically accelerated phenomenon of religious disaffection (which seemed at first to resemble the re-emergent revolutionary secularism of *Liberté* which Pierre Maheu foresaw as being nothing but a straightforward phenomenon of deculturation) gave no proof whatever that the people of Quebec had automatically become more highly political or suddenly more receptive to dialectical materialism, the preachy preachings about class struggle, guerilla warfare, and so on. This was clearly shown in the October Crisis, with its enormous undercurrents of collective guilt, together with the symptoms of depression and the swing to the right that followed it. Actually, the problem of violence as a response to colonial domination has remained central, and has not been solved despite invocations to Marx or prayers to Althusser. It is also quite striking that the most audacious spokesmen for *Parti pris* have finally turned their revolutionary tactics towards fields of cannabis and daisies, of naturistic mysticism, 'peace and love' movements, and universal poetic liberation. This is not very far removed from *Refus global*, which makes us wonder whether revolutions in Quebec can only be spiritual in nature and very personal and interior even then ... Even if the ex-members of *Parti pris* have maintained their social awareness, it seems that they have not been able to realize their goals in truly political terms or to sacrifice their intellectual purity to support the basic objectives of the PQ (Parti québécois), and thus have not been able (even with a Leninistic, long-range vision) to enter into the great daily arena of popular ideas. Of course the individual evolutions of the *Parti pris* writers would be significant only as anecdotes did they not coincide with the vaguely depoliticized and universalist attitudes of an important segment of the young intelligentsia. Meanwhile, the *Liberté* group, also anxious to formulate a revolutionary morale to follow up its patient cultural psychoanalysis of the sixties, has taken refuge in a sort of concrete internationalism, as evidenced by its organization of the Quebec International Writers Meetings, its publication of foreign authors, and so on. Thus, from the sombre backwaters of the local intelligentsia, it holds high its little humanist flame of opening unto the world.

On the whole, the intellectuals have more or less failed in their task of articulating in genuinely autochthonous terms a theory and an ethic of decolonization. (Curiously, those who have felt the need of doing this, with the means available to them and the guidance of their own cultural heritage – writers like Vadeboncœur, Bouthillette, or Grand'maison, to name only a few – have not succeeded in establishing an influential school of thought and have attracted infinitely fewer followers than those who have stumbled into the ideological shoes of Mounier, Marx, Marcuse, and *tutti quanti*.) All things considered, the intellectuals have more or less abandoned the Parti québécois to its task of sensitizing, psychoanalysing, and re-educating the masses, without having fully understood that the problem of the PQ's so-called 'electoral' prudence is fundamentally a problem of language, that is, to formulate an unmistakable, original conception and historical comprehension of our particular colonial situation. On the other hand, deprived of their genuinely creative contribution and instinctively rejecting a less perfect instrument for popular consciousness-raising, the PQ has maintained, behind a benevolent exterior, a scrupulous mistrust of leftist intellectuals; in the process it has also underestimated their possibilities.

By way of conclusion, let me simply point out the absence of a philosophy that can be called determinedly Québécois, centred upon the problematics of alienation, and clearly rooted in the experience, the sensibility, and the cultural and historical heritage of the Quebec people. It may be hoped that such a philosophy will emerge, just as in earlier times a national literature emerged from the melting pot of outside influences. (On this point I must make a final observation: while giving expression to the critical thinking of an entire decade or generation, *Refus global, Liberté,* and *Parti pris* left in their wake a bulk of important creative writings. The achievements of the Automatists are impressive; the magazine *Liberté* is directly or indirectly associated with the dynamism of the Hexagone poets and the flowering of the new Quebec novel; and the commitment of *Parti pris* directly stimulated the production of a vigorously national and contestatory literature, heralding for better or worse the era of writing in a proudly vernacular language, and making way for the current explosion in Quebec theatre. Yet there is no evidence of such creative fervour in the evolution of *Cité libre,* and it appears to be only incidental in the case of *Maintenant.* Is it simply a coincidence that these are both magazines which have explicitly honoured the Christian tradition, although in very different senses, and that have particularly encouraged theological commentaries or socio-political studies in the academic vein without either directly challenging the whole question of language or even implying, through an examination of the perilous dialectic of form and content, the necessity of a totally revolutionized Québécois mode of expression? Lacking sufficient space to deal with this question more fully, I shall have to be content with pondering the conditions for a revolutionary aesthetic ...) Although I do recognize the specific function of the intellectual, I do not overestimate his role as a leader, and even less his 'avante-garde' mission – an inflated myth if ever there was one. Actually, the course the Quebec intelligentsia has followed, and which has been reflected over the years by the publications discussed here, seems to me to correspond very closely to an objective, historical course: beginning with the struggle against Duplessis, the Quiet Revolution and the general effervescence of the sixties, it wobbled through Bill 63, the War Measures Act, Bourassa's 'sovereignty' and Bill 22, finally staggering off in the direction of an immense, collective abandonment of the ship. Buffeted by adverse winds, Quebec is in the trough of the waves. The creative vitality of its intellectuals is also at a very low ebb, it seems to me, with each one keeping afloat as best he can and clutching his own little lifebuoy: some hold to the catechism of class struggle, others to a messianic belief in *joual,* and still others are adrift in the vapours of Oriental or American counter-cultures and other trips or mini-trips. In relation to the determining forces of History, it is tempting to define the Quebec intelligentsia as a class of people who are endlessly thimking, dessertating and anulyzing* – and actually are of no real importance to anyone. In spite of

*In the original, the author makes ironic reference to a famous phrase used by Charles de Gaulle during his visit to Quebec in 1967. (ed.)

their light-weight status, however, their undertakings are significant. And in order to evaluate the progress of the collective conscience, we have little choice but to look back at them, for when all is said and done, it is the writings that remain.

THEMES AND GENRES

JEAN-CHARLES FALARDEAU

The Evolution of the Hero
in the Quebec Novel

A pioneer in the study of sociology in Quebec, Jean-Charles Falardeau has had a brilliant academic career. The first director of the Department of Sociology and Anthropology of Laval University (where he still teaches), co-founder and co-director of the magazine *Recherches sociographiques*, and president of several academic and cultural associations, Falardeau has also published an impressive number of books and articles dealing with Quebec society. Like Fernand Dumont, Marcel Rioux, and Yves Martin, he is a distinguished sociologist whose interest in Quebec culture goes beyond the strict limits of his discipline and whose work has had a considerable impact on the intellectual life of the society on which it is based.

Falardeau has long been interested in what literature can tell us about society. *Notre société et son roman* (HMH, 1967) approaches the Quebec novel from the point of view of social topography, examining its reflections of the family, social classes, professions, institutions, and ideology, and exploring its predominant symbols and myths. Here the focus is primarily sociological, although the author makes it clear that the world created in novels is connected with real society but not entirely dependent upon it. A thorough and thoughtful study, it also provides detailed analyses of the works of Robert Charbonneau and Roger Lemelin.

A later collection of essays, *Imaginaire social et littérature* (Hurtubise-HMH, 1974), reveals that the author's interests have shifted more in the direction of literature than of society. Preoccupied with questions of literary theory and methodology, Falardeau reviews the critical approaches of various Quebec writers as well as of theorists like Goldmann, Lukács, and Sartre. He also proposes his own methods for investigating literary texts and their relationship with society, advocating a multidimensional approach which takes into account the immense role played by the imagination in any literary creation. This same concern explains his mild anti-Marxist bias and his conviction that sociology is only one of many valid tools for literary research.

Jean-Charles Falardeau is generally considered the dean of sociological criticism in Quebec. His dual interest in literature and society, his pervasive humanism, and his sober, weighty style are all apparent in the following article, first published as a brochure by Les presses de l'Université de Montréal in 1968 and reprinted in various collections since then.

THE EVOLUTION OF THE HERO IN THE QUEBEC NOVEL

It is not inconceivable that the novel might one day disappear. Its present condition would seem to indicate that it has exhausted all available forms and techniques. The fictional hero has long been considered by Lukács to be rather doubtful; in several literatures, he is being atomized by his own questioning, or helplessly transformed by his creators' aesthetic preoccupations and formal considerations. And now we are seeing the structures and aesthetic concerns of the novelist being adopted and surpassed by such things as 'happenings,' experimental theatre, and cinema.

The Quebec novel has perhaps not yet reached this stage. Its evolution, like our society's, has been less spectacular. And also like our society's, an important phase of its growth has short-circuited, so that it has many of the characteristics of an unfinished symphony. This is how the Quebec novel is seen in the summaries and analyses of those critics who have provided the best discussions of it. On reading such studies, it occurs to us that the critical appraisal of French-Canadian fiction is moving in directions that are increasingly difficult to reconcile, and that any attempts to carry on with such appraisal are futile.

Nevertheless, examining our novels remains one of the best ways of reaching a clearer awareness of the evolution of French-Canadian society and culture. A sociological study of the novel, although it does not pretend to an exhaustive treatment of the literary object, can be responsive to the groups of themes on which it is structured, to the underlying concerns which have perpetuated these themes, and to the various forces that have transformed them. In this way sociology is indicative of the continuities and discontinuities of culture, and it leads to a wider viewpoint from which to consider the similarities, divergencies, and interpenetration from one culture to another.

It is in this perspective that I once again approach our novel, examining certain important aspects of the visions of the world it contains. I shall deal most specifically with the characteristics of the fictional hero and with his attitudes towards life: how he perceives and uses time; what he aims for and achieves in his life; how he relates to his setting, communicates with the physical world, and communicates with others. Sartre writes that 'a novel is made with time and free minds.'[1] If we plan to deal effectively with these two fundamental dimensions, we shall be led to an examination of the density of the fictional worlds and the intrinsic nature of their heroes.

Thus my principal concern is not with the novel's form and structure (composition, technique, style), although I am aware of their relative importance. Until very recently the significance of the Quebec novel did not depend on structure and form. Nor am I sure that it ever does so completely. Can style alone reveal the 'true content' of a work of literature, as Réjean Robidoux would have us believe?[2] I do not think so. To quote from Sartre again, 'a fictional technique always derives from the novelists' metaphysics. The critic's task is to define the latter before evaluating the former.'[3] Rather than 'metaphysics' I would say 'vision of the world,' and rather than searching for this in the novelist, I would look for it in his characters: a vision of the world composed both of the visions of the novelist, and of the society and age he lives in.

CLASSIFICATION OF THE QUEBEC NOVEL

Various attempts to classify the Quebec novel according to genre correspond to similar attempts to identify specific stages in its evolution. This coincidence is revealing and worth a closer look.

Jeanne Lapointe's still relevant study from 1954 does not aim to propose an actual typology.[4] Nevertheless, it constitutes a first attempt at dividing the contemporary novel into categories based on what the author calls 'lines of force.' This term implies such diverse criteria as the dominant themes, the groups of themes, the nature of space in the fictional worlds, the psychological make-up of the heroes, and their criticism of or protest against social institutions. Thus Jeanne Lapointe distinguished among: (1) novels dominated by the themes of an idealized past and loyalty to France; (2) realistic novels of farm life; (3) novels with bourgeois settings; (4) a sub-category of the preceding division, including psychological novels that deal with internal breakdown; (5) the urban novel of everyday life; and (6) novels that emphasize clerical themes or criticism of institutions. Most of these categories overlap one another in time, although the later ones are concentrated in the contemporary period. It is significant that Jeanne Lapointe sees the publication of Les demi-civilisés* in 1934 as the 'first attempt to make a break' between the first two categories of novels (those dealing with loyalty to tradition and with life on the farm) and the later categories; these she considers a true turning point 'with insurrectional overtones.'

Nor does Henri Tuchmaïer present a typology in his patient study, Evolution de la technique du roman canadien-français.[5] He limits himself to a summary of the novelists' use of narrative methods, certain traits in their characters, the nature of time in the novels, and so on. In this historical account, he chooses 1930 as a date which marks a change in every level of fictional technique. Tuchmaïer classifies all novels prior to 1930 as 'novels of fidelity,' a fidelity that applies equally to the themes and the manner of writing. After 1930, the novelists 'confront the major problems of fictional creation,' using internal narrators, witness-narrators, and interior monologues; the triumphant, idealized hero is succeeded by a free character whose incipient transformation is made evident in the plot, and whose manipulation of time is carried out with greater vitality.

For Gilles Marcotte, our novel 'was not born until about 1925,'[6] when it began to draw closer to 'its own reality as a work of art' and 'the reality ... of the milieu' that had produced it. He notes two key dates in this first phase: 1933, with Un homme et son péché, and 1934 with Les demi-civilisés. Félix-Antoine Savard's Menaud, maître-draveur,† which is more an epic poem than a novel, marks, together with his other works, the end of regionalism. In 1938 another important period begins with our four 'classic' authors: Ringuet, Roger Lemelin, Gabrielle Roy, and Germaine Guèvremont. These novelists bring about a revolution of observation, realism, and faith in the present.[7] However, this stage is really more like a hiatus since, simultaneously, in the decade from 1940 to 1950, a new current takes shape, showing what is to become the main thrust in the evolution of the novel: novels of personal adventure, and novels of passion. A whole generation of young novelists who are spiritually related, Charbonneau, Langevin, Cloutier, and Giroux, are all engaged in an experience of recognizing and transcending their anguish.[8] For their immediate successors, Jean-Jules Richard, Yves Thériault, and Jean Simard, this investigation takes on a more instinctive and direct form. In thirty years, suggests Marcotte, the novel has experimented with and experienced everything possible.[9]

---

*By Jean-Charles Harvey, translated by Lukin Barette as Sackcloth for Banner (Toronto: Macmillan 1938) (ed.)

†Translated by Alan Sullivan as Boss of the River (Toronto: Ryerson 1947) (ed.)

Meanwhile, Réjean Robidoux and André Renaud make their own survey in *Le roman canadien-français du vingtième siècle*,[10] in which they are particularly concerned with questions of style. Borrowing Tuchmaïer's term, 'novels of fidelity,' they consider that this tradition survived into the forties. This category includes both the historical novel and the novel of farm life, and 'reflects the social and religious context'[11] in a style that has remained conventional. The 'social novel,' by which they mean the 'novel with social implications,' first appears with Roger Lemelin and Gabriélle Roy. It can be recognized 'by the modern age and modern spirit' that it depicts,[12] and is also characterized by the use of more varied techniques, the renewal of artistic methods, and by its satirical bias. A third category impinges chronologically upon the previous one; this is the 'interior novel' where the writer must deal with the problem of the autonomy of the character. In a final stage, Robidoux and Renaud see the novelists as changing from passivity to action, bringing to their work an aesthetic approach based on questioning. This is a period in which the novel creates its own form, the 'poem-novel,' and in this category we find the first signs, in the sixties, of our 'new novel.'

As varied as these points of view may be, they do concur on certain points: the authentic Quebec novel began to emerge between 1925 and 1940; the years 1933 and 1934 marked a decisive turning point; until then our novel was one of fidelity to a traditional thematic and stylistic framework. Their views are less in agreement as to the directions the novel has taken since then, but they do quite clearly point out several of its principal characteristics: the emergence of realism; a wider field of vision, now including urban social milieux; the predominance of the so-called interior novel, whose hero is beset by what Gilles Marcotte has called 'vertigo';[13] and the recent appearance of unfamiliar and experimental forms for the novel.

THE FICTIONAL HERO AND ITS MODELS

Such statements do not give a full account of the evolution of our novel. It is possible, by placing ourselves in the centre of the fictional worlds that have followed one another in the course of this evolution, to learn still more about them. Let us observe the fictional hero as closely as possible and attempt first to discover the models that have guided his behaviour.

The hero in the traditional novel – novels of farm life or historical novels – is a hero who is or who is meant to be exemplary. He has had a vision of the world presented to him, and he would like to live up to this vision. He is preoccupied and often obsessed with conforming to an abstract, ideal model, a model that has been set out *a priori*, from outside him and above him, removed from any existential experience. Often the priest is at his side as a representative of supernatural power, proposing a model or reminding him of one. Even when the priest is not there, the hero, within himself, lets him have the final word. The hero lives within a clearly defined concept of time, one that is steeped in nostalgia for the past. The past itself is ideal, heroic, and exemplary. The space in which he lives his life extends only as far into the countryside as he can see with his own eyes. This space is Québécois and rural.

It is the non-Québécois writers who have set their imaginary worlds in the vast spaces of Canada and Northern Quebec: Maurice Constantin-Weyer, Louis Hémon, Louis-Frédéric Rouquette, Marie Lefranc, Georges Bugnet, and, more recently, Gabrielle Roy. Quebec novelists have generally set their stories within familiar horizons, horizons that nevertheless are constantly beckoning towards the distances beyond: the land of the voyageurs, the storytellers, and the men from the *'pays d'en haut'* – a hinterland whose nature and attractions have been analysed by Jack Warwick.[14] Actually, the heroes in this fiction live with a constant urge to get away, and they almost all question whether they should stay or leave. Many of them leave for fascinating and dangerous places, while the others remain behind and dream. In any case, the city is a perilous or nefarious place: the letters from Montreal written by Gustave Charmenil to his friend Jean Rivard are worth remembering in this regard. The countryside and the land are desirable microcosms, and are associated with fidelity. However, they are almost always places that have been recently settled or acquired. The hero of the land is a pioneer-hero, clearing the land but still very close to the forest. The countryside and the land seem insufficient as soon as they are possessed. They cause boredom or nostalgia.

Menaud, maître-draveur must be considered the apotheosis of the exemplary hero, with Menaud attaining truly mythic dimensions. He has an irrepressible faith in the ideal of fidelity to the call of duty, duty that demands he win back the mountain his people have been dispossessed of. He personifies a desperate effort to overcome the physical dispossession of the forest / land. He is a dramatic hero, expressing himself on the level of poetry. He has kept the faith.

In the traditional novel, however, Menaud is the final incarnation of the hero preoccupied with an ideal model. This concern with having a model to imitate first begins to disappear in the so-called novels of the land. With the publication in 1918 of *La scouine** and then *Un homme et son péché* in 1933, we

*By Albert Laberge, translated by Conrad Dion as *Bitter Bread* (Montreal: Harvest House 1977) (ed.)

begin to see a progressive moral dispossession. The former heroes are disenchanted. Their lives are bound to a landscape that traps them, hopelessly and fatefully, behind a wall of time. The setting too has a fateful quality about it. Here, however, it is important to distinguish between the country and land bordering the river and the other places further inland. Life is peaceful for those living along the St Lawrence and on the islands; sometimes there are even visits from the occasional 'outlander,' bringing with him the fascination of the beyond and the unknown. Tragedy is associated with the settlements in more isolated country, with settings that are closed in upon themselves. (Later we find an equivalent of this situation in the 'urban' novels; just as the 'land' is more tolerable if it borders on water or if it is an island, so the city is more tolerable for those living in the suburbs, close to rural spaces. The land needs the complement of water, and the city needs the complement of neighbouring countryside.) The characters' relationships and actions are emptied of meaning. Filiatrault reminds us that, like the space they inhabit, these characters have become 'barren lands,' destined for misery, mourning, and destruction.

The extreme example of this type of hero can be seen, I think, in the fictional world of Yves Thériault. Although each of the worlds described by Thériault is exotic, this does not detract from their significance. In essence, the hero finds himself in a universe stripped of all value. The male confronts a natural world reduced to an elemental state, from which he must learn everything all over again. Lacking a human model, he himself is reduced, it would seem, to his blind nature: to a nature that expresses itself in arrogance and in a need for physical domination, violence, and destruction. Without conscience and without duration, he exists essentially as a brutal force. His time and space are those of combat. He has no past and he is from no place. He is the last descendant of Séraphin Poudrier.[15]

However, heroes who are preoccupied with models have not entirely disappeared. We find them as early as 1922, in Jean-Charles Harvey's character Marcel Faure, and we continue to find them in novels by Desmarchais, Desrosiers, Charbonneau, Giroux, and several others. It is their *status* that has changed. Beginning with *Marcel Faure*, and later in *André Laurence* by Pierre Dupuy and *L'initiatrice* by Rex Desmarchais, the hero is a city dweller. He has had a classical education, he is part of the bourgeois or semi-bourgeois 'class,' and he belongs or would like to belong to the category of 'intellectuals.' His models are heterogeneous. The word model implies superior standards, values that provide the standards with content and prestige. Although the new, intellectual type of hero remains possessed by a need for models, he no longer looks for them among models based on the old values. He has begun to say 'I' and he poses problems that originate in himself. And thus a great variety of differing attitudes develop. In novels by Harvey, the hero is ardently dedicated to an ideal of freedom while at the same time aspiring to combine it with traditional values in which he believes strongly but confusedly. The heroes in Desmarchais's and Charbonneau's novels speak out against the traditional values. They are looking for 'real life,' but they seek it in models of excessive purity, abnegation, and renunciation – new models that are more demanding than the old ones. The characters of Robert Elie and André Giroux are frustrated at not being able to reconcile Christian values with the hypocrisies of concrete existence. The questioning of traditional values is more radical with Langevin's heroes, but they eventually find that they have been defeated by tradition and drawn back into it.

Like variations on a basic theme, these are the destinies of such characters as Max Hubert, Julien Pollender, Marcel Larocque, and Denis Boucher. The hero's conflicts stem from his incapacity either clearly to define the new values – political involvement, economic activity, intellectual life, friendship – or to confront and dominate the representatives of the old values: the priest, the grandfather or the mother of the family. In each case, he feels himself somehow victimized from the very beginning. He lives in the damning gaze of others, and his career is a failure. This failure is most clearly seen in his attitude towards and communication with women. Women are not so much human beings as symbols of the two extremes of his dilemma. On the one hand, they are angels associated with an otherwordly absolute, agents of atonement whose prototype is presented by Rex Desmarchais in his character Violaine Haldé: 'her arms cross-like in front of the open window ... her chest bare ... the cruel North Wind [freezing] the virginal flesh offered in a holocaust.'[16] Or, conversely, they are ripe for intrigues and debauchery, associated with human turpitude.

Space and time, too, draw away from the world, or into zones of introspective awareness. Although we refer to these heroes as being 'urban,' it must also be said that 'the city' for them is an uneasy place, whose nebulous streets all lead back to an area of inner anguish. The hero seeks metaphysical or intellectual escape, and he ultimately takes refuge in the act of writing.

With Gabrielle Roy and Roger Lemelin, the city for the first time becomes an actual setting that influences the fate of their characters; it is a difficult, human, and demanding setting in which they are forced to define and defend their existence. Within the cities of Montreal or Quebec, the characters live in a particular neighbourhood. For the first time, the urban hero comes from a working-class area, and he is directly involved in a conflict between the traditional values of his place of origin and the new values: money, freedom, conquest, love, and success, all of which are associated with the more prosperous neighbourhoods and the upper levels of society. In *Bonheur d'occasion*, Jean Lévesque conforms to the cruel demands of social mobility, thinking that this will open his way into the level of society and the residential areas owned and inhabited by others: the élite, the oustiders, and the 'English.' As for Lemelin's Jean Boucher, he openly renounces his neighbourhood, wanting to gain access to the Upper Town, a symbol of political and intellectual power and of wealth. However, his impatience and naïveté with regard to the 'mysterious powers' condemn him to failure, and he can rise no further than the Latin Quarter, an ambivalent area surrounded by that fortress of ecclesiastical power, the Archbishop's palace and the Grand Seminary.

This need for a model for the urban fictional hero continues, through *Mathieu* in 1949 right up to Bessette's *La bagarre** in 1958 and Marcotte's *Le poids de Dieu†* in 1962. At the same time, however, from about 1939 on, we see it begin to disappear. This disappearance is marked by novels in which the conventional fictional forms are more flexible: *Le beau risque* (1939) and *Anatole Lapointe, curieux homme* (1944) by François Hertel, *Les médisances de Claude Perrin* (1949) by Pierre Baillargeon, *Les hypocrites* (1949) by Berthelot Brunet, *Le poids du jour* (1949) by Ringuet, and *Neuf jours de haine* (1949) by Jean-Jules Richard. Little by little, the fictional hero no longer has the same voice or the same attitudes. He becomes more lucid and more critical, surrounded by lives of disillusionment. He himself becomes disillusioned, casting a lucid glance at the problems and turpitudes of others, taking pleasure in his own bemused lucidity.

LANGEVIN'S HEROES

It is in the work of André Langevin that the urban fictional hero appears for the first time without a model and, consequently, that he attains the extreme limits of solitude, the greatest distress, and the most absolute destitution. For this reason, Langevin's work is an important landmark, perhaps the most revealing in the history of the contemporary novel. Let us consider its basic elements.

---

*Translated by Marc Lebel and Ronald Sutherland as *The Brawl* (Montreal: Harvest House 1976) (ed.)

†Translated by Elizabeth Abbott as *The Burden of God* (New York: Vanguard Press 1964) (ed.)

One and the same hero moves through these three novels, although under different names and with different variations. Jean Cherteffe in *Evadé de la nuit* is an orphan; his drunken father had been an absent God. Beginning his existence without an identity, and unable to create one for himself, he seeks unsuccessfully to build himself up through others, to find in others the answers to his own questioning. Dr Alain Dubois in *Poussière sur la ville** is also an orphan, and he lacks both vitality and virility. 'Engulfed in the gaze of others,'[17] he is unable to face up to the men of this small city who have sensed and judged his deficiencies. Above all, he is unable to face his wife, Madeleine. In *Le temps des hommes* the ex-priest, Pierre Dupas, is also an orphan. Having grown up in the bell-jar of the seminary, he finally breaks out of it in order to go out into the world of men and become a man himself. He is too taken aback by suffering and evil, unable to respond with anything more than his silent pity and the spectacle of his own deficiency. In all three instances, the hero is dominated by a relentless fate that overwhelms, paralyses, or destroys him. The monstrous enigma of children's suffering contradicts all justice, turning birth into a kind of death. Life begins in a coffin.

In this world, time and space resemble and reflect the hero: a hero whose past was a catastrophe, a hero without a past, a hero whose past was not of this world. He lives compressed in a present with no future, and as his tragedy progresses, the present clamps down on him like a vice. The first hero lives in an indefinite setting, 'the city,' composed of a series of lugubrious micro-settings: the funeral parlour, the tavern, the hospital, and the squalid bedroom. The second is pursued through the small city that spies on him, a city alternately covered by dust and snow, shakily constructed above a mine full of underground workers. The moral drama of the third hero takes place in the hostile and limitless forest, a place of snow and cold, a landscape from before the beginnings of the world, as overwhelming as the wickedness of men. The hero is left alone in this setting, as the other human beings die. They exist only in the plural, amalgamated into an invincible generic type. The men are as elemental as the forest that shelters them; like the forest, they are from before the beginnings of the world. Such are the three faces of the hero: despairing of reconstructing others, too weak to affirm himself against others, and incapable of understanding and helping others. Women are even further out of reach, and any attempt at love brings dispossession. Total failure leaves the hero at death's door, or

*Translated by John Latrebe and Robert Gottlieb as *Dust over the City* (Toronto: McClelland and Stewart 1955; rpt. in the New Canadian Library 1974) (ed.)

as with Dr Dubois, prepared for one last attempt at making a new start, this time in the light of pity. So far, however, none of these new starts has lasted.

OTHER INCARNATIONS OF THE FICTIONAL HERO

In the novels that have followed Langevin's, we hear echoes of this same anguish. The fictional characters of the next period no longer know where they are going; thus they head off in all directions, searching out their own identity, a father, a husband, a substitute for God, or reasons to go on living. The worlds they move through change like the patterns in a kaleidoscope. What common denominator can there possibly be in the worlds of Wilfrid Lemoyne, Claire Martin, Marie-Claire Blais, Gérard Bessette, Jacques Ferron, and Louise Maheux-Forcier?

In some of these worlds, as in *Les témoins* by Eugène Cloutier, the hero is discountenanced or distorted by the perceptions of others. More and more frequently, the hero himself becomes the perceiver and, standing back from his own milieu, he subjects it to an eager and surgical examination, as is the case in *La bagarre, Le libraire,** and *Cotnoir.†* The hero grows increasingly detached, becoming an object of humour; in *Simone en déroute*, for instance, we see the mother's family 'empire' come tumbling down about her. Thanks to the women writers, female characters have descended from a purely symbolic level and have taken form as human beings who will more openly express their desires and their plans for living. Several of these heroines seemed, from the very beginning, to be more advanced than their male protagonists. We see woman as nature in Claire Mondat's *Poupée*, woman as inspiration in *Les hauts cris* by Suzanne Paradis, and the woman as artist in *Amadou* by Louise Maheux-Forcier. But above all, in the novels of Claire Martin, we see women in love: wanting to love, knowing how to love, and wanting to teach men how to love. Like the young characters from an earlier period, several of these female characters have been victimized; and they too are seeking, in a difficult and magical rediscovery of their childhood, a way to come back into contact with the physical world and the world of man. Not all of them are as deeply involved in eroticism as

---

*By Gérard Bessette, translated by Glen Shortliffe as *Not for Every Eye* (Toronto: Macmillan 1962) (ed.)

†By Jacques Ferron, translated by Pierre Cloutier as *Dr. Cotnoir* (Montreal: Harvest House 1973) (ed.)

Nathalie in *Amadou* or Isabelle in *L'île joyeuse*, but they all affirm the importance of love.

Thanks to the heroines in these novels, love is identified and experienced as a positive value, one that sends fresh air through the ancient labyrinths. We have difficult love in Claire Martin's novels, fantasy love with Réal Benoît, and protean love with Jean Basile. Very often, the object of love is a foreign woman, preferably Jewish. And very often too, sex, love, and marriage with a foreign woman are the results of having travelled. In so far as the hero can escape his immediate confines and venture into new areas, he is able to draw nearer to women. In his usual surroundings, love is a source of conflict. The automobile has entered the picture, and it quickly becomes a frequent and regular element in the fictional landscape. The accordion of time can still be expanded. The vision of the world begins to take on a cinematic appearance, although the penchant for looking towards the past is maintained.

CLAUDE JASMIN AND JACQUES GODBOUT

Let us now look at the work of two other writers, Claude Jasmin and Jacques Godbout, to see how their fictional worlds have grown and changed in a number of significant ways.

In Jasmin's world, space, time, and the destiny of his characters are modified by brusque transformations in the setting. In his first novel, *Et puis tout est silence...*, the hero is trapped in the collapsed scaffolding of a barn. In the second, *La corde au cou*, he is trapped by a circle of policemen closing in on him. In the third novel, *Délivrez-nous du mal*, the car takes over the setting, which includes both Montreal and vast spaces around the city, stretching out towards all four compass points and as far as the ocean. In *Ethel et le terroriste*,* it is New York that has been taken over by the highways. His latest novel, *Pleure pas, Germaine*, is nothing short of a geographical rediscovery of Quebec, from Montreal to the Gaspé; it is a discovery that signals a final abandonment of the poverty-stricken areas of Montreal and a decision to settle in the edenic maritime area where the mother originally came from. Time is theatrical or cinematographic, marked by movements through space. Time is frozen or breathless, mixed with memories in the first two novels and becoming a time of anxiety and impatience, an automotive time in the third novel. A time of fantastic and mythical flight in *Ethel et*

*Translated by David S. Walker as *Ethel and the Terrorist* (Montreal: Harvest House 1965) (ed.)

le terroriste, it finally dilates into a time for relaxation, gentleness and *joie de vivre* in the endless family picnic of the last novel.

At the centre of this increasingly relaxed world, the hero moves successively from non-existence to self-affirmation, and finally to a full possession of his life. In the early novels, the young hero is overwhelmed by an unknowable evil that has been destroying him from within ever since he came into existence. The mask of death rules over the theatre of life; those we love must be killed; the hero himself must die. In the last two novels, the hero progresses from an obsession with evil to a desire for liberation. There is an eloquent symbolism in the actions of Gilles Bédard who, on the dock at Percé, throws into the water all the old things he has carried from Montreal in his trailer, even including 'a useless monstrance.'

Godbout's first hero in *L'aquarium* lives in a sodden world in which all values are breaking apart. The setting for him is a suffocating goldfish bowl. His protagonists too are breaking apart and only he, thanks to a woman, is able to escape. *Le couteau sur la table** introduces a hero who has come back to a familiar setting. Dreaming of the tropics and sunshine, he has to face the snow and cold of a land that is not his own: the endless reaches of the Canadian West. He must also confront a sensual doll-woman who is apparently without soul, the incarnation of the foreign *Anglaise*. He returns with her to a familiar setting, Montreal, but life there is denuded of meaning: his relationship with the woman is essentially false, and his activities are ridiculous, although they are brightened for a time by an authentic and eventually tragic love affair. Having lost all patience, he finally decides on a complete break with the Englishwoman. He is perhaps not a rebel, but he knows what obstacles must be eliminated so that life can be made possible. The hero in *Salut Galarneau!†* lives and has always lived in a Montreal setting. He writes about his life, the life of a man who has made a success of his modest business: a restaurant in the suburbs where he sells hot dogs. He is, in fact, the hot dog 'king.' When his mistress, Marise, leaves him, he falls into a deep depression. He has a huge wall built around his property from which he will not come out alive: an ambivalent, phoney, life-denying civilization is not worth living for. Once before, however, as a child, he had emerged victorious from an initiation rite his grandfather had subjected him to – he had 'conquered the dragon.' Life is made of effort.

---

*Translated by Penny Williams as *Knife on the Table* (Toronto: McClelland and Stewart 1968) (ed.)

†Translated by Alan Brown as *Hail Galarneau!* (Toronto: Longmans 1970) (ed.)

François Galarneau will finish his book and go on to write others. He will go on living. After all, as he points out, his name does mean 'the sun.'

RECENT MUTATIONS

This long account of the fictional hero's progress does not completely account for his most recent metamorphoses, which have been closely associated with the fragmentation of form in the novel. The kind of writing that used to be called the novel corresponded to a literary type whose conventions and rules were carefully respected. Now the appellation 'novel' is no longer a precise term, and it is applied, in Quebec as elsewhere, to all makes and styles of writing. The novel has crept towards something quite different from itself. It has been transformed into a narrative that is increasingly dreamlike, as with Réal Benoît, or fantastic, as with Marie-Claire Blais, or almost delirious, as with Hubert Aquin and Réjean Ducharme. It has become a monologue in which the novelist-narrator speaks for himself, seeking himself through self-expression; thus one of the constants in our novel is given a contemporary twist: the hero as writer. Writers have increasingly adopted Gide's technique in *Les faux-monnayeurs* and have incorporated into their narrative a description of the genesis of the novel they are actually writing; as examples of this, see Réal Benoît's *Quelqu'un pour m'écouter*, Hubert Aquin's *Prochain épisode*,* Laurent Girouard's *La ville inhumaine*, and Jacques Godbout's *Salut Galarneau!*.

One cannot avoid some mention of the most striking characteristic of recent novels: the writers' language. Commentaries on this phenomenon are more numerous than all the novels they are based on. There can be no doubt that *joual* is an extreme form of cultural disintegration. There is little doubt either that the young writer's use of *joual* is symptomatic of a fundamental attitude of radical protest against all the values of earlier generations. This is a phenomenon that leads nowhere, and sooner or later it must come to an end. More worthy of our attention than their use of *joual* is the verbal virtuosity of certain recent novelists; with Hubert Aquin and Réjean Ducharme, although at different levels, this virtuosity reaches its highest point of effervescence. Such an overabundance of language, whether in waking dreams, retrospection, or in a theatrical type of monologue, is a sign of new inner resources and a new self-possession. However,

*Translated by Penny Williams as *Prochain Episode* (Toronto: McClelland and Stewart 1967; rpt. in the New Canadian Library 1973) (ed.)

I am less sure that it can be seen as a sign of a need for communication with others.

In view of the frequent identification of the novelist with his hero, the preceding observations are applicable to both the former and the latter. In a situation like this, can we still say that the fictional hero exists in the old sense? We should not forget that in *La ville inhumaine* by Laurent Girouard we see the spectacle of a hero being destroyed by his own creator. Nevertheless, there are still cases in which the characters carry on an autonomous existence. We find certain of them, as in *Ce maudit soleil* by Marcel Godin, returning to a forest and a natural state that are reminiscent of Thériault's world. Otherwise, they decide to go on living a doubtful urban existence. The most striking characteristic of the recent fictional worlds is that they are again becoming inhabited by adolescent heroes. This process began with Marie-Claire Blais, continued with Claude Jasmin, expanded with Jacques Renaud and André Major, and reached its apex with Réjean Ducharme. What is the explanation for this phenomenon? Does it have something to do with the age of the writers? If so, are we seeing a final liquidation of the deepest taboos that previous heroes only appeared to surmount, a final putting to rest of a residual fear of the city?

This question becomes clearer when seen in terms of the very recent evolution of the setting in the novels. The setting becomes increasingly cinematic as it casually shifts to different levels and locations. Some are settings of escape and return, of new beginnings, as in *Le poisson pêché* and *L'aquarium*; some are dream settings, mingling memories from the past with dreams of the present, as in *Quelqu'un pour m'écouter, Prochain épisode,* and *L'avalée des avalés,** and some are labyrinth or underground settings, as in *L'incubation.†* Writers still frequently retreat into childhood memories that provide meticulous and tender evocations of places long since part of another world. Such is the case in *La nuit* and many other narratives by Jacques Ferron, for whom the illusion of going back to the land is a persistent obsession. The fictional world is also often located, as with *Les terres noires* by Jean-Paul Fugère, in settings that I would describe as 'stopping-places' on the outskirts of Montreal.

These latter cases are exceptions, however. Most of the fictional heroes now live in Montreal; it is their setting, their place of origin, their city.

---

*By Réjean Ducharme, translated by Barbara Bray as *The Swallower Swallowed* (London: Hamish Hamilton 1968) (ed.)

†By Gérard Bessette, translated by Glen Shortliffe as *Incubation* (Toronto: Macmillan 1967) (ed.)

Montreal has become a presence in the lives of these characters; in novels by Claude Jasmin, Jean Basile, Jacques Renaud, André Major and several others, Montreal is a way of life – a life of combat, of struggle, and of joy. In a recent interview published in *Culture vivante*,[18] André Major, referring both to recent novels and to French-Canadian society, declared that 'we have not yet accepted the city.' This statement needs clarification on two accounts, the first being that this non-acceptance of the city is not, in itself, peculiar to Quebec fictional heroes; the same phenomenon may be found in all occidental literature. One of the profound reasons for this is probably that the city, as Sartre notes, 'is a social and material organization which derives its reality from the ubiquity of its absence...it is always elsewhere...the myth of the capital with its 'mysteries' clearly demonstrates that the opacity of direct human relationships comes from this fact, that they are always conditioned by all others.'[19] Also, if one compares the present state of the Quebec novel with its earlier stages, one is struck not only by the dynamic presence of the big city but also by the positive ways in which the characters perceive and inhabit it. Of course, not everyone accepts it without reticence, but most of them carve out their own particular spaces in it, and they all accept the rules of the game.

Whether the characters reluctantly accept the city or euphorically take possession of it, Montreal is more than merely described in these novels; it is a living protagonist which determines and shares in the actions of its inhabitants by contributing to and meeting their needs and expectations. The characters in Jean Basile's *La jument des Mongols* bathe in Montreal as in a paradisiacal world perfectly attuned to their jauntiness or their cynicism: it is a full-flavoured world, a world of discoveries, surprises, and relaxations. In *La ville inhumaine* by Laurent Girouard, Montreal resembles the 'Catholico-Franco-Canadian' character whom the author destroys under our very eyes. And in *Le cassé*,* a first-person narrative by Jacques Renaud, the young hero has been maddened to the point of bloodlust by the painful chains that bind him to Montreal:

It's summer. Montreal is a bruised and battered, seared and wounded town. A moving and resonant isle like a sea being slaughtered. The river has settled around it like cast iron. The river wants to sleep. Nothing will stop it. The St Lawrence is an anarchist. When it feels like invading the island, it will... The only difference in the orgies between East and West is that in the East it's a butchery and in the West it's a party...Montreal is a death-rattle...Montreal is a tortured island, knocked out,

*Translated by Gérard Robitaille as *Flat Broke and Beat* (Montreal: Bélier 1964) (ed.)

hideous with poliomyelitis. Montreal stretched out with its wounds in the moonlight.
Montreal fed up.
Montreal sold out.
Montreal mad as hell.[20]

And finally, we should note one part of Montreal that is considered to be very special by the characters in several of these novels: 'la Main.' Victor, in *La jument des Mongols*, says 'You know, if it weren't for the Main, I really think I'd hate Montreal.' The 'Main' (or Saint Lawrence Boulevard) is seen as an almost exotic little island, an ambiguous, deceptive, enticing, anonymous centre for the big city: the starting point of the old line of separation between French and English Montreal...

THE FICTIONAL HERO AND QUEBEC SOCIETY

This rough outline enables us to see more clearly the decisive moments in the evolution of our novel: Laberge (1918) and Grignon (1933); Harvey (1922); Langevin (1951); and the new novelists, circa 1960. Above all, this sketch of the destiny of the French-Canadian fictional hero suggests the image of a line of development which splits into two sections, each one superimposed upon the other. The hero of fidelity, whose life is based vaguely on absolute values and models, is succeeded rather abruptly by a hero who has freed himself of these values and models. No longer having any particular status, this hero has lost the ability to play any particular role. He is followed by a primitive sort of hero who is struggling in a natural world devoid of meaning. The heir to these models is an urban, intellectual hero from the middle or working class or the bourgeoisie. It is at this level of society, at the same time as the hero is being affirmed, that new models are sought out and the old values are called into question. The hero lives on tensions and anxieties, and his inner emptiness increases as he enters 'the time of men.' Thus begins a long series of incarnations, which leave him oscillating between anguish and satire, revolt and cynicism. He is like Sisyphus or Daedalus, groping his way through inner or outer labyrinths and reconciling time with the memories of his own past. Women happen along, offering him the possibility of regaining control over himself and his life. He ventures into unfamiliar settings, begins to discover love, and marries a foreigner. His protest fails to gain a foothold on a reality he would like to change entirely. However, he accepts the city and uses it to create a new setting for himself. Unsure of the future, he forges himself a present.

He is finally transformed into a young person who is enchanted with his own voice and who, in more ways than one, rediscovers some of the themes of the hero living in the primitive world of nature. More often than is normally the case, this hero is a writer faced with the dilemma of choosing between living and writing. From now on he will both live (*vivre*) and write (*écrire*), or as Godbout's character François Galarneau ambiguously puts it, he will *vécrire*. Any models will have to be invented from experience. Will the hero remain a Sisyphus or will he become an Icarus?

Pierre Desrosiers has lucidly noted certain general characteristics of our fictional heroes.[21] I am afraid, however, that he may be guilty of oversimplification in reducing them all to a single type who is caught 'between dream and failure, between vacuousness and escape... attached to a world that no longer answers,'[22] or when he telescopes all the heroes' visions of the world into a single one, of which *Un homme et son péché* would be the prototype. Séraphin Poudrier's vision of the world is no doubt of capital importance, and Pierre Desrosiers has summed it up as follows:

a historic universe, lost values, omnipotent and alienated power, disintegrated collectivity and fixed temporality; power without rational foundations reduced to the mere exercise of itself, impossibility of going beyond what is immediately necessary, hopeless search for values bereft of meaning.[23]

Authoritative though it may be, this vision is not the only one. Nor am I convinced that it should even be seen as the primary one.

Succeeding this vision of the world and the abandonment of its traditional models, we have a series of visions which are more than mere variants; each in fact is worthy of being analysed individually. Equally revealing and conclusive are visions of the world which aspire to integrate the new values with the old ones: some of these express an agonizing awareness of a loss of values, while others reveal a desperate eagerness to define values that are original and lasting, as in the works of Charbonneau, Langevin, Jasmin, and Godbout. In any case, I am not convinced by attempts at 'explaining' these successive visions exclusively in terms of the ideology of 'a social class particular to Quebec history: the nineteenth-century liberal bourgeoisie.'[24] We do not yet know enough about the ideological beliefs or the degree of awareness of this group, which constitutes not so much a 'class' as a political, intellectual, and economic élite. To say that it was modelled on any one ideology would be rash and presumptuous.

Our novel *has stuck very close to reality*. There is a break in the evolution of the fictional hero: we see him suddenly stop believing in his models, burn himself out in his distress, and then give way to a new kind of intellectual and urban hero. This break coincided with a growing awareness in society of the fact that our society no longer conforms to traditional ideals and that in the future it will have to adapt in its own way to the demands of urban civilization. *La scouine* and *Un homme et son péché* are in line with this break-up, and subsequent visions of the world correspond to the various stages of 'coming to the city' that Georges-André Vachon has referred to.[25] Coming to the city brought with it a deconsecration of social models and objectives. The evolution of religious thought and attitudes is just as likely – or more likely – to have been responsible for the social elements that have influenced our creative writers. For above all, our novels express the crisis that results from a shift from the sacred to the profane, from the intemporal to the temporal. The 'dispossession' or 'alienation' that the French-Canadian hero is trying to overcome is no doubt economic and political in nature. But in my opinion, it is also – if not more – a 'religious' dispossession and an alienation from the physical and human earth.

At another level, these reflections invite us to make comparisons with other literatures. Let us again examine the fictional hero's attitude towards women. Until recently this attitude divided the woman into two paradoxical images as opposite as day and night: the angel and the courtesan. We have always tended to think of this as a typically French-Canadian attitude, a specific characteristic of our culture. It is obvious that the women in our fictional worlds do not resemble all women, and that the men often behave rather strangely with them. However, it is also true that Freud regarded this attitude towards women as being a characteristic phenomenon of Western civilization. Western man shares a common psychological make-up which results in women being perceived as bipolar beings. Men see women as having two different faces, the one that of a creature who is above the world and the other that of a creature who is too deeply within the world. Denis de Rougemont, in *L'amour et l'occident*, has attempted to present evidence of an analogous phenomenon, and like Freud has interpreted it as a cultural trait.

In terms of our fictional heroes' most common attitude towards time, it is difficult not to compare them to the characters of Faulkner. Speaking of these characters' feelings of time, Sartre remarked:

Faulkner's vision of the world can be compared to that of a man sitting in an open car and looking backwards...the past takes on a sort of super-reality; its contours are hard and clear, unchangeable. The present, nameless and fleeting, is helpless before it. It is full of gaps, and through these gaps, things of the past, fixed, motionless and silent as judges or glances, come to invade it ... The present is not; it becomes. Everything *was*.²⁶

Does this not sound like a description of the novels of Quebec? Would it be possible, by analysing different aspects of Faulkner's world, to discover some unexpected points of comparison between the cultural make-up of the American Deep South and Nordic Quebec?

We might also suggest an interesting comparison between the world of Joyce and the world of our novels. Joyce's characters actually live in a state of tension between the past and the elsewhere; the destiny of Joyce's central cultural hero, Stephen Dedalus, is to cope with this dilemma – and the paralysis represented by Dublin – by creating a work of art which will transcend, by eternally animating it, 'the uncreated conscience of the race.' Like the work of Joyce, many of the Quebec novels are in the category of the *Bildungsroman* or the *Kunstlerroman* – stories of the formative experiences of the artist-hero or the writer. Unlike Stephan Dedalus, French-Canadian heroes now accept the big city and construct themselves in a space in it, planning for the future. Like Dedalus, however, they get involved in an aesthetic activity that shatters language and transforms it into a wild rush of symbols, that, to judge from Ferron's *Papa Boss*, is rather accurately expressed in a philosophical tale of supreme irony. Their aesthetic attitudes include every possible cinematic technique; like many others, our novelists could not resist borrowing from the cinema, even though it remains far in advance of them. We are no longer surprised by the great alternative that is already before us; our answer to it will be largely responsible for the kind of cultural future we will have: which will win out, the written word or the living image?

As far as I myself am concerned (and this may be only a question of generation and of cultural models), I know that I shall continue to read the novels written here. Especially if, like Godbout's Galarneau, they opt for the world we live in – and the sun.

NOTES

1 Jean-Paul Sartre, *Situations I* (Paris: Gallimard 1947) 56 [tr. Annette Michelson, *Jean-Paul Sartre: Literary and Philosophical Essays* (New York: Collier 1955)]
2 Réjean Robidoux 'Le roman canadien-français de demain' *Le roman canadien-français, évolution, témoignages* (Montreal: Fides, 'Archives des lettres canadiennes' 1965) III, 241–56
3 Sartre *Situations I* [tr. Michelson 71]

4 Jeanne Lapointe 'Quelques apports positifs de notre littérature d'imagination' *Cité libre* No. 10 (October 1954) 17–36; rpt. Gilles Marcotte, ed. *Présence de la critiqe* (Montreal: Editions HMH 1966) 103–20

5 Unpublished doctoral thesis, Université Laval, 1958.

6 Gilles Marcotte 'Brève histoire du roman canadien-français' *Cahiers de l'Académie canadienne-française* No. 3 (1958) 44–80; rpt. *Une littérature qui se fait* (Montreal: Editions HMH 1962) 11–50

7 Marcotte *Une littérature* 37

8 Marcotte *Une littérature* 45

9 Marcotte *Une littérature* 49

10 (Ottawa: Editions de l'Université d'Ottawa 1966)

11 R. Robidoux and A. Renaud *Le roman canadien-français du vingtième siècle* 24

12 Robidoux and Renaud 73

13 Gilles Marcotte "L'expérience du vertige dans le roman canadien-français' *Ecrits du Canada français* XVI (1963)

14 Jack Warwick, 'Les pays d'en haut,' *Culture*, XXI, No. 3 (September 1960) 246–65; 'Les "pays d'en haut" dans l'imagination canadienne-française' *Etudes françaises*, II, No. 3 (October 1966) 265–93; see Jack Warwick *The Long Journey: Literary Themes of French Canada* (Toronto: University of Toronto Press 1968)

15 This statement may seem rather strong; I offer it as an hypothesis that has resulted from the perspective with which I approach the subject. It also enables us, I think, to see Thériault in a new light without contradicting existing interpretations of his work. For example, it corroborates at least one of André Brochu's opinions, to the effect that 'whether he is writing about Eskimos or Spaniards, Yves Thériault never stops exploring the reality of Quebec.' 'Yves Thériault et la sexualité' *Parti pris* 1, Nos. 9–10–11 (Summer 1964) 155; rpt. Gilles Marcotte, ed. *Présence de la critique* 243

16 Rex Desmarchais *L'initiatrice* (Montreal: Lévesque 1932) 165

17 Jean-Louis Major 'André Langevin' *Le roman canadien-français, évolutions, témoignages* (Montreal: Fides, 'Archives des lettres canadiennes' 1965) 216

18 *Culture vivante* No. 5 (1967) 69

19 Jean-Paul Sartre *Critique de la raison dialectique* (Paris: Gallimard 1960) I 57 [tr. Hazel E. Barnes *Jean-Paul Sartre, The Problem of Method* (London: Methuen 1963)]

20 *Le cassé* (Montreal: Parti pris 1964) 86, 87 [tr. Gérard Robitaille *Flat Broke and Beat* (Montreal: Bélier 1964)]

21 Pierre Desrosiers 'Séraphin ou la dépossession' *Parti pris* IV Nos. 5–6 (January-February, 1967) 52–62

22 Desrosiers 58

23 Desrosiers 59

24 Desrosiers 59

25 G.-André Vachon 'L'espace politique et social dans le roman québécois'
Recherches sociographiques VII No. 3 (1966) 261
26 Jean-Paul Sartre 'A propos de *Le bruit et la fureur*. La temporalité chez Faulkner'
Situations 73–4 [tr. Michelson]

GILLES MARCOTTE

The Poetry of Exile

In addition to being one of the most prominent literary critics in Quebec
today, Gilles Marcotte is also one of the most prolific. Beginning his critical
career as a book reviewer for the newspaper *Le Devoir*, he soon expanded his
activities to include contributions to literary magazines and radio programmes as well as producing a whole series of books – of which five (to
date) are critical studies of Quebec literature.

In many ways, Marcotte's writings reflect the course of Quebec criticism
in the past quarter-century. Placing his faith in the values of international
humanism rather than in the moral dogmatism of his predecessors, he
seeks to explain Quebec literature in 'universal' rather than 'provincial'
terms. In *Une littérature qui se fait*, published in 1962, he uses archetypes and
themes as unifying structures for his discussions of various movements
and characteristics of the literature. The following selection, for example,
traces the theme of exile through the full range of Quebec poetry, and thus
manages to account for a number of its particular qualities. This is of special
concern to a literature preoccupied with the question of its own existence,
and we see a similar thematic approach used extensively by critics who
wish to single out the unique aspects of Quebec writing.

Marcotte's criticism is also typical in that it shows a strong sociological
bent. The conviction that literature reflects the society that has produced it
is apparent in his most recent work *Le roman à l'imparfait* (1976), as is the
increasing attention he devotes to considerations of form in the writing.
Even the shifting of his interest from poetry to prose is indicative of a
changing emphasis in Quebec letters generally, where poetry no longer has
the ascendency it enjoyed for so long.

Although his methods and his interests often anticipate or coincide with
general movements in the same directions, Marcotte's criticism does stand

apart in several respects. His prose, for instance, is clear, concise, and effective, and he seems to have a special ability to detect the significance of specific events or developments. Whether discussing an individual author or work, or writing about the overall evolution of Quebec culture, he quickly pinpoints the essential qualities of his subject and then goes on to explore its larger implications. This ability to move easily from the particular to the general, and back again, is most characteristic of Marcotte's criticism.

All these qualities are apparent in the following article, in which the author immediately identifies one of the quintessential aspects of Quebec poetry. First published in 1958, it has since become one of the classics of Quebec criticism.

THE POETRY OF EXILE

French readers of contemporary French-Canadian poetry will not generally find that it seems foreign to them. They might read a collection by Anne Hébert or Alain Grandbois, for example, and never suspect that it had been published on the other side of the Atlantic, in a physical and spiritual climate very different from their own. Certainly there are no hard and fast divisions between the poetry that is being written in Paris and that being written in Montreal: the same literary influences are to be found in both centres, and if it is possible to distinguish a common poetic experience for French writers, the same experience is being shared by the poets of French Canada.

We may thus ask ourselves whether it is legitimate to refer to French-Canadian poetry as such – and if so, in what sense. As recently as the early years of this century, several of our poets still stood out as being conspicuously different, with their bric-à-brac of patriotic and regionalistic themes grafted more or less successfully onto completely ambivalent forms. These outwardly visible signs have now been abandoned, and it is generally agreed that with Saint-Denys-Garneau, French-Canadian poetry turned resolutely towards the human and the universal. This comes dangerously close, however, to saying that there is no longer anything particularly French-Canadian about it. But to say this would mean ignoring the very close connections among the most significant works of contemporary French-Canadian poetry as well as the bonds between this body of poetry and the most authentic contributions from the previous century. Our poetry is no longer imprisoned behind its own borders, but the very freedom it has won has led it to a more conscious and more rigorous exploration of a spiritual landscape that is entirely its own. In this sense it reveals, beyond any variations in form or literary affiliation, a very profound unity. In so far as it avoids the easy temptation to be merely local and picturesque, French-Canadian poetry reverts to its basic preoccupation: the questioning of its rootedness and its human achievement in a specific locale.

This questioning can be heard all the way back to Crémazie, one of the forefathers of French-Canadian poetry, who in the years around 1850 was writing poems that were dreadfully ponderous, stuffy, and smothered in convention. Still, in the verses of his 'Promenade de trois morts,' however awkward they may be, he gives sincere expression to a *difficulté de vivre* that has been too readily attributed to personal temperament and to difficult circumstances in his own life. The first poetic voice to be heard in French Canada speaks of death: death not as repose, tranquillity, or the hereafter, but death that keeps eating away from the inside at any hope of becoming rooted to one's place, death as an interdiction to live here. Crémazie's testimony, moreover, is soon corroborated by other witnesses. His contemporary Alfred Garneau shows the same obsession with cemeteries, the same disaffection with existence. Several years later, Albert Lozeau would write: 'I feel the soul of a stranger growing within me.' Whenever the poetry of this period abandons its patriotic, sentimental or religious façades, this is what remains: a feeling of being estranged from life, of being in extreme exile. The most telling words in this poetry are those of terror, regretfulness, and despair, and, in the guise of a variety of literary conceits, it falls prey to some strange maledictions.

This may strike one as being surprising or even scandalous. It does not seem normal that the first songs of a young nation reputed to be jovial, healthy, and engaged in a robust adventure of survival should be anything but heroic. This, however, is to form a rather simplistic notion of the French-Canadian reality. Our first poets were anything but primitive: they were simply uprooted Europeans. In all their cultural attitudes and in the essential fibres of their moral being, they still belonged to France. And yet they were no longer totally French. A different life-style, different allegiances, and a different soil all laid claim to them. They lived in a different 'landscape' which they had not yet accepted, and in which they had not yet found themselves. Canada, for these poets, could not be completely sufficient human dwelling place. Building a country does not involve only clearing away the forest, raising cities and formulating laws; it also – and especially – involves reinventing man within a network of new values. The

American had yet to arrive. Alfred Kazin, in a recent essay on American literature, speaks of an 'impression of being adrift in our own land.' If Americans still suffer today from such a feeling of homelessness, what must it be for the French Canadian facing the same task of humanizing his environment, but turned in on himself, isolated in North America by his very language, and deprived of the security of the numbers and wealth of his neighbours to the south?

It is not surprising, therefore, that our poetry should question its state of exile with a very particular constancy and anguish. It is not so much that it makes frequent references to the outward appearances of this exile, or that it turns back nostalgically to what until quite recently in French Canada was called the 'motherland.' This poetry cannot be given its humanity from elsewhere – and France, to some degree, is an elsewhere. The exile that French-Canadian poetry must contend with is faceless and formless; it lodges in the heart and nurtures the temptation of absence – absence from both external reality and social reality. In the measure that it breaks free of patriotic and regionalistic clichés, this poetry finds itself voiceless before the men and the landscapes which should belong to it. Rare are the French-Canadian poets who have really confronted the great spaces of North America, and those few who have done so have drawn from the experience only a recognition of the void, the 'silence of snow in its arid nuptials with nothingness,' as expressed in the poetry of Yves Préfontaine. Most often, however, landscapes and things are barely expressed at all. The poets remain aloof, in the painful privacy of their being, where the external is allowed in only after it has lost its quality of otherness. What is usually called reality here becomes a series of pure images, with no other connection and no other claim to existence than their own inner resonance. To take an extreme example, look at Anne Hébert's *Le tombeau des rois*:* here are references to fountains, birds, trees, houses, and villages, but the images evoked by these words are devoid of individual colouring. The particular, for this poetry, does not exist; only the most general things are named and possessed, things that have barely begun to exist. This poetry takes its birth at the same time as a new world is born; or rather it is reborn, in the feeling that everything has been taken from it or denied it, that everything must be learned all over again from the elemental beginnings.

One must learn everything all over again – especially oneself. For if the possession of things seems threatened, the poet finds it no less difficult to possess himself and achieve his own unity. Here we find the definitive

*Translated by Alan Brown in *Poems by Anne Hébert* (Musson 1975) (ed.)

image of absence, in an inner alienation that has always been apparent in French-Canadian poetry. One thinks of the following lines by Saint-Denys-Garneau:

I walk beside a joy
A joy that is not mine...
[Tr. John Glassco]

The decisive influence of Saint-Denys-Garneau on the recent evolution of French-Canadian poetry stems from his having experienced this alienation and having expressed it with such overwhelming sincerity, for having brought it bursting through into the light of day. Many things had been said before him, but only in bits and pieces, with much reticence and hesitation; also, one must add, they had been said in outmoded poetic forms that were ill suited to liberate poetic expression. In Saint-Denys-Garneau's work, the freeing of form goes together with the freeing of speech. From now on, it becomes much more difficult to avoid a bruising confrontation with reality. French-Canadian poetry has found its centre: above all else, it acknowledges an inner division, a profound malaise in living. From Anne Hébert to Alain Grandbois, from Jean-Guy Pilon to Roland Giguère, there is no poetry worthy of mention in French Canada today that does not pit itself against the peril of absence. In this combat it affirms its ever-increasing humanity, and this too is where it connects with the most significant of contemporary poetry.

It becomes apparent, in fact, that many of the characteristics attributed to French-Canadian poetry could be applied equally well to certain postwar French poets. There is a difference, however, and this means that the same words in France and in Canada have the same meaning... and yet that the meanings are somehow different. The French poet is equipped with weapons that the French-Canadian poet does not have: he possesses a language, whatever his difficulty in recreating it, and a culture, whatever the trials it may have endured. The house he lives in, though it may be threatened with ruin, is one in which he knows his way around, one in which the smallest objects have an immediately accessible meaning for him. The French-Canadian poet begins from further back, in a position of more naked poverty. His pessimism – or what is often referred to as such – is not a European pessimism. He is still in the process of discovering the place he inhabits, and of winning his right to life, his freedom with himself, and his freedom with things. French-Canadian poetry is a poetry of first steps.

PAUL CHAMBERLAND

Founding the Territory

Paul Chamberland is best known as a poet. Collections such as *Terre Québec* and *L'afficheur hurle* are among the most eloquent expressions of the current of revolt that swept through Quebec culture in the sixties, and they are paralleled in prose by Chamberland's many contributions to *Parti pris*, which he helped found in 1963.

Although *Parti pris* began as a magazine, by the time it folded in 1968 it had also become a publishing house and a burgeoning political movement. Concerned to combat Quebec's material, cultural, and spiritual alienation, *Parti pris* called upon the Québécois to reject the past, to assume the present, and to create their future in the form of an independent, secular, and socialist republic. While its inspiration was largely Marxist and its aims revolutionary, it is *Parti pris*'s nationalistic preoccupations that now seem to have had the greatest impact; their importance in the evolution of Quebec culture has been documented in several studies, including *The Shouting Signpainters* by Malcolm Reid (McClelland and Stewart 1972).

Chamberland played a central role in the protest movement, and his writings in *Parti pris* deal with an astonishing range of issues: constitutional reform, economics, trade unionism, colonialism, revolutionary morality, cultural alienation, and so on. Providing much of the theoretical support for the movement, his articles show him to be intellectually rigorous, emphatically articulate, and deeply committed. 'The only style is to shout,' he wrote; 'the only ethic is violence.'

A 1967 issues of *Parti pris* celebrating the *'centrentenaire'* of the Patriots' Revolt in 1837 reveals yet another facet of Paul Chamberland: the literary critic. In the article translated below, published in *Parti pris* in 1967, he shifts his attention from social concerns to their imaginative counterpart in the thematic evolution of Quebec poetry. As in his political writings, Chamberland pays careful attention to questions of methodology and definition, and as always his style is expressive and concise. By combining insight, documentation, and a thorough comprehension of his subject, he makes a perceptive and wide-reaching analysis of one of the central currents of the Quebec imagination.

In the 'Manifeste des enfants Libres du Kébec,' Chamberland relates that one night in January 1969 he died and was born again, an experience that marked an abrupt change in the direction of his writing. Having turned away from political and social issues in order to investigate questions of a more cosmic, mystical significance, Paul Chamberland has since conducted a series of communal writing projects in Montreal, and has published several more volumes of poetry.

FOUNDING THE TERRITORY

METHODOLOGICAL FOREWORD

The following article may give a false impression of order; in fact, it is really just a collection of notes. At the outset, I cannot insist too strongly on its fragmentary nature, this being a result of hesitations and even disarray in my methodology. The article is one stage, and certainly a beneficial one, in an extended study of Quebec poetry – a study that gradually proved to be a very risky business indeed. The benefit stems from the communication of various results, so that they can be appraised by those who are interested in similar investigations.

I had in mind an area of investigation extending approximately from Grandbois to Péloquin, and I started out confidently, convinced that my insights would serve, like Ariadne's thread, as a guide through my survey. Now, however, I find that I have become entangled in a vast web of rambling, detailed studies.

What was the nature of my original intuition? I set out to discover a common 'poetics' in the writers I had selected, with the present article being the first draft of this. However, I was soon brought to the realization that, in looking for common features, the 'basic precaution' of setting aside anything too particular or individual amounted to a rhetorical refrain. Since the only way to reach a final synthesis is to pay close attention to an exact knowledge of the particular, this explains why the following notes can only be conjectural.

This is a first point of methodology. There are others. I discovered that attempting to interpret Quebec poetry along thematic lines was to risk imposing on the object of my study a predetermined direction that would be 'clever' enough to make it all look convincing; it is not very difficult to end up discovering something if one starts out with it in the first place. This is the 'essayistic' easy way out.

And finally, the problem of critical method must be dealt with – and clearly. The use of several notions that I felt should be retained is justified later in the article. What might be called a 'poetology' still remains for the most part to be established, for in order to be able to advance an hypothesis, one has to have found the means of really *knowing* the object one is examining. This amounts to questioning oneself as to the concepts and investigative procedures of criticism, and it must be noted that the various currents of criticism are notoriously inadequate when it comes to poetry. Marxist criticism, for example, is strangely silent on this subject, and the Althusserians do not seem to be an exception to this general rule. As for the 'thematic' school, particularly Richard's approach, it at least has proven that its methods are efficient. But, I might add, they are also wide of the mark. Actually, Richard's thematization, although it is very rigorous, deals only with the lexical and stylistic dimensions of poetic language: the image, for example, is seen only in its role as the signified (*signifié*), and the versification is examined only for substantiating material. Genuine structuralism in the criticism of poetry remains in the realm of good intentions.

Perhaps the most interesting discoveries now are coming to us from structural linguistics.[1] The application of linguistic methods to poetry has the major advantage of drawing attention to the material body of the poetic language, no longer in terms of a 'musicality of the verse' reinforcing the meaning, but for once as an element that is directly required in the production of meaning. Thus the image, which is the principal source of the poetic function, is approached not only in its lexical and stylistic dimensions but also in its prosodic, grammatical, and phonological dimensions. In this way it is possible to grasp the poetic message in the full complexity of its various expressions.

I thought it necessary to preface my article with these theoretical considerations in order that its limits be carefully defined. There is always a great temptation to come up with an hypothesis large enough so that one's interpretations can be based on a poor knowledge of the writings. Now, however, I do not think that I can 'know' Paul-Marie Lapointe's poetry unless I can explain, for example, the primary role played by nouns in governing his syntax.

THE POETIC FIELD

What I refer to here as *poetic field* occurs when a certain combination of forms is commonly found in the work of a certain number of poets. For the moment, I shall have to be content with describing this combination as a 'thematic ensemble,' even though such a term is not sufficiently accurate. Such a thematic ensemble might be thought of as the orientation that informs the production and presence of the images. I am tempted to think of this field as being *structural* in that it constitutes a mode of organizing poetic discourse, a mode that would be defined in terms of the (structural) properties governing the appearance and articulation of the images. However, since I am unable to provide a clear definition of the concept of structure, and since I am not able to assign it a precise theoretical role, I shall refrain from using this concept in my discussion. As for the notions of a poetic field and a thematic ensemble, their purely descriptive functions allow me to use them without such reservations. The idea of a field, even in a metaphorical sense, does help to clarify one's thinking in this respect. A field, for instance, includes or excludes, and so certain works or writers may be contained or shut out by its perimeters. However, as Althusser notes, we must be wary of the spatial 'realism' implied by such notions: for example, that which is excluded from the field is still in some way a part of it and is contained within it as its invisible or 'repressed' side.[2]

I could also talk of a *code* that is common to these poets and which seems to have connections with the same thematic ensemble. A code can be defined as a system of elements and relationships presiding over and governing the utterance of the *message*. This notion too must be taken metaphorically. At the present stage of my investigations, I can only *describe* forms and themes, and *make connections* among them in a very empirical fashion, as they appear in the light of careful reading.

Once my work had begun, I thought I had discovered a basic thematic ensemble that was common to one period of Quebec poetry, that formed a field in the sense that it determined what was to be included and excluded. This second aspect I shall deal with later. Although as yet I offer it only as an hypothesis, I would describe this thematic ensemble as having to do with *founding* and *belonging*. In other words, this poetry is cosmogonical and territorial, stressing the theme of origin, the *in illo tempore* of acts of foundation. The primacy of the founding act, opening and open to the timeless time of origin, informs a number of specific spatial and temporal structures that I could only begin to describe here. Thus the poetry can be seen in terms of a mythic ensemble, often accompanied by ritual and liturgy.

The boundaries of this thematic field can be quite clearly identified. I would first of all point out that the accepted procedure for this excludes any linear or chronological progression: by definition, the thematic field is necessarily and in all ways identical to its 'surface,' and the development and dynamism over which it has control can only be explained in terms of the relationship of the elements and forces of which it is the expression or the product.

One very clear and concrete way of defining the field, and consequently its limits, is to name the poets or works which are in it, to indicate what is included and what is excluded. The field begins to take form with Grand-bois, in several of his poems or from a certain dimension of his poetry as a whole. It also takes form with Anne Hébert, and in this regard it is interesting to specify two points in particular. The first is that the field emerges with *Mystère de la parole;** thus the boundary runs between this collection and *Le tombeau des rois,** the final poem of which constitutes the dividing line. Secondly, the fairly close connections between the poetry of Anne Hébert and Saint-Denys-Garneau become strikingly clear when considered in terms of the unity of the field. Curiously, Saint-Denys-Garneau is excluded from the field for reasons of a thematic ensemble that is completely similar to the one in *Le tombeau des rois*. I shall comment further on this at the end of the article.

It will be apparent that this central theme of foundation is primarily associated with the 'Hexagone poets,' by which I mean the Hexagone† generation. In particular, this includes Gilles Hénault, Roland Giguère, Maurice Beaulieu, Jean-Paul Filion, Gaston Miron, Yves Préfontaine, Michèle Lalonde, Fernand Ouellette, Paul-Marie Lapointe, and Jacques Brault. There are others, of course: I would also include Michel Van Schendel, whose work can be seen as being very indicative of the particular strength of the field. Actually, though, it is only in *Variations sur la pierre* that Van Schendel's poetry becomes clearly a part of this central theme of foundation.

What has been called the 'poetry of the land' is only an apparent variation on the central theme of foundation, with Miron and Brault being its foremost practitioners. In their poetry the field is modified, reaching what seems to be its outermost boundaries: the movement from the time of origin to historical time.

---

*These two collections are translated by Alan Brown as *Poems by Anne Hébert* (Toronto: General Publishing 1975) (ed.)
†Name of a Quebec publishing house prominent in the sixties (ed.)

Later I shall come back to a discussion of what is excluded, and thus complete the definition of the thematic field. In all probability, contemporary Quebec poetry is deeply involved with a new problematical context, which, because it is just in the process of taking form, is difficult, if not impossible, to define. This, however, only makes the old problematical context stand out more clearly. It is important to point out that the passage from one field to another, because of what a field essentially is, cannot be gradual and gentle, but must rather be brusque and total.

It is now time to explain the motif or theme on which this study is based: founding, belonging to, and taking possession of the territory. It might be tempting to make a connection with myths, since we will be dealing with poetry that is cosmogonical; however, since I am unable to find a theoretical justification for doing this, once again I shall have to resist and to limit my references to those of a purely metaphorical nature.

What distinguishes this current of Quebec poetry is that the acts and movements conveyed by the web of images take place in a time of origin, *in illo tempore*. They are acts and movements of founding: being born, beginning, conquering, naming for the first time, taking possession of and inhabiting the territory, and experiencing the ordeals of initiation that are a necessary part of any founding. The essential condition of the protagonist, of man as he is presented in this poetry, is one of dispossession as well as primordial bleakness.

To be born, to found, to conquer, to possess – these verbs form a primary series of images related to everything implied by *birth*, emergence, and beginning: dawn, spring, thawing out, and an explosion of plant life. This accounts for the insistent return to things that are *elemental*, basic, and earth-related, so that the resultant enracination can bring fertility. It also accounts for the appeal of the *primitive* in the form of prehistory, Amerindians, animals, the wilderness, and so on. The definitive act being one of founding *ab origine*, the search here is for a *central place*, the 'ultimate setting' that is the only location worthy of the act of foundation. By virtue of its position, the central place dominates the space around it: to be in it is to be able to participate in the world, to plunge into the stream of universal life.

The time of origin opens up vast new spaces. Taking their orientation from the various acts of foundation, these spaces are revealed through the kind of movements that might be described in terms of an *ordeal of initiation* or ritual of passage. Its essential characteristics include an isolated retreat, an adventurous expedition, an ordeal or confrontation with hostile forces, and being stationed in the central place. The wandering and exile caused by deracination and dispossession are transformed into a passionate search for signs and for a centre. Very often this takes the form of climbing to the summit or plunging into the depths of the earth or sea.

Temporal structures also play a role in the voyage of initiation and the foundation *ab origine*. Time is expressed in terms of a dialectic relationship (often in the form of a reversal) between an idyllic, distant time and a more immediate, desolate time. Thus the idyllic past (golden age or primitive time) is opposed both to the individual, historical past (which is stagnant and in ruins) and to the present (a time of poverty and nothingness). In the same way, the future is presented as being unforeseeable or idyllic. The decisive, a-historical moment of the founding act (*in illo tempore*) is sustained by the negation and repression of an intolerable present and is projected into the idyllic realm of the past or future.

The process of founding, claiming, and exploring eventually becomes an act of settlement, of taking geographical possession of the territory. What had been a basic, mythical space becomes a country, a native land. To Miron and Brault, for example, the treatment of the land theme itself is actually a variation on what I have referred to as the process of settlement or geographical appropriation. This may sometimes be expressed without any explicit references to the natural world: as a celebration of the Quebec landscape or territory (to use a better word), with all its particular qualities and all the different species (of trees or people) who live in it.

In order to be convincing, my discussion should be based on the complete body of writings that deal with the same general theme. Since this article is of a purely conjectural nature, and in order to keep the number of references to a workable minimum, I shall limit my discussion to those texts that seem particularly relevant. These include:

ANNE HÉBERT 'Mystère de la parole' (*Poèmes* p. 73), 'Naissance du pain' (Ibid. p. 76), 'Alchimie du jour' (Ibid. p. 80)*

GILLES HÉNAULT 'Je te salue' (*Totems*), 'No Man's Land' (*Sémaphore* p. 53), 'Bestiaire' (Ibid. p. 55), 'Saga' (Ibid. p. 58)†

ROLAND GIGUÈRE 'Midi perdu' (*L'âge de la parole* p. 79), 'Yeux fixes' (Ibid. p. 87), 'En pays perdu' (Ibid. p. 143)‡

MAURICE BEAULIEU 'A glaise fendre' (in *A glaise fendre*)

*Translated by Alan Brown in *Poems by Anne Hébert* (Toronto: General Publishing 1975) (ed.)
†Most of these poems are translated in *Ellipse* 18, 1976. (ed.)
‡See translations of poems by Roland Giguère in *Ellipse* 2, 1970. (ed.)

JEAN-PAUL FILION 'La grand-gigue' (*Demain les herbes rouges* p. 5), 'Terre de miel' (Ibid. p. 26)
PAUL-MARIE LAPOINTE 'Arbres' (*Arbres, choix de poèmes*)*

TO BE BORN, TO ESTABLISH, TO POSSESS

The world is not beautiful, François, You must not touch it; renounce it, right now, freely. Don't lag behind...
   I had never possessed the world, but there was a change now: part of the world possessed me. The stretch of water, mountains and secret hollows came to me with a sovereign touch. I believed myself to be free of my mother, and I discovered a new kinship with the earth.
(Hébert, *Le torrent*† pp. 19 and 29) [tr. Gwendolyn Moore]

In *Le torrent* by Anne Hébert, François becomes deaf after his mother strikes him with a bunch of keys. This deafness consummates the separation from the world; symbolically, the bunch of keys locks him out totally. The 'objective' sounds of the world are replaced by the 'inner' rumbling of the torrent; once it has become irreparable, noncommunication is transformed into a communication with things that are subterranean, profound, and mute. However, the dispossession is such that it soon changes into 'possession' and 'being possessed.' All awareness moves back towards the 'interior,' which is immediately revealed as being more 'profound' than an awareness of oneself. Totally repressed desires do not die out but rather surge back with greater violence in a 'rapturous' relationship with the world, with things in their elemental state: the torrent too is desire. The son / mother relationship, which is violent and destructive, is changed into a son / earth relationship. This latter relationship is in a sense analogous to the former, or rather determined by it; however, it also results from its suppression, a suppression of others and a disintegration of one's self into one's surroundings. In other words, it is a form of alienation.
   Such is the fate of François. However, I detect another lesson in the mutation of the son / mother relationship into a son / earth relationship: it creates a distance between dispossession and foundation, between closed

*Selections translated in *Ellipse* 11, 1972 and by D.G. Jones in *The Terror of the Snows, Selected Poems by Paul-Marie Lapointe* (Pittsburgh: University of Pittsburgh Press 1976) (ed.)
†Translated by Gwendolyn Moore as *The Torrent* (Montreal: Harvest House 1973) (ed.)

time and primordial time. In poetic discourse, alienation is transformed into the root of a new re-possession. It is a well-known fact, even in a clinical sense, that unfulfilled desire can build up to the point where, unknown to itself, it becomes neurosis or psychosis. Poetry offers it a different fate: certainly it may result in alienation and 'possession,' but it may also lead to hypnosis, animistic participation, magic, exorcism, and incantation. This is clearly the thrust of the movement in Hébert, but it is also the basic impulse in writers like Hénault, Giguère, and Miron. In Hébert's writings, this movement is accomplished by such sure means as dreams and *enchantment*. Enchantment resolves the conflict of desire (between attraction and repulsion) by precipitating their interchange. Thus in the following lines by Anne Hébert,

> We must not go into that deep wood
> For the great fountains
> Sleep there behind
> (*Poèmes* p. 17) [tr. Alan Brown]

the unfathomable is imposed through transparence, attraction through defence, and presence through absence. Enchantment is what creates the distance between these two poles by bridging the gap it has opened: enchantment causes a break or *rupture* in the fabric of time / history, so that one finds oneself *in illo tempore*, in the time of origin. The meaning of the initiation rite is also one of rupture. Here the distance, the break, are considered possible only because they are imaginary. But this is precisely the possibility of the poem: the imaginary is just that – a division or rupture – at least in this specific kind of poetry of foundation that I am dealing with here.

In the end, François dies in the 'sealed / profound / interior' whirlpool of the torrent. Conversely the 'plunge' that takes place in the poetry of foundation opens up the full new space of birth and beginning. This does not negate the conflict of desire and dispossession but invests it with a new meaning in which the opposites become part of one another:

> Life and death within us received
> right of asylum, looked at each other
> with blind eyes, touched each other
> with careful hands.
> (*Poèmes* p. 73) [tr. Alan Brown]

One characteristic of the imagination is that the extremes of dispossession are absolute only in the sense of a possible rebirth; the 'abolition' of opposites can only be the abolition of time, which activates them, in that timeless instant that inaugurates a new history.

A whole fabric of images captures the impulse of beginning and emerging: dawn, morning, spring, thaw... In Hébert we see a rush of vegetable power and animal passion:

Raw shoots slit the countryside,
underearth life lets its green hair
pierce through. The world's womb
shows off its flowers and fruits in
the high sun of midday...

All forms and colours called-up
rise from earth like visible and
measured breathing.
(Poèmes p. 77) [tr. Alan Brown]

Let the awakened gift ripen its
strange alchemy in high-mettled steeds.
(Poèmes p. 82) [tr. Alan Brown]

Whether in the form of passion or as an instantaneous surge, the beginning or birth is effectively prepared for by a slow process of maturation in the womb of the land or the 'primitive night':

O the long first night, face
against cracked soil spying the
beating of given blood...
(Poèmes p. 77) [tr. Alan Brown]

Following this passage there is a clear description of the condition of bareness, of 'enchantment' (changed into 'attention'), a condition presented as being necessary for rebirth. 'Face against cracked soil, spying.'* This attraction towards the depths, towards 'the world's other side,'* is

*Tr. Alan Brown

what motivates the plunge, the burrowing into the ground; it also heralds fertility, so that already in the next stanza, 'raw shoots slit the country-side.'* For Hébert, then, the beginning is above all a birth, with the earth-mother producing her children.

For Gilles Hénault, birth and beginning are typically 'the thaw and its violent cleavages' (*Sémaphore* p. 53), the break-up of the ice. Spring is seen as an irresistible force that overcomes all obstacles in its path, with 'geysers of boiling words spurting against the sclerotic borders' (*Sémaphore* p. 53). The rebirth of vegetation is itself a 'fire damp burst of green' (p. 12) [tr. C.R.P. May]. This is the 'heroic,' warlike treatment of the theme, and it plays a large role in Hénault's approach.

In this context we can talk about a cosmogony only if it is understood as being the basis for an anthropogeny, since the study of man's origins is seen as its necessary complement. If at the end of 'Naissance du pain,' 'God can be born in his turn, a pallid child,'* he is clearly seen as a human prototype. The same is true with Giguère:

A thunderbolt shatters
the obscurity: in the flash of
lightning a human face
emerges from the block of basalt,
ten times larger than life, a face
without scars or wounds,
ready to suffer the assaults
of time; silent but
terribly meaningful, its
eyes peer into the
inevitable.

So it is that we have
a right to expect
disfiguration to be followed by
complete transfiguration...
(*L'âge de la parole* p. 144)

For Filion too, in his poem 'La grand-gigue,' fire is the moving force for emergence and transfiguration.

*Tr. Alan Brown

In Hébert's poem, 'Mystère de la parole,' a striking cosmogony is presented in which man is able to participate precisely because of his power of speech. This power is conferred upon him because he is still in the time of origin and because he has been reintegrated with the earth-mother. Thus the poem hinges on one passage in particular: 'In a single dizziness, the instant was.'* Everything before that instant will now be distinguished from everything that comes after; and so passivity is distinguished from active participation, a teeming chaos of sensations is distinguished from a neatly ordered world, and an investment (fecundation) with tellurian powers is distinguished from a domination of the world through the power of words. These contrasts are only another way of giving a double expression to the unique act of being born, of being born in order to found. 'Arrows of colour reached us, uniting us to the earth...like a wedding marked by its excesses,'* 'colours and sounds visited us in numbers and by small stunning groups...';* the binding, carnal, 'participatory' function of the senses is clearly emphasized in the preference shown for the sense of smell: 'all our riches bleed their fragrance, animal musk beside us.'* In other words, sensation, as it appears here, is less a question of perception (knowledge) than of identification and fusion with matter and with the earth – for which the blood acts as an intermediary. This same kind of sensual, violent celebration of the world will be found in Hénault, Giguère, Lapointe, and Beaulieu. It is a celebration through which blood, as in Beaulieu's work, is contrasted with bone in the same way as a fruitful appropriation of the land is contrasted with dispossession and destruction.

THE ELEMENTAL

Like the act of founding, the act of being born (or reborn) is obviously interpreted as a preliminary reintegration with one's origins, with the body of the earth / mother and the 'primitive night.' We notice the various forms it takes as an *obsessive return to the elemental*, where, for example, such primary substances as earth, clay, and rock are evoked.

Hénault writes:

We have no limits
And great plenty is our mother...
("Je te salue,' *Totems*) [tr. Al Poulin, Jr.]

*Tr. Alan Brown

And Giguère:

> Coming out of the ether dream, I
> steer into a tattered harbour – another
> place where I shall have to make my
> own fire – and I discover that I am
> every bit as naked and destitute
> as the rocks I see about me...
> Everything must be tamed:
> air and wind, words
> and the song foaming on
> frost-laden lips.
> ('En pays perdu,' *Totems* p. 143)

We should note here that the return to the elemental has two essential properties: the nudity of man and the fertility of the land. In the poetry of Paul-Marie Lapointe, great emphasis is placed on horizontality, the proximity of the soil, enracination, tenderness, warmth, and fertility. His poems worship the bountiful earth by celebrating her fruits and her changing seasons. To take two examples:

> I write tree
> tree spinning rings into cones sap into light
> roots of the rain and of fair weather   animate earth...
> ('Arbres') [tr. D.G. Jones]

and

> each day astonished you land up on earth
> this night was not the last.
> (*Pour les âmes* p. 70) [tr. D.G. Jones]

The almost sacred sensuality that begins to become noticeable in *Mystère de la parole* marks the full range of Lapointe's poetry. Its admirable radiance of happiness and light is very much in evidence, and in 'Arbres' his attitude toward the act of founding is deeply influenced by this sensuality: to feel is *immediately* to be born and to found.

On the other hand, 'A glaise fendre' by Beaulieu invites us to return to the elemental in the form of a harsh divestment which is heroically accepted because it is quite properly recognized as being primordial:

I use few words.
Deliberately. Some people
criticize this, speaking of
breath, of austerity.
No, no, no! Being is
what's at stake. How
can you name something
...without being? What
good are words that are
...empty? I like people
who live in themselves
and their words.
(*Journal d'A glaise fendre*)

For Beaulieu, these 'few words' are central to the 'art of poetry': the very form of the poem – short, intolerably concise, hard, stemming from the spiralling succession of a few nouns and adjectives – 'signifies' (even more than it expresses) the elemental bareness that must precede enracination and birth; the *human being* is a hard core modified by primary nouns:

Man, here is a naked man,
A man naked as his hunger.

'*A glaise fendre*,' cleaving the soil, ploughing furrows, wounds, sowing seed: the archetypal nuptials. Man here is naked man; his language is naked – the language of his raw desire and hunger. The vocabulary too is proper to an austere anthropogeny, and to violence. It is a universe whose 'elements' are blood, soil, night, wind, and cold, whose characteristics are harshness, nakedness, blackness, and elevation. Everything is reduced to essentials. Man is blood and soil; the setting is night, wind, and cold – hostile forces, and the forces of complicity as well. Although this reduction to essentials originates in privation and separation from the world, it does not amount to destruction; rather it is 'heroically' transformed into resistance, recalcitrance, a recuperation of energy, which is not very far removed from possession and inhabitation. And so man has to take on the same characteristics as his surroundings; he must 'become' the landscape – closed, hard, opaque, upright ('the black earth of my veins'). It is a narrow, patient transfer – a veritable ritual of initiation. And it is very much a transfer, since the reduction to essentials is not made into a theme as with the bone imagery of Saint-Denys-Garneau of Hébert in *Le tombeau des rois*. Here the imagery is of blood: life, strength, energy concentrated and 'reintegrated' into the 'strong veins,' with the indomitable resurgence of hunger and desire:

> Howl my blood howl
> In the nor'west of my veins.

What is possible – and achieved in spite of 'all the nights' – is the most demanding form of inhabitation, the inhabitation of oneself:

> My pain is so close to me
> that I inhabit my soil.

The transfer that takes place in the root is precisely this: to invoke and inhabit one's flesh and body as one's soil, as a participant in the heart, substance, and womb of the world. A transfer implies affinity and connection. The ploughing, wounding, seeding (cleaving…the soil) really take place on the inside; man's bleeding is an opening, a fertilization and enracination; the cycle of the transfer has come full turn.

The central image, the cornerstone of this genesis is Christ crucified – archetypal man at the founding moment of death and rebirth:

> O my soil intermingled with
> the body on the cross.

The full meaning of the poem is focused in the vertical body on the cross, which is hard, still, upright, living, and enracinated, all at the same time. Emerging from the primordial bareness and exclusion, it gives a centre to the landscape and conveys its full dimensions. To coalesce with Christ is to attain the moment of origin, the 'equinox of silence.'

RETURNING TO THE PRIMITIVE

The appeal of the primitive, which can be perceived in Beaulieu's work ('I am an Amerindian'), is another form of returning to the elemental. The primitive is expressed in such forms as the prehistoric, the Amerindian, the savage, and the animalistic.

Take the following examples from Anne Hébert:

Joy set to crying out, a
new mother smelling of game-
birds among the reeds...
(*Poèmes* p. 74) [tr. Alan Brown]

Let no serving-woman serve
you this day in which you
bound your savage sorrow, a
beast of blood, to the low
branches of a black spruce.
(*Poèmes* p. 80) [tr. Alan Brown]

Amid the smoke of burning
flesh, on the blackened stone,
among wild, upturned
banquets, see the gleam
in the primitive dark of
the watcher's fire...
(*Poèmes* p. 78) [tr. Alan Brown]

In Hébert's poetry, the primitive is very often associated with an outbreak of violence – an ambiguous violence that is both destructive and liberating.

The return to the primitive is very important in Hénault's poetry, and is given threefold expression in the images of primitive hordes (*Sémaphore*, 'L'invention du feu'), the fauna and flora of the wilderness, and the Amerindians. It brings substance to his celebration of the origins and helps invest it with that warlike, 'heroic' quality so characteristic of Hénault's work:

Red-Skins
Tribes vanished
in the conflagration of fire-water and tuberculosis
Tracked down by the pallor of death and the white-Face
Carrying away your dreams of spirits and manitou
Your dreams exploded by the fire of hackbuts
You've left us your legacy of totemic hopes
And now our sky is the colour
of the puffs from your peace pipes.
(from *Totems*) [tr. A. Poulin, Jr.]

In Giguère's poetry, the return to the primitive is made into an especially important theme in one passage from 'En pays perdu,' (pp. 145–6). Here the 'archaic hamlet' 'in the heart of the city' is given a particularly elaborate treatment. However, I will simply refer to it here, since I plan later to deal with the whole poem from which the passage is taken.

One could also seek evidence of this motif in Lapointe's poetry, where references are frequent but discreet; animals, for instance, are often found, and the celebration of basic, everyday actions is one of its main components.

BEING IN THE CENTRAL PLACE

To found is also to be founded at one's highest point, in a central place. The place is central because it in some way radiates time and space. For Beaulieu, this place is the one in which the cross has been erected; it is the tree bearing archetypal man, and the centre assumes a vertical character.

The centre (of space and time) is also the equinoxes and solstices ('solstice of the earth,' writes Anne Hébert, and also 'in the complete centre of the world...at the point of the world.') For Hébert, it coincides with the 'primitive night' and the underground world ('tomb of the kings,' 'the world's other side'); this is why the 'profound, transparent' source is a place of magnetism and 'enchantment.'

The poetry of Hénault often leads to a long period of patient waiting in a place where the world can be directly apprehended and listened to – in other words, a confluence. Later I shall attempt to show the meaning of this, but for the moment I shall simply give an example:

Motionless, deep in the hold,
there came to me the dull
sound of blades, the
immersed thud of the
icebergs (cunning mines
laid by the Gulf-Stream)...
(*Sémaphore* p. 58)

The quest for the central, founding place also plays a determining role in Giguère's poetry, taking the form of a volcano, the interior of the earth, a keystone or cornerstone, the sea bottom, the water source, or the 'archaic hamlet.' We shall come back to this.

As an incidental note, I notice a similar quest being undertaken in Van Schendel's poetry, with its dialectic of movement and immobility (wind and stone). In this vein too is his marvellous revival of the Phoenix myth, apparent in numerous passages from *Variations sur la pierre*.

COSMIC PARTICIPATION

> If suddenly I feel the
> vastness come over me,
> my veins intertwined
> with the rivers of the world,
> it is because my body is the
> tide, because I am bathing
> in universal liquidity,
> because the fibres of my
> being are immersed in the
> passing of physical time,
> because my pores are open.
> (*Sémaphore* p. 40)

We have seen in Hénault's poetry how the beginning is conveyed through images of thaw and the spring break-up; this is the break-up of those obstacles the cold and the North have placed in the path of the vital ebb and flow. Hénault's poetry is 'energetic' and warlike. This time I would like to examine more closely the particular form he gives to the general theme of foundation. The passage quoted above is a good place to start. Here the search for a central place does not lead to the secret places which, in Hébert's poetry, require above all that one remain motionless in the priestlike posture of a half-sacrificed officiant. Nor is the search enlarged, as we shall see with Giguère, to the labyrinths of the initiating expedition, where the wanderer must undergo the ordeal of disorientation. For Hénault, the search is a call for breathing space, for vast expanses, radiant mobility, and a liberating immersion in both the billows of life and the streaming source of cosmic energy. Openness and availability are rendered above all as 'porosity': Man must be invested with the current of life right down to his most secret being, and he must give himself up to it.

Now I am
assailed by the four winds

of desire, feeling myself
tossed about in the midst
of the seven seas
by all their combined forces...
(*Sémaphore* p. 58)

The 'swimmer's' immersion in the confluence explains the frequent recurrence of the river image. With particularly poetic logic, however, the river is replaced by a tree motif which combines flowing sap, a proliferation of vegetation, and the triumph of the vertical position. In 'No Man's Land,' the two images are expressed simultaneously:

But already the rivers are
snaking down towards the
mouth of the sea – rivers
with and without names,
tree-like rivers fed by
their streams. In vain
the ice-jams try to
staunch the flow of
time and water; everything
gives way to its molecular
thrust.
(*Sémaphore* p. 53)

Another poem from the same collection, 'Le temps s'arborise,' may be examined from this same point of view.

The first two poems in *Voyage au pays de mémoire*, 'No Man's Land' and 'Bestiaire' begin with the lines 'to say it all' and 'one cry.'* A careful reading of the latter poem reveals that the flow of life symbolized by the tree / river is informed by an urgent need to name; therefore it too must flow from the founding confluence. The poem is structured on the opposition between the 'one visceral cry'* of the animal and the 'dumbness'* of the spoken word. In the opening stanzas of the poem there is a celebration of the 'visceral cry,' which, because of its authenticity, is taken as a model for poetry. Thus poetry is thought of as a language of foundation and is said to 'bray, crush, make heard.'* This is precisely why the animal cry is emphasized here, because it is 'natural,' immediate, and generally 'original.' It is

*Tr. D.G. Jones

one, inclusive, transparent, efficient, creative, and directly grafted onto the world that produces it. This problematic dimension of language is curiously close to Rousseau's in 'L'essai sur l'origine des langues.'

> One must find the cry
> that will call up all anguish,
> that will express all joy, that
> will communicate from man
> to man a gut response
> from the most secret springs
> of his desire.
> (*Sémaphore* p. 156). [tr. D.G. Jones]

GIGUÈRE AND THE ORDEAL OF INITIATION

It is in Giguère's poetry that we find one form of the creation myth given its most complete expression. Here, the rites and trials of initiation can be traced through three long poems, 'Midi perdu,' 'Yeux fixes,' and 'En pays perdu.' Giguère's general thematic framework, particularly in these selections, is steadily attracted to the initiatory experience; it is a poetry of space and movement, 'concrete' and 'visual,' and it reminds us that Giguère is not only a graphic artist but that he also runs his own publishing house, Erta. There is, for example, a constant transposition of the temporal into the spatial, which takes the form of expeditions or material changes in the landscape. Thus the past is what is 'behind' and the future what is 'ahead.' Quite literally, this transposition is the source of a complete new set of circumstances:

> ...coldly watching
> the spectacle of a
> past being put to the
> torch does not necessarily
> mean turning into pillars
> of salt. What is ahead
> of me, coming, or what
> I imagine to be ahead has
> always had the strongest
> attraction for me...
> (*L'âge de la parole* p. 143)

The image here distinctly recalls the biblical prohibition (in the story of the destruction of Sodom), which we know is linked to a sort of ritual of passage, similar to the Passover rites. With Giguère, the 'road' of time is clearly based on a repulsion for what is behind and an attraction for what is ahead – in this way similar to the 'hero' off on a trail of adventures. The repulsion for what is behind even takes the form of a prohibition against turning back or retracing one's step (see *L'âge de la parole* pp. 94-5).

Prohibition is the definitive characteristic of the past. However, a very important distinction must be stressed in this regard: this prohibition is less a moral stricture than one of the properties of the 'landscape' through which man 'walks' and makes his way; the past, what is behind, is absolutely beyond recovery. The prohibition is determinant, especially because it is based on a *cut* that breaks the line of time; it is an incursion against the time of origin, the *in illo tempore*. Turning away from the past is not the result of a determined resolution but rather the resolution is only an acceptance of the abrupt revelation of the break. What this adds, in a sense, is the weight of a particular fate. Hébert's emergence from 'The Tomb of the Kings' into a new, first morning and Beaulieu's movement from the naked, hard, high place to the 'living soil' stem from the same preoriginative prohibition. Prohibition is the fall ... or dispossession, which the break with the time of origin transforms into a nakedness that is sacred and associated with birth; see, for example, the passage cited above from *L'âge de la parole* (p. 143).

Here we should again note the primary meaning of the expedition. Emerging from the dream is directly associated with emerging from the womb, but it is conceived as being one of the ways in which a break is effected and the time of origin inaugurated.

The past is a time (the 'hind side') of ruins, chaos, *'ronces et roses,'** and shadows. The present is a naked time, and 'poor' (as described by Van Schendel in a similar problematic context), a time of 'heroic' wandering.

The weight of the prohibition and the power of the 'enchantment' or spell are experienced here – as we might have guessed – in the form of *disorientation*, which is necessary in the quest for a new *direction*:

> we no longer knew
> where to fling the white
> sticks we had been using for
> compasses
> (*L'âge de la parole* p. 79)

*Title of poem by Roland Giguère, meaning 'thorns and roses' (ed.)

To this is added the 'disorder' of the landscape:

> the animals were disturbed and howling
> the sky was growing red
> the virgin forest shrieked with pain
> the sand absorbed as many waves as it could
> and then drowned
> let itself drown
> exhausted
> (*L'âge de la parole* p. 82)

This is a passage strangely similar to Saint-Denys-Garneau's description of the 'end of the world.'

It is logical that the loss of the old, habitual points of reference should be paralleled by amnesia, whereby memory becomes unintelligible (see *L'âge de la parole* pp. 80 and 97). The entire poem, 'Midi perdu,' takes place in this period of break-up. Literally 'Lost Noon,' the title suggests the loss of the median hour which 'divides' and governs the temporal order.

In this poem, the hour of noon is experienced as disintegration, crumbling into ashes, vacillating memory, 'repetition,' and the invasion of shadows. At this moment, the major symptom of disorientation becomes clear: the reversal of opposites and the disquieting vertigo of contraries which bring about the destruction of established order and familiar dimensions. Both the monstrous and the marvellous surge forth: noon/midnight, day/night, high/low, and so on. Such is the principal law of Giguère's world; whether beneficial or harmful, it is always supreme.

> disquieting darkness of broad day
> (*L'âge de la parole* p. 80)

> it was noon
> as we shall remember
> it was noon
> the noon was already high above our foreheads
> white weapons in hand
> night was attacking on all sides
> day was diminishing
> (*L'âge de la parole* p. 82)

We shall see this law of opposites reappear in a variety of forms; the real key to the 'heroic expedition,' it provides a measure for its different stages and a form for the various ordeals. This alternance between occultation and illumination is clearly the very essence of an 'initiation.'

The new time is founded in disorientation, which is an indispensable condition for reorientation. The wanderer must both make sure he is on the right road and allow or expect that the road will itself indicate the important landmarks; the result is both surprise and challenge.

> I am more and more
> perpendicular to the
> ground, perpendicular to
> the ground and at the same
> time parallel to the road
> leading back towards the
> heartlands. I AM THE
> MINISTER OF INTERNAL
> AFFAIRS, obscure and
> convoluted affairs, and
> the game involves
> alternately losing and
> finding myself in them
> – as long as it lasts –
> being found so that I
> can be lost again –
> as long as I can stand
> it – being lost and being
> found, diving and coming
> back to the surface (the
> sky is right where it should be)
> and diving deeper, always
> deeper...
> (*L'âge de la parole* p. 91)

In this passage we are given the fullest explanation of the meaning of the initiatory venture. Throughout the initiation there is a succession of the prominent features of the world, in which the keys to a new world are alternately revealed and obscured. The road is marked with malefic and beneficent signs, with meanings which may be ambushes, mirages, or life rafts.

Nevertheless, the adventurous voyage maintains its commandment-like power, and the poem 'Yeux fixes' is punctuated by the line 'Continuing. Continually,' revealing both the traveller's need to move on and the incessant metamorphosis of the landscape. As if to distinguish clearly among the different stages – and also to underly the adventurous character of the expedition – the poet constantly marks his progress with the words 'I turn around' (*L'âge de la parole* pp. 92–3); this phrase acts as an almost magic key to a new sequence of images which impose themselves by breaking with the previous sequence.

Superimposed upon the horizontal motif of the expedition, which is implied by the image of the road, we find a double vertical movement of ascension and plunge, as if to suggest a testing and reinforcement of the earlier motif. Actually, the vertical movement is what determines the 'meaning' of the quest, since it is the road, the obstacles, the ordeals and the metamorphosis all at once.

> Now I turn towards the
> heights, climbing. The
> cold peaks fix my
> eyes on the storm.
> Surely I will discover
> the altitude of man,
> where he can soar
> indefinitely, discharging
> ballast until he himself
> becomes a vast current
> of air, a terrifying
> thunderhead or simply
> a little white cloud...
> (*L'âge de la parole* pp. 93–4)

This passage clearly reveals the meaning of the ascension: to attain the pride and dignity of a victorious and sovereign mankind, possessing and surveying from above. The same ideal is to be found in Ouellette's work, although the limits of this article allow me only to mention it. It is an ideal that is too easily 'forced,' too rectilinear on the whole, and one which is in danger of detracting from the first rule of the ordeal: disorientation and the loss of oneself. The sky, at the beginning of 'Yeux fixes,' is presented in terms of its relationship with man; it is said to 'unfold and gently infiltrate the open wounds, the bleeding cuts of man' (*L'âge de la parole* p. 89). During the ascent, the sky seems to be the goal of the voyage. There is an association with the ideal of hardness, autonomy, and also of explosion.

> Soon the volcano will
> strike noon and I shall
> be in its mouth spitting
> fire myself...I shall
> be at the fire's centre,
> exploding like a
> grenade, on all sides
> spurting forth the blood
> I have swallowed for the
> past twenty years.
> (*L'âge de la parole* p. 90)

> They would like to make
> me into an amalgam,
> but I intend to
> remain pure and
> simple mercury...
> (*L'âge de la parole* p. 92)

The summit of the heroic ascension is reached when the traveller

> heaves into the Void a
> cornerstone...which bursts
> out into bloom, while
> all around its multicoloured
> ramifications spread out
> like interlacing crystals
> that soon form a
> whirling platform expanding
> endlessly into space in a
> geometric progression.
> (*L'âge de la parole* p. 95)

There is no better way of showing the act of founding or the establishment of the central place than by first stationing oneself in it and thus dominating time and space – so that the ensuing, irrepressible growth of the nucleus seems to satisfy the demands of desire. It happens, however, that this 'platform' or 'base' is revealed as being only a 'wretched illusion, a treacherous layer of neon light' which the 'body flies right through.' Then comes a dizzying fall. In the inverted illusory centre and the brusque reversal from the climb to the fall, we recognize the primary law of Giguère's world; here it must be seen as the decisive ordeal in the process of initiation. Until now the initiation, in its ascending form, was only a preliminary step; in its second phase, it completes the liberating disorientation. Although getting stuck is accepted as part of the trial ('I am sinking down because I want to sink down,' p. 96), it is radically opposed to the ascension in that it leaves no room for initiative ('now I can only let myself sink down'). This time the loss is total, the vertigo uncontrollable (p. 97).

The dizzying, blurring plunge is really a reintegration with the origins, which may be symbolized as the sea bottom, a mine, a fountainhead, or a swamp. We find the major expression of this in the poem 'En pays perdu,' with the 'episode' of the 'archaic hamlet' previously quoted from pages 145–6. The revelation of the centre of origin is preceded by the 'disorientation necessary for a renewal of strength.' It is while he is 'lost in the heart of the city' that the poet suddenly discovers the 'archaic hamlet, a sort of primitive tribal village.' This discovery is strangly similar to an hallucination, or to Rimbaud's 'deliberate disordering of the senses'; it also has affinities with the search for wonderment as practised by the surrealists: Aragon's *Le paysan de Paris* or Breton's *Nadja ou la nuit du tournesol*. The drily narrative and descriptive style paradoxically produces an effect of extreme density: the discovery leaves one breathless. The architecture of the 'well / hut' is remarkable in that it accurately conveys the very structure of Giguère's world, with its rigorous relationship between the high and the low always allowing the possibility of a reversal. In the same manner as with Hébert's work, the birth of speech takes place in complete silence: 'silence, unmoving, unspeaking, the word takes form...' (*L'âge de la parole* p. 74); with Giguère, the instant of origin, the decisive moment of initiation, occurs in the 'silence favourable to all presence,' *dum silentio*. At this moment the question 'Where was I? Where am I?' crystallizes in a supreme moment of vertigo and potential; time does not yet exist in this central 'nowhere.'

Dum silentio: here the wanderer reaches the meridian hour of night, of primeval shadow, the 'heart of darkness.' This reintegration is fraught with the greatest possible risks; however, since it is a sacred act, it is inexplicably regulated by secret powers ('the black sorcerer' who 'guides and exorcises me') that operate by casting and controlling various spells. And now for the first time the ideal that was sought in the ascension is shown to be attainable:

I glimpse the possibility
of reincarnation in a
happier form, as a cloud
or a flame, always on a
human scale.

From this moment on, the march, the advance, pushes resolutely ahead; radiantly liberating, it moves on to experience the joy of 'levitation,' which is an unquestionable form of successful initiation.

SETTLEMENT

I see the act of *settlement* as progressing from the pure act of beginning or being born, as being a change from the single to the multiple, from the abstract to the concrete, from the nocturnal, central 'nowhere' to a full possession of the territory in broad daylight. 'Progress' here should not be taken as implying that the 'land poetry' is somehow superior, but rather as indicating one step in the process by which each phase is based on its necessary connection with the others. To show the pattern of this would have meant giving the structure of the 'poetic field' that I had intended to identify. By settlement I mean a deliberate taking possession of the land one was born in. Since it is rooted in them, this act in no way causes a break with the acts of founding and beginning; rather it assumes their previous existence and sweeps them along in a renewed time of myth and origin. Historical time, meanwhile, increasingly assumes the proportions of a happy, forgotten, successful time of origin. However, the time of dawn and the frontier remains a period of severe wrenching apart, as is shown by Miron and Brault. The nocturnal, central 'nowhere' of the origins, which we must remember is 'outside time,' is transformed by the act of settlement into a specific geographical territory: the land. Even now the time of origin is not left behind; rather, the territory, as a specific space, must itself be founded and mythically created, itself becoming the source of a 'myth of origin' and developing its own cosmogony.

This is why the land, the geographical territory, is perceived in its 'natal,' virginal condition, in a time of dawning in which it remains as yet unexpressed and unchanged by history. Thus it is not surprising that it is perceived in its guises as the Amerindian land or a sylvan setting. To settle it is to give oneself a wild, virgin land that still must be 'colonized': the land remains primal and elemental. Settlement is the supreme form of overcoming the initial 'dispossession'; it is conquering, appropriating, making it one's own and similar to oneself. Once the world has been created in its abstract simplicity, progress (in the relative sense I suggested earlier) consists of taking possession of it by means of subduing its multiple (particular) features: the geography, the fauna and flora, the seasons, climates, landscapes, and the features of its human inhabitants. After all, to be dispossessed of the world is to be dispossessed of a *particular* land or country. The return to the origins is justified and sought after only if it provides for the emergence of man in an harmonious relationship with the land. (Even if it were a question of the whole planet, one still could not ignore its particular features or the rhythmical arrangement of its continents. Besides, to inhabit a particular territory, as Miron and Brault make abundantly clear, is the best possible way to inhabit the world.)

This progression from 'nowhere' to one's native land and country does not, as we have said, constitute a break with the past; in fact it heightens and sharpens the basic tension between desire and its repression (through obstacles or dispossession). Here history, and 'impoverished' time, must finally be created and renewed; the appropriation of the territory is also a reappropriation of time – the call of a history that is yet to be made and enacted. Turning to a myth of origin was the result of being totally dispossessed and particularly of being expelled from history, which had since assumed the dimensions of an absolute interdiction. This accounts for the obsessive recurrence of amnesia, whose harmful effects Giguère, Miron, and Brault all recognize and try to overcome. Ultimately, returning to one's origins can have no meaning unless it allows for the establishment of time. In short, settling the territory is to invest it with a history, to shape and humanize it. 'Natal' dispossession is continually frustrated in its encounters with the curses of geography and memory.

Giguère's 'disorienting' expedition furnishes an appropriate symbolic balance in the myth of origin. Unlike Hébert, his search for the founding centre abandons gravity and ritual immobility and takes the form of extreme uneasiness and mobility. The course of this search recalls both the flowing rivers of Hénault and the tragic, patient, or turbulent agitation of Miron, Brault, Filion, and Lapointe. The search both opens up the spaces of the native territory and establishes its boundaries. Its horizontality, implying combat, inventory, and 'design,' has replaced the vertical quality of the ritualistic enchantment found in Hébert and Beaulieu.

The project and process of settlement may take a variety of forms, with the two major ones having an heroic or Dionysian bipolar relationship. The 'heroic' mode emphasizes the obstacle that must be overcome, and more or less sets itself the goal of surmounting the double dispossession, geographical and historical. For Hénault and Miron (actively seconded by Brault), the accent is placed on history; thus the memory functions as the site of the struggle for appropriation. Hénault, and especially Préfontaine, project into their bitter landscapes of ice and tundra, of North and Cold, the tangle of obstacles and interdiction that must be surmounted by *l'homme québécois*. For Préfontaine, the image is 'overdetermined' and is elevated to the level of a myth of origin. Once again in the confines of this article, I must unfortunately be content simply to make passing reference to this. (A methodological note. The act of settlement is to some extent implied in all poetry of foundation, as shown by the North or the appeal of the primitive; thus, if the article were longer, we would examine the settlement theme in the works of all these poets. I think I have sufficiently shown the close continuity between the 'beginnings' and the 'settlement' to be justified in otherwise making a distinction between them.)

With Hénault we find a remarkable passage illustrating for the first time what might be called the geographical lyricism of settlement; here the poet gives particular expression to the desire for possession:

> Country belted in steel
> With large eyes of lakes
> And a rustling resinous beard
> I salute you and I salute the waterfalls of your laughter.
> Country capped by polar ice
> Haloed by the northern lights
> And offering future generations
> The sparkling wreath of your uranium fires.
> Against those who pillage and empty you
> Against those who parasite your huge body of humus and snow
> We hurl the thundering curses
> That issue from the throats of storms.
> ('Je te salue,' *Totems*) [tr. A. Poulin, Jr.]

If we remember that the publication date of *Totems* is 1953, we can only be amazed by the prophetic scope of this poem. The eleventh and twelfth lines have an astonishingly Mironian cast to them, and the whole stanza is built on the emergence of the warrior-country: 'country belted in steel'... 'rustling resinous beard'...'country capped in polar ice...' This is the warrior-hero whose time of glory is yet to come (with future generations). The humanization of the landscape conveys the very qualities of the man whose goal it is to take possession of it: the conquering hero. This is made explicit in the closing lines of the stanza.

Come, with your lovely sparkle of spruce
Red land of joy
O world of heroic euphoria.
(Jean-Paul Filion, 'La grand-gigue,' *Demain les herbes rouges*)

There is a clear similarity between these poems by Hénault and Jean-Paul Filion. Moreover, 'La grand-gigue,' which opens the collection *Demain les herbes rouges*, is dedicated to Miron, another sign of their closeness. This poem, together with 'Terre de miel' from the same collection, constitutes one of the high points in this poetry of investiture and settlement. The two poems form the two sides of the appropriation and conquest: the first in a heroic mode and the second in a mode of nuptial lyricism.

There is a common trait in the two texts that is somewhat bothersome: the annoying inclusion of inverted commas around such 'French-Canadian' words as *chassis-doubles* (storm windows), *battures* (sand-bars), *coulées* (ravines), *trécarrés* (boundary lines) and *drave* (log-drive). This has the effect of impeding the full thrust of the joyous and turbulent process of appropriation, like the hesitations of a lover who wants both to keep his distance and at the same time to express his joy. The presence of the 'French-Canadian' words is only reinforced by this, and it would seem that the use of inverted commas is not a very effective way of indicating their actual foundation in the language of poetry; in fact the inclusion of these words illustrates and initiates the process of assuming control over and taking command of the territory and people of Quebec.

'La grand-gigue' is a celebration of 'heroic euphoria' in the same manner as in the passage quoted from Hénault. In this 'natal' cosmogony, the creative force is fire: subjugation, purification, transfiguration, and delirium. And above all, *celebration*: 'Thousands of torches stowed in the holds of a new Saint-Jean Baptiste Day.' The dynamism of the fire is unmistakable: light, heat, and energy, called forth as it were by the antagonism of the North and the Pole.

Dance, oh dance
So long as the high walls of the Far North
May once display your fiery phantom

The first three parts of the poem celebrate the exploits of the warrior-fire, which is charged with transforming the territory, its inhabitants, their goods, and their daily life:

> I welcome you
> so that our land
> might be filled with people.

There are several reasons for placing this poem in the 'heroic' dimension of conquest. First, fire mythically magnifies the energies that have been mounted against the obstacle, whether in the form of boredom, ruins, stagnation, exile, or ice. Secondly, the action and triumph of the fire are announced in the future tense, and in this way chanted like a warriors' song. The poem's finale clearly recalls this, suddenly stopping in the minor chord of a 'long stroke of the bow,' at which the euphoria gives way brusquely to the 'sombre day of our melancholy.' However, its projection into the future carries the poem off on waves of triumph, and by harking back to it, emphasizes its celebration and joyfulness in the noon of time and of space:

> Your dance this July gives me joy
> at being in the world.

Thus we have a metamorphosis of the territory into a 'dance floor' for the fire dance: horizontality and triumphant expansion have mythically succeeded subterranean expeditions, dangerous ascents, and plunges. This progress, from plodding along in the same old ruts to the spreading out of a fiery country, is described with remarkable complexity in the lacerated/radiant poetry of Miron.

'Arbres' by Paul-Marie Lapointe is surely one of the most beautiful poems in Quebec literature. For the purpose of this article, I shall propose it as a central text. Although the appropriation of the world one was born into, which I defined as 'settlement,' is not made into a central theme as in the work of Hénault, Filion, or Miron, nevertheless the entire poem constitutes a multiple, joyful act of taking an inventory of the territory by enumerating its riches and its essences.

Conquest and appropriation in Lapointe's poetry are quite different from the 'heroic' mode of Giguère or Hénault; they do not involve clearing or overcoming obstacles (such as the cold), but rather are cast in a predominant mode of embrace, inclusion, nuptiality – a Dionysian delirium. All of

Lapointe's work exudes a happy and radiant sensuality: things such as salmon, furs, and cupboards are given a strong and simple existence and bask in the glow of an inventive embrace of the senses. This can be seen in the emphasis placed on nouns, which constitutes (rather than conveys) the immediate presence of the objects being described. More than sight, which is captured distance, the sense of touch is the primary, founding sensation; thus we have closeness, contact, caress, and penetration:

> Do we ever live but at night
> in your mauve caresses
> in the pink melon fruit
> of your lips and your sex?
>
> do we ever live but in love
> my hands caught in the gloves of your skin
> in this suppressed anger of the cry?

In this passage, the caress is quite naturally associated with buccal and oral qualities, thus forming an erotic cycle, a veritable network that achieves the union of man and things. This is a relationship which is principally effected through all forms of welcome and inclusion, creating spaces of closeness and intimacy: hospitable lands or nests of warmth.

It seems to me that Lapointe's world can also be defined as a world of 'between,' of bridges between all things, between things and men. The emphasis placed on this preposition is a grammatically verifiable sign of this. 'Between' implies passage, communication,and changes, a continuous circulation which produces an endless chain of relationships:

> on nylon gangplanks
> between the worlds
> sway the tender hips of girls
> ('ICBM,' Pour les âmes) [tr. Ben-Z. Shek]

To be more explicit, it is Lapointe's use of language – actually his very particular syntax – that gives immediate expression, in the 'body' of the writing, to the processes of exchange and metamorphosis. Without fail, the adjacency of the nouns itself forms the image of the connecting relationship; things come together not in a process or movement but rather through the respective position of their presence in a founding co-presence. This, to the highest degree, is what happens in the poem 'Arbres,' which I shall now discuss.

The form of the poem clearly commands attention; it is a long litany, a sort of ritual enumeration or eulogy of the tree in all its variety. The effect it produces is one of assembled multiplicity which results, literally, in a universe. It seems to me that the appropriation of the territory, to begin with, is carefully carried out at this first level: the diversity is a form of taking an inventory of the land, the place and birth. By means of a prodigious metonymical survey, the tree is accorded the function of 'representing' the territory in its full variety. We should note that in this case the multiplicity reinforces the singular, determined, and specific character of each individual item.

On a second level, the appropriation of the territory is clearly presented as a form of geography. Listing things is a way of naming them, and the representation itself is marked by what it represents: the territory. These are the essences of a specific country. It is perhaps useful to list them in their order in the poem: pines, cedars of all kinds, junipers, spruces, balsam and fir, birches, sapwood, poplars, nutwoods, willows, hickory, alders, oaks, beeches, chestnut, cherrywood, sumac, elms, plum trees, hawthorns, sorb apples, crab apples, magnolias, tulip trees, sassafras, witch hazel, rowanberry, apple trees, ash, linden, and maples.

The 'representative' function of the trees in the poem (the details of which we can appreciate as the poem moves along) proves to be remarkably fertile. As the various faces of the tree succeed one another, they set up strings of associations that widen endlessly and form a close network that reflects the features of the total field: the land. This associative mechanism produces three sets of ripples which intersect with one another in concentric circles. To illustrate this, I shall limit myself to the 'pines' passage at the very beginning of the poem.

An initial series of associations is formed from the simple juxtaposition of the 'objective' natural properties of the tree. Notice that it does not proceed in a descriptive manner but rather is expressed through the impulse of a quick and careful sensuality, guided by the thread of 'correspondences':

> pine   the white and the red   norway and jack pine
> tough heavy-wooded pine   pine with long twisting
> needles   pitch pine
> [tr. D.G. Jones]

On the whole, this first series forms a basic, 'natural' background from which the others can issue.

At a second level, we find a vast network of 'analogic' associations, remarkable both for their daring and their accuracy:

> lordly pine
> pine with tender pores   pines traversing time
> wrapped in their snows   proud masts stretched
> sails dry-eyed and remorseless   armed companies
> [tr. D.G. Jones]

It seems to me that this second series is basically intended to establish a 'correspondence' *between* the tree and the world around it. However, the process of expansion is always centred and rooted in the tree itself, which acts to some extent as an 'indicator.'

This 'secondary' level of associations is strategically crucial to the poem's economy and to the unfolding of its meaning, since it necessarily and 'naturally' leads to a third series of associations. These are highly analogical associations, and they complete the meaning of the poem by revealing the 'kinship' of the (Québécois) tree with (Québécois) man in his laborious or joyful appropriation of matter or territory (metonymically, the tree):

> pine of quiet cupboards   of simple houses
> wood for tables and for beds
> wood for paddles frames and beams   men's bread
>   rising in your squared palms
> [tr. D.G. Jones]

To continue reading the poem in this sense reveals an astonishingly rigorous recurrence of the structure I have just attempted to describe. In the opening passage from which I have just quoted, the development of the three networks of association is carried out in a clearly linear manner. Further along in the poem, however, the three levels tend to merge with one another in vividly abbreviated form:

> juniper keeping the plumb of alphabets.
> [tr. D.G. Jones]

The full meaning of the poem is focused in one line:

> I write tree
> tree for the trunk and its leaves.
> [tr. D.G. Jones]

Here the kinship of tree and man is captured in a flash of identification.

This example of the general theme of the land poetry being used in a 'political' sense may mark its high point, its culmination. However, this does not mean that it should not be considered as a phenomenon within the poetry itself, in which case the political aspect is justifiable only if it is integrated into the poem and made part of it. Otherwise, we would have to denounce it as false representation, both poetical and political. In Miron's work,* for example, the political element is an integral part of the poem; this is forgotten when Miron, the political activist, is shown as a poet whose writings might easily lead to a vital political commitment. I shall not attempt in a few lines to unravel a problem that Brault's excellent study[3] revealed to us in its full complexity, warning us of the dangers of getting involved in it. In any event, Miron in the poem is above all a poet; this in no way sacrifices his other 'causes,' but rather grafts them onto the poetic act, revealing their profound relationship with the love from which all poetry emerges. The incomparable 'naturalness' of Lapointe's poetry should in turn clarify the no less sure 'gushing source' that identifies Miron's poetry and such verses as the following in which we can feel its centre of attraction:

dawn and the crackling branches
through the opacity and my ignorance
mark me with hawthorns and epiphanies
ah poetry my resting place
my sweet svelte and fresh revelation of being
('Monologues de l'aliénation délirante' from *La vie agonique* in *Liberté* no. 27, May-June 1963, p. 219)

It will no doubt be considered surprising that in the chapter on settlement I have not dealt with the works of Miron and Brault, which provide important illustrations of this theme. This present article, however, would not have done them justice. The study of Miron's poetry suffers, albeit less than others, from approximative analyses which perpetuate certain of the misconceptions it usually causes and which I have just discussed. Miron's poetry is pre-eminently one of inhabitation, both of impulse and reflection. It is geographically definite and at the same time involves a precise anthropology of suffering mankind. It is 'politicized' poetry, stemming from a vital, internal movement that has led it from the 'no where' of origin to the

---

*A selection of the poetry of Gaston Miron was translated in *Ellipse* 5, 1970. (ed.)

country and history. The same movement gives to it the extremely harsh quality of a conflict that is correctly perceived and experienced as being a non-poem.

Perhaps Brault,* especially in his long poem 'Mémoire,' offers us the living, armed synthesis of the different aspects of the foundation of the territory. Similar to the poetry of Miron in this respect, Brault's work moves through a maze of memory, effecting an irreversible passage from the time of origin to historical time.

EXCLUSIONS

The presence of a definite thematic field can be established – and the characteristics of the field better defined – by examining what it excludes. An examination of what is excluded, however, can only be relevant if it is based on a detailed analysis of the field itself. In lieu of such an analysis, therefore, I can only indicate some very rapid perspectives for marking out areas of further research.

With Anne Hébert's poetry I have interpreted the break between the poems in *Le tombeau des rois* and those in *Mystère de la parole* as being a particularly striking indication of the frontiers of the general theme of foundation, a process that begins with dispossession. The radical change in the meaning of this dispossession, as privation is transformed into the starkness of birth and origin, is the strategic result of the metamorphosis of the field. No comparable event ever took place in Saint-Denys-Garneau's poetry and this is no doubt the reason it remains outside the thematic framework of foundation. However, the experience of dispossession is initially similar with these two poets – the role of the *bone* images is an obvious indication of this. Thus, by making a close comparison of these two bodies of writing, the thematic framework of foundation can be quite clearly determined. In the work of Saint-Denys-Garneau, dispossession ends in disintegration, decomposition, and self-destruction. A planned foundation and invention of the world is present in the poetry only as an image of what might have been – and it is searing in its perpetual failure. A random poem (p. 126 in the *Poésies complètes*,† second edition) gives clear proof of this:

---

*A selection of Brault's poetry is translated in *Ellipse* 7, 1971. (ed.)
†Translated by John Glassco as *Complete Poems of Saint-Denys-Garneau* (Ottawa: Oberon 1975) (ed.)

There, out there, you shall awake
Convulsing all my universe
Before me and building it again
In an overflowing of every form and flame.
[tr. John Glassco]

Even more troubling is the unfinished quality of Saint-Denys-Garneau's poetry, as if the very letters were exhausted in their efforts to express the effects of erosion: this is not only a poetry of failure, but failed poetry as well, which no doubt partly explains the painful impression caused by reading it. The poetry of Saint-Denys-Garneau would be excluded from the field precisely because it constitutes its counter-thematic opposite; thus it is connected to the field only in that it shows what the field *excludes* – or in other words, it belongs to the field only in a purely negative sense. This problem shows up the insufficiency of such concepts as field and thematic framework; nevertheless, these concepts have been useful to us, provided that we have clearly indicated the problem here.

The poets of the Hexagone generation were unanimous in recognizing Alain Grandbois as one of their 'masters' and 'precursors.' His famous poem 'Ah toutes ces rues'* may be seen as a symbol of all of Grandbois's work, centred mainly on exile and wandering throughout the world. This wandering movement is somewhat analogous to the initiatory excursion in the important poems by Giguère. In Grandbois's poem, as in several others, wandering is ultimately defined as a failure to find the central place where the dispersion of time and space is brought to an end. Certainly there is no lack of attempts to plunge towards reintegration with the bowels of the earth or the bosom of the seas; here the 'purple star' plays the role of a captivating mirage, just as the keystone does in Giguère's work. Time in Grandbois's poetry strikes me as being exactly the same as in Giguère's 'Midi perdu,' a moment or point of break-up, close to the time of origin and the act of foundation. In this particular respect, Grandbois's poetry unquestionably belongs in the thematic field of foundation.

The development of Quebec poetry has been marked by a major event, Borduas's *Refus global*, which has also determined the overall direction of ideas in general. There is no need to mention the thrust this movement gave to painting. In 1947, the then young Paul-Marie Lapointe 'privately' published a collection of 'automatist' poetry of very high calibre: *Le vierge*

*The translation of this and other poems by Alain Grandbois appears in *Ellipse* 14/15, 1974. (ed.)

incendié. * It would also be easy to establish the thread of influence connecting the productions of such publishing houses as Erta and L'Hexagone to
the 'Automatist' movement.

Such historical considerations, however, do not take account of – and
indeed make it more difficult to understand – the rather rapid eclipsing of
both the ideas and the literary production of the 'Automatist' movement (at
least in poetry, for the case of painting is quite different). The principal
victim of this eclipse was Claude Gauvreau, whose work, from what we
know of it today, reveals a poet of the first order. The eclipse also affected
the scant but brilliant production of the poet Jean-Paul Martino. It seems
likely, however, that this period of silence is nearing its end, as plans have
been announced for the publication of Gauvreau's work.† This comes of its
own necessity, but that it should be happening now is highly indicative of a
change in the direction of Quebec poetry, the benefits of which seem to be
evident in recent work of Claude Péloquin and the activities of the group he
directs, 'le Zirmate.' With Péloquin there has been a reinstatement of the
value, as much in the 'moral' as in the 'technical' sense, of the automatism
and experimentation introduced by the surrealist movement. From the
perspective of this study, the double phenomenon of the eclipse and reap-
pearance of a certain form of poetry might be explained in terms of a
transformation of the field. Certainly Gauvreau's poetry appears clearly
excluded from the thematic framework of foundation (I have opted here to
define it only in negative terms in order to avoid any imprecision). The
work of Péloquin and certain young poets who have been swiftly classified
as formalists is also clearly outside the thematic field of foundation. In
addition, since their work shows a definite kinship with Gauvreau's writing, we might predict the creation of a new thematic field that would
resuscitate the work of some of those who have been 'excluded.' It is almost
as if their writings have become 'unintelligible' to an audience raised on the
mass of literature belonging to the poetry of foundation. If this poetry
reaches its full development, it may yet bring an end to the 'jamming of the
signals' and the eclipse of the 'doomed' writers.

NOTES

1 Jean Cohen, *Structure du language poétique*, coll. 'Nouvelle bibliothèque scientifique'
  (Paris: Flammarion 1966)

*See translations in *Ellipse* 11 and in Jones's *The Terror of the Snows*. (ed.)
†Gauvreau's *Poésies complètes* was finally published in 1977 by Parti pris. (ed.)

2 '... the seductive metaphors of the terrain, the horizon and hence the limits of a
visible field defined by a given problematic threaten to induce a false idea of
the nature of this field, if we think of this field literally according to the spatial
metaphor as a space limited by *another space outside it*. This other space is also the
first space which contains it as its own denegation; this other space is the first
space in person, which is only defined by the denegation of what it excludes
from its own limits. In other words, all its limits are *internal*, it carries its
outside inside it ...' Louis Althusser *Lire le Capital* 1, p. 29. [tr. by Ben Brewster as
Reading Capital (London: NLB, 1970, rpt. 1972) 26–7]

3 'Miron le magnifique,' no. 6 in the collection *Conférences J.A. de Sève*, published by
the Département d'études françaises de la Faculté des lettres de l'Université de
Montréal.

GÉRARD BESSETTE

Psychoanalytic Criticism

The critical writings of Gérard Bessette show a steady evolution towards psychocriticism (or psychoanalytic criticism, as it is usually called in English). *Les images en littérature canadienne-française*, published in 1960, examines not only the frequency of certain images in Quebec poetry but also their kind (technique) and their content (subject). We also see the author's careful methodology, his concern for precise definitions, his meticulous attention to detail, his painstaking analysis backed by numerous textual references, and his frequent value judgments. These characteristics have remained constant in his criticism, and with the exception of the value judgments, can be considered particularly useful adjuncts to his later practice of psychocriticism.

While this first book attempted to apply the techniques of the social sciences to the study of literature, Bessette's later work is more concerned with the methods of the human sciences, particularly psychology and psychoanalysis. His *Histoire de la littérature canadienne-française*, published in collaboration in 1968, organizes Quebec literature according to what might be called 'psychological themes' such as fidelity, solitude, and 'man and his ego.' The psychoanalytic bent is more apparent in *Une littérature en ébullition*, published the same year. Here he presents both a formal and a psychocritical treatment of the writers he discusses, stressing the need for extensive textual analysis and providing an example of it in a forty-page study of a single poem by Nelligan. *Trois romanciers québécois*, which appeared in 1973, shows the full scope of Bessette's psychoanalytic approach. It allows the critic to investigate both individual novels and the entire *œuvre* of a particular author, and it enables him to interpret the unconscious motivations of both the characters and the writer who has created them.

Bessette is something of a pioneer in his attempts to use the concepts and methods of psychoanalysis to illuminate Quebec literature. As he suggests in the following article, his efforts have met with resistance, partly no doubt because of the esoteric nature of psychocriticism itself, and partly, one suspects, because of his insistence on making judgmental pronouncements. Bessette argues that a young literature in particular needs evaluative criticism, however unfashionable it may be; yet by its very nature, psychocriticism is non-evaluative.

Psychocriticism is also, by nature, closely directed towards a particular piece of writing. Because it was impossible to include a representative sample of Bessette's criticism in a general anthology such as this, the following article reveals Bessette's concept of psychocriticism rather than his practice of it. The 'oral' quality of the text is explained by the fact that it was first presented as a paper at the Learned Societies meetings in Toronto, 1974.

Gérard Bessette is well known for his novels as well as his criticism; he teaches in the French department of Queen's University.

PSYCHOANALYTIC CRITICISM

Taking it for granted that any cultivated French-speaking Québécois would be aware of the existence of psychoanalytic criticism, I learned the hard way that such is not the case. Indeed, the mental obduracy with which my book *Trois romanciers québécois* was received by certain reviewers has led me to the conclusion that fossils can be discovered in all age groups.

Now I am told that psychoanalytic criticism is little known or practised in English Canada. This has come as something of a surprise, since Northrop Frye, one of the few English-Canadian critics to have gained so great an international reputation as to be known even by a few Québécois, has always seemed to me to be something of a Jungian – not that he is a psychocritic in the strict sense of the word, but simply that he has been influenced by psychoanalysis. Nevertheless, Frye's approach to criticism (and I must confess that I have not read all his work) does strike me as being considerably different from that of Charles Baudouin, in his *Psychanalyse de Victor Hugo*, or from almost all the writings of Charles Mauron.

Actually, Frye's *Anatomy of Criticism* is defined more in terms of collective myths than of 'personal myth.' Still, it would be interesting to make a comparison between *Anatomy of Criticism*, on the one hand, and *Psychocritique du genre comique* and *Le triomphe du héros*, on the other. In each of these latter works, Mauron and Baudouin deal simultaneously, as Frye does, with a great many works by different authors, in the hope of discovering or elucidating their underlying structures, or, to use Frye's metaphor, their common 'anatomy.'

In any event, and in spite of the divergencies in their methodological approaches, Frye, Baudouin, and Mauron all seem to make a basic distinction between the latent content and the apparent content of a work of literature. The apparent content, we know, is the one that the author has thought about, while the latent content has escaped his awareness, or at least his active awareness. Of course the lack of precise and direct indications from the creative artist often makes it dangerous to try to establish a clear line of demarcation between these two 'territories,' these two 'poles' of a work of literature. And in this regard, the following quotations from Mauron seem to me to be admirably adroit and precise:

...psychocriticism claims to increase our knowledge of literary works simply by discovering in them facts and relationships that have hitherto remained unnoticed and that can be attributed to the author's unconscious. The method is justified if there is agreement that it has reached its goal.[1]

The second quotation deals in part with these same concerns:

Psychocriticism attempts to increase our knowledge of literature first by discovering and then by studying relationships which can reasonably be thought to stem from the author's unconscious, if they cannot be explained by his intentions or by chance.[2]

Mauron, in these two excerpts, implicitly recognizes that psychocriticism is a *partial* form of criticism, and that as criticism it deals with only one part or one aspect of a work of literature. In many other passages as well, Mauron provides a full, straightforward explanation of the partial nature of psychocriticism:

Let us first of all define the position of psychocriticism: it must be considered an adjunct to classical criticism, one that – far from replacing it – adapts and must adapt to it. By widening the horizon, the psychocritical study of texts permits us to gain a clearer comprehension of the object to which classical criticism itself is addressed.[3]

It is curious that in spite of such forthright statements as this, a great many opponents of psychocriticism turn a blind eye to these passages and accuse Mauron of pretending to explain *everything* by his method of approach. Other objectors (as in 'conscientious objectors') are less scotomatical (that is, selectively blind) in their reactions, but they do question Mauron's motives. One of the phrases used by Serge Doubrovsky in a paper recently delivered at Queen's University is particularly striking. I quote from memory: 'Of course Mauron claims that he restricts his analysis to one single aspect of the work, but we know that, deep down, his brand of criticism, like all brands of criticism, is totalitarian and inclined to imperialism, wanting to explain everything.'

Well, enough polemics (even indirect ones), *pro domo*. We should now ask how – by what means – psychocriticism claims to scent out and unearth the unconscious aspects of a work (and of its author). Actually, unlike the psychiatrist with his patient stretched out on the proverbial couch, psychocriticism cannot ask the writer to try making free associations, saying whatever comes into his head. For in fact the literary text – with the exception of what in the Bretonian period was called automatic writing – is usually the very opposite of free association. It is language that has been watched, weighed, and worked on, and that has gone through many different forms and many 'conscious' corrections, with the author presenting us with only the final version of what he has written.

Now, there are two 'methods,' as it were, of detecting or tracking down the presence of the unconscious in literary texts. The first method I shall call 'intuitive,' for want of a better word. It is unfortunate that Mauron does not have more to say about this. The quotation below, taken from *L'inconscient dans l'œuvre et la vie de Racine*, is, to the best of my knowledge, the only instance in which the father of psychocriticism indicates what it is he proposes to observe. Having just spoken of the field of forces that underlies every work of literature and 'arranges its ... lines of invisible forces,' he adds:

How are we to recognize, in a given piece of literature, the elements that are dependent on this field of forces and on which we must therefore base our knowledge of it? Let us say that, in general, they can be recognized in those features that are characteristic of any product of the unconscious: fatalism, obsessive repetitions, very pronounced presences or absences, strangeness, bizarreness, double meanings, ambivalence, primitive functions, magical thinking, dream symbols, and so on. Naturally, this is where a knowledge of the human unconscious becomes indispensable.[4]

Here, as we can see, Mauron is directing the reader or the aspiring psychocritic back to a basic study of the unconscious (that is, the theory of psychoanalysis and the works of Freud). Actually, although a newcomer to the field might conceivably recognize signs of fatalism or obsessive repetitions in a particular piece of writing, he would certainly wonder which cases of 'bizarreness' should be investigated and interpreted.

In this respect, the two books that I have found most helpful, together with such works by Freud as *Introduction to Psychoanalysis, Five Case Histories*, and *Three Essays on the Theory of Sexuality*, are Marie Bonaparte's study *Edgar Poe, sa vie, son œuvre* and above all *L'âme enfantine et la psychanalyse* by Charles Baudouin. This latter work contains the most complete list I know and also the most brilliant description of the complexes discovered by Freud, Jung, and by Baudouin himself.

In considering the 'very pronounced presences and absences' in works of fiction that involve a story (particularly drama and the novel), it is useful to compare the protagonists' family situation or 'group' with a situation that could be considered 'normal': one in which the subject has both his parents as well as brothers and / or sisters. Thus the startling number of orphans in Quebec literature is surely significant, being a reflection of the feeling of orphanhood which, in both a familial and a political sense, affects the entire community. It also reveals a parental complex that I have detected in both Nelligan and Yves Thériault, as well as in Gabrielle Roy and André Langevin.

Let me digress for a moment here so that I can reply to an objection which has often been raised in more or less the following terms. 'If, as Baudouin affirms, complexes are only networks of tendencies and if they are to be found in varying degrees in all people (including, of course, writers), what is the use of wasting one's time enumerating or analysing them in such and such a work?' This recurring objection, I must say, strikes me as being very strange. Would anyone ever think of blaming a classical critic for writing about love and jealousy in a study of Racine, or heroism and duty in an analysis of Corneille, with the pretext that most people have similar feelings or have to contend with some of the same obligations? Why then should it be considered any more surprising for a psychocritic to point out an Oedipus complex in Hamlet, a birth complex with Agaguk or to analyse a castration complex in Jos Connaissant?

Just as we may suppose there was once a time when it was an achievement for the critic or reader even to be able to identify feelings of jealousy or envy, for example, in an oral or written narrative, so it may now seem difficult for various reasons to detect signs of the oral stage, a Diana complex, or even a parental fixation. Perhaps future generations will be able to do this almost automatically, although I somehow doubt this. But whatever the case, one has to begin with the task of detection and discovery, and this is surely what Mauron means in the preceding quotation when he states that 'a knowledge of the human unconscious becomes indispensable.'

Of course, this is only a first step, however indispensable it may be. The next task is to analyse the specific appearance and form of the various libidinal stages or the various complexes found in a particular work. Pure and simple detection, however – and this cannot be stressed too strongly – is not always easy. Actually, the genetic development stages (oral, anal, and phallic) give rise to complexes which are expressed through oneiroid fantasies. After following a long chain of connecting symbols, such fantasies often show no apparent resemblance to their starting point (the incident or trauma that triggered them).

The starting point is usually found in early childhood, and this explains why one of the books I have found most useful, along with *L'âme enfantine ...*, is *Psychoanalysis of Children* by Melanie Klein. As well as showing us that, for children, all games are symbolic, this important study also abundantly describes the most common infantile fantasies having to do, for the most part, with birth, sexuality, and interpersonal relationships among the family and siblings. In this connection, *Narrative of a Child Analysis*, also by Melanie Klein, lets us put our finger, as it were, on the workings of the creative imagination in children, with its constant play of introjections and projections. Also, this infantile creative imagination bears a striking resemblance to the creative imagination of the artist.

It has frequently been said that writers play with words as children play with blocks or with the parts of a Meccano set. Even the lugubrious Saint-Denys-Garneau, who never said much of anything interesting, still knew enough to describe this similarity in his childlike poem 'Le Jeu.'

Whatever the case, we can see how a psychoanalytic critic working with a writer and his text is in some ways similar to an analyst working with an adult patient doing free association or a child patient involved in his play. Let us repeat, however, that the disadvantage of the psychocritic in comparison with the analyst is that the writer is absent and can neither be questioned like a patient nor encouraged to pursue his fantasy along a particular course.

This is where the second method comes into play, using a technique that is the cornerstone of psychocritical methodology: *the superposition of texts.* An analyst listening to his patient's monologue with 'floating attention' is eventually able to discover certain hypersensitive poles or themes around which his patient's fantasies are centred; and so the psychocritic, by superposing metaphors or groups of images or characters, is able to detect in a piece of literature the underlying tendencies and directions that are dictated by the author's unconscious affectivity.

Again, let me quote from Mauron:

The superposition of different texts by the same author jumbles the conscious relationships and reveals the unconscious ones. The latter, which are actually more obsessive and less rich (because removed from reality), are bound to emerge more clearly from the jumbling. In literary analysis, the superposition of texts thus plays the essential role that free association does in psychoanalysis. In both cases, it is by muting the voice of consciousness, as it were, that one is able to perceive the voice of the unconscious.[5]

Let us note in passing that, as far as verbal association is concerned, the psychocritical practice of superposing metaphors is actually closer to the method of Jung, in his first period, than of Freud.

This is how Dr Roland Cahen describes the Jungian experience:

The experimenter is equipped with a chronometer and a list of, say, one hundred words. He advises the subject that he is going to speak a word and asks him to reply as quickly as possible with the first word that comes into his head. The experimenter keeps track of the average amount of time, in fiftieths of a second, between the stimulus word and the response word...[6]

When the subject takes an unusual amount of time to react (or to associate), or when one or another of the response words deviates so far from the norm that it has no apparent connection with the stimulus word, this was found by Jung to indicate that the subject had a complex.

If, for example, a patient hearing the word *black* were immediately to associate it with *white, snow,* or *coal,* then everything would be in order. But if he hesitated and replied *chair back* or *brassiere,* then something would be the matter: there would be a complex to deal with. Jung would then have experimented further, presenting the client with a new list of words in which *chair back* and *brassiere* (and other related terms) would serve as springboards for new associations. (Jung might eventually have discovered that the patient had in his childhood frantically clutched the back of a black chair while feasting his eyes on a woman dressed in a white gown with a wildly plunging neckline revealing a traumatizing brassiere! *Quod erat demonstrandum!*)

But enough of this libidinal (or libidinous) speculation! Let us return to the white sheep of psychocriticism and the technique of superposition.

We all know that with every poet or fiction writer there are key words, or rather interconnected groupings of words (which are often figures of style). We also know that these same writers often have recurring scenes that are highly charged with emotion. Using the technique of superposition, these recurring groupings and patterns can be precisely and objectively identified. Actually, any reader would then be in a position to check whether the elements of the grouping can in fact be found in the texts that the psychocritic has superposed. The subjective element comes into play only during the interpretive stage.

I earlier used the Freudian expression 'floating attention' to describe the frame of mind with which the psychocritic should approach his work. But why should this sort of 'detached' attention be more effective than 'regular' attention, which is concentrated and focused on the text? This is because a psychocritical reading, at the stage of detecting groupings, must disregard the connection-words and the logical structures of discourse (especially prepositions and conjunctions) which express relationships of cause or consequence. A psychocritical reading should in fact concentrate on the nouns and verbs expressing action and emotion, and also on the actual sequence of images or emotional states. Acquiring this 'aerial' manner of reading (if it can be so called) requires even more perseverance and training because it takes an approach that is directly contrary to traditional textual analysis, in which the emphasis is placed precisely on the connection-words and the logical structuring of speech.

Mauron is quite correct in affirming that psychocriticism provides a new adjunct to traditional or classical criticism, for we are dealing with another world entirely. This explains the necessity of the new approach for anyone who wants to deal with a work of literature – not in its entirety, which is impossible – but at least in the recognition that there are two sides to it, with the apparent content and the latent content corresponding to the two poles of the human psyche, the conscious and the unconscious.

If such is the case, and if psychocriticism (or criticism that is based on psychoanalysis in general) proposes only to aid or complement traditional criticism, why should it provoke such stubborn reactions of mistrust, animosity, and anger in its adversaries? It would be too easy for psychocritics simply to argue that their opponents are using resistance (in the Freudian sense of the word) and are suffering from repression – even if these two psychic phenomena often do have some role to play in such attitudes.

Nevertheless, psychocriticism is not beyond all reproach. Still smitten with its own (relative) novelty and a certain penchant for the esoteric – which is exacerbated by the fierce opposition of its detractors – psychocriticism has a tendency not to pay enough attention to classical criticism and formal analysis in the traditional sense. In doing this, it denies itself the possibility of making any value judgment as to the strictly literary quality of the work; nor can it reveal the beauties that arise from full consciousness and deliberate composition.

The fusion or rather the synthesis of these two methods of approach has still to be accomplished. Marie Bonaparte gives us a glimpse of how this synthesis might be achieved when she speaks of the 'massing of affects' (here 'massing' must be understood in its mathematical sense of addition or totalization). Although her terminology may be difficult for the uninitiated, Marie Bonaparte thus explains what she means by 'massing':

In dreams and their elaboration, we regularly find that the unconscious affects originally bound to significant but repressed representations, are transferred to representations which have generally arisen during the foregoing day. Often, it is as though their very unimportance determined the selection of the recent representations to which such affects are transferred, a phenomenon which, for ages, has attracted the notice of those interested in dreams. Freud has demonstrated that such a choice, in fact, appears to be determined by the moral censor, in order that the latent meaning of the dream be concealed. None the less, what remains of the day's experiences and links up with our earliest, strongest and most repressed wishes, must conceal some associative bond with the deeper desires which are seeking expression.

In Poe's works, as doubtless in creative art generally – where the artist's purpose is, as it were, to instil his own unconscious affect into the unconscious of his audience or, more exactly, to make both unconsciouses vibrate as one – what is of prime importance is that, as perceived, this transposition should be as close as possible, in affect, to the degree of affect it is intended to pass on. A *massing* of affects then takes place, a massing utilised by the censor to distribute affect as it will. No instance better reveals this mechanism than *The Pit and the Pendulum*, where the deep and unconscious affects which are to enter the very unconscious of the reader are, in effect, linked with representations of an especially infantile and deeply repressed nature; wish-phantasies to possess the mother in intra-cloacal fashion and passive homosexual wish-phantasies towards the father.[7]

What is needed here is more meticulous and more textual analysis so that the critic can show us in detail how, in *The Pit and the Pendulum*, the unconscious and the conscious are (unknowingly) co-operating with each other, both in the writer and in the reader...

In the course of this brief outline I have been obliged to fly rather quickly over some aspects that, in contrast to the psychoanalytic approach, should have been treated in a strictly discursive manner. Lack of time has prevented me from dealing fully with a great many aspects, explanations, and general ideas.

In closing, let me console myself by pointing out the recent publication of an excellent reference book on the subject of psychocriticism. *Psychanalyse et critique*, by Anne Clancier, provides a complete account of all French literary criticism that has been influenced by psychoanalysis.[8] I commend it to you.

NOTES

1 Charles Mauron *Des métaphores obsédantes au mythe personnel* (Paris: José Corti 1963) 13

2 Charles Mauron *Psychocritique du genre comique* (Paris: José Corti 1964) 141

3 Charles Mauron *Phèdre* (Paris: José Corti 1968) 9

4 Charles Mauron *L'inconscient dans l'œuvre et la vie de Racine* (Aix-en-Provence: Editions Ophrys 1957) 18

5 Mauron *Psychocritique du genre comique* 7

6 C.E. Jung *L'homme à la découverte de son âme* (Geneva: Editions du Mont Blanc 1962). 'Note' by Dr Roland Cahen, p. 192

7 Marie Bonaparte *Edgar Poe, sa vie, son œuvre, étude analytique* (Paris: PUF 1958) 3, p 791. [tr. John Rodker, *The Life and Works of Edgar Allan Poe, a Psychoanalytic Interpretation* (London: Hogarth Press 1971) 661–2]

8 Anne Clancier *Psychanalyse et critique littéraire* (Toulouse: Privat 1973)

LOUIS FRANCŒUR

Quebec Theatre:
Stimulation or Communication?

Semiotics, the science of signs, may be said to have its immediate antecedents in French structuralism, which in turn grew out of Russian formalism. In the past decade, however, it has become a truly international movement, with scholars all over the world engaged in establishing its theoretical foundations and its practical applications.

As a science, semiotics is closely related to modern linguistics, from which it has taken many of its basic concepts and much of its vocabulary. The semiotic approach is to view literature as a system of communication in which form conveys meaning. The signifying structures and components of literary discourse are thus submitted to detailed analysis in order to determine the role played by language in the literary process. Contrary to traditional forms of criticism, in which the dangers of subjectivity are always present, semiotics strives for complete 'scientific' objectivity, using the tools of linguistics to 'prove' its conclusions.

Both because of its level of abstraction and because of its highly specialized vocabulary, semiotic criticism is likely to appear of difficult access for the uninitiated. In this, though, it may be compared to several other kinds of contemporary art, such as painting, dance, or music, in which a growing self-consciousness and preoccupation with its own form result in ever-increasing conceptualization. As the medium becomes the message, the message becomes harder to grasp.

A professor at Laval University and one of the leading semiotic critics in Quebec, Louis Francœur has been involved in applying semiotic theory to the study of Quebec literature. Several of his articles have dealt with two particularly prominent features of recent Quebec literary production: the monologue and the theatre. With his wife, Marie, Francœur has also published a comparative study of the tales of Sherwood Anderson and Yves

Thériault, in *Etudes littéraires* 8, No. 1 (April 1975). The advantage of using a semiotic approach in making such comparisons is that Quebec literature is viewed in exactly the same light as any other literature; thus it becomes possible to point out what is specific about Quebec literature by means that are quite independent of the national context.

In the following article, Louis Francœur uses communication theory to propose a theoretical model for Quebec theatre. The text was originally presented as a paper at the ACFAS conference in 1974 and was subsequently published in *Voix et images* 1, No. 2. (December 1975).

QUEBEC THEATRE: STIMULATION OR COMMUNICATION?

'Official' critics are often surprised by the growing interest shown in Quebec theatre over the past few years by a numerous and varied audience, both here and abroad. As always with theatre, the audience is right. And perhaps one of the reasons Quebec theatre has attracted a faithful audience, apart from its powers of identification, entertainment, and imitation, is that people have realized that a 'message' is being communicated to them. The audience receives this message and responds to it in its own way, by regular attendance, tears and laughter, applause, or in some cases, even by words and actions. Certain productions of *Medium saignant, Double jeu,* or *Les belles-sœurs,* not to mention the more recent spectacles at the Théatre du Même Nom or the Grand Cirque Ordinaire, have accustomed us to these kinds of interaction between Quebec audiences and Quebec plays.

The phenomenon of theatre communication in Quebec provides a double challenge for the critic: on the one hand he has to work out a theoretical model which will enable him to make a thorough analysis, and on the other hand he has to analyse the polysemia in order to isolate its signifying structures. Since theatre today is considered to be a means of mass communication, it must therefore be given as much attention as any other 'communication procedure or method used to influence others and recognized as such by those it intends to influence.'[1] In his work on *La communication et l'articulation linguistique,* Eric Buyssens defined semiology as the study of these very procedures, this being a refinement of Saussure's tenet that semiology, as defined in the *Cours,* is 'a science which studies the life of signs within society.'[2]

These preliminary considerations enable us to make three propositions: first, that Quebec theatre, like any other theatrical production, is a sign system and an intended communication process, and not only a means of signification; second, that the semiology of communications, in so far as it can be considered to have sufficiently solid bases, will furnish the descriptive and analytic elements required by theatre communication; and third, that the use of a theoretical model becomes necessary as soon as we claim to be dealing with a particular process, which is really only a specific instance of a more general and more abstract process.

Before going any farther, however, it might be appropriate to recall Jakobson's dictum concerning the dissension that often prevails among the research community. 'Very fortunately,' he writes, 'scientific and political speeches have nothing in common. The success of a political convention depends on the agreement of most or all of the participants. On the other hand, the use of votes and vetoes is foreign to scientific debates, in which disagreement is usually more productive than agreement.'[3] This has been our attitude in approaching the present article, which, as will become apparent, places us in disagreement with a certain number of researchers, notably Georges Mounin, who wrote in his *Introduction à la sémiologie* that 'what happens in the theatre is better explained in terms of 'stimulation' than in terms of communication.'[4]

If we take a closer look, however, and consider the constituent elements in any linguistic process or act of verbal communication, as identified by R. Jakobson in his *Essais de linguistique générale,*[5] we shall find that dramatic writings contain very similar constitutive elements. We discover, for instance, that there is a sender (or encoder) who is the speaking actor / character, and that he sends messages to a receiver (or decoder) who, at an intradiegetical level, is the listening actor / character and who, at an extradiegetical level, is the 'fictitious intermediary' for the spectator sitting in the theatre. In order to be transmitted and perceived, this message requires a context to which it refers; in theatre, this will be verbal or scenic, or some combination of these two groups of referential elements. A message also presupposes a common code for the sender and the receiver; in theatre this code is composed of all the signs of dramatic language – verbal, physical, and scenic. And finally, according to Jakobson, the message requires a contact, a physical channel and psychological connection between sender and receiver so that communication between them can be established and sustained. To say that such contact exists in dramatic writing is hardly enough, since without it there would be no play, no re-presentation.

Theatre, then, is far from being simply a means of stimulating the spectator; in fact, it would appear to have all the characteristics of a veritable intended communication process which functions according to a system of signs. That theatrical language is made up of signs and not only of symbols is evident from an examination of the arbitrary, linear, and discrete character of its components. Actually, there can be little doubt that with such things as costumes, sets, gestures, and the characters' names there is no necessary motivational connection between the signifier (*signifiant*) and the signified (*signifié*) and that they can thus be considered as signs. Similarly, although certain elements occur simultaneously in theatre, some combinations are also linked to the irreversibility of time, which clearly indicates that dramatic utterance is also a series of signs 'proffered in time and perceived in time.'[6] Finally, connected with the linear character of the sign is its discrete or differential character, 'the property of being able to be distinguished by yes or no.'[7] Like linguistic signs, dramatic signs are usually either similar or different, as dictated by the decoding of the message – a process in which the spectator is invited to participate.

In many cases, then, we are dealing in theatre with authentic signs, signs which are 'clearly defined units combined or structured according to defined or known rules';[8] in other words, these units are part of a system. Later, we shall have occasion to define these rules more clearly. At this point, however, we can advance the idea that theatre, as a sign system and an intended communication process, is to be distinguished from those 'means' of communication or signification that are asystematic, such as 'plastic arts, advertising, direction signs,'[9] fashion, or cuisine. In this sense, theatre can be considered as a phenomenon that depends upon a semiology of communication, and not only upon a semiology of signification as described by R. Barthes in his *Eléments de sémiologie*.[10] Thus it is the concepts proper to the semiology of communications that will be used here to formulate a descriptive theoretical model for dramatic writings. For if all science is general and all objects particular, any analysis which attempts to render a strict account of a system or a particular structure must be based on a theoretical model that is pre-existent to the work being described. This model, 'the symbolic representation of a process that one is attempting to describe,'[11] is not, as is often thought, a strait-jacket into which the spectator or the reader is expected to fit; on the contrary, it is a clear guide to the discovery of its deepest structures and a tool to be used in identifying and describing the work in question.

We shall attempt to provide a rough outline of this theoretical model, based on a synthesis of contemporary semiological research, by referring as often as possible to its applications in Quebec theatre.

1 TITLE

First of all, we must examine the title. The relation between the title and the play is one of opposition. The title is opposed to the play as a noun is to a sentence (*Florence, Ben Ur, La Duchesse de Langeais*), as a summary is to a narrative (*Encore cinq minutes, T'es pas tannée Jeanne d'Arc?*), or as the signifier is to the signified (*Wouf! Wouf!, Au retour des oies blanches*). Through this opposition, the title names, summarizes, and orients the dramatic action that will ensue.[12]

2 DIVIDING THE DRAMATIC TEXT INTO MINIMAL UNITS

A second step is to divide the dramatic text into minimal units, unless this has already been done by the author. Analysis consists in articulating the text in terms of its discrete units.[13] For purposes of dividing the text, we shall adopt the criteria proposed by Steen Jansen,[14] who follows the practice of eighteenth-century writers in looking to the staging for the characters' entrances and exits as well as for changes of scenery. Each unit, which we propose to call a sequence, is simultaneously an integrated element of a larger unit (the dramatic work) and an integrator of the smaller units within the whole (the 'functions'). As an integrated element, the sequence may or may not assure the work's coherence as a sign system; as an integrating element, the sequence may or may not allow the production of 'functions,' the constituents of the drama / narrative.

In this way, a breakdown of the text of *Encore cinq minutes* allows us to identify nine sequences in the final act and eleven in the second. Thus we find approximately the same balance between the acts as in classical plays of the same dimension.

3 IDENTIFYING THE INITIAL SIGNS AND THE FINAL SIGNS

Our third step is to identify the initial signs and the final signs in the dramatic process / system. 'The task of scientific description is to explain how the movement from A to B occurs and how the two entities are connected.'[15] To take one of many examples, in *Encore cinq minutes* we can identify the following initial signs: 'An empty white room in which Gertrude is pacing about. On the smooth surface of a wall, a crack is deepening and lengthening, causing the spread of other, smaller cracks – almost invisible little fissures that will soon cover the whole wall.' Gertrude is the only character: 'A sigh of anguish. A moan of oppression. – "What can I do?" – "What?".' Thus a question is asked by the initial signs. And the final signs? 'The same room, now overrun with incongruous objects (furniture, knick-knacks) in great disorder.' Four characters are on stage, including Gertrude who is preparing to leave the room and her family. The combination of signs in the final sequence provides the reply to the question asked in the first sequence. How have we gone from the question to the answer? This is precisely what is revealed by the description that will emerge from the theoretical model.

4 AND 5 INVENTORY AND CLASSIFICATION OF DRAMATIC SIGNS

Before any attempt is made at analysis, it is first necessary to effect a complete inventory and classification of all the signs in the dramatic text. None of these signs should be left aside, since for the analyst they all have the same value *a priori*. Only their role in producing 'functions' will enable us to make distinctions and establish an order of importance among them. Several methods of classifying signs may be considered. It seems to me, however, that any classification must take into account the heterogeneous nature of dramatic signs, with some, like the speeches and stage directions, stemming from the purely textual level, and others, like the characters and settings, belonging more specifically to the scenic level. The classification should also make provisions for the permanent character of some of the dramatic signs and the transitory character of others. Table Ia may be consulted as an illustration of this.

This inventory and classification in themselves provide the analyst with information that is sometimes very useful. For example, a simple classification of the signs in *Encore cinq minutes* enables us, among other things, to state that the proportion between the number of speeches and their length (1153 responses for a length of 1911 lines) indicates that, in the play as a whole, the dialogue is quick and long conversations are rare. It also shows that the only character who is given autonomy on the stage is Gertrude, and that, conversely, her husband Henri never appears on stage alone with one or another of his children.

6 TABLE OF DRAMATIC SIGNS

All dramatic signs will appear in a table compiled from the stage directions. (See Table Ia.)

Quebec Theatre: Stimulation or Communication?

TABLE Ia
Dramatic Signs, Graphs, and Functions
Encore cinq minutes by Françoise Loranger

ACTS/SEQ		STAGING UNITS	CHARACTERS (Attitude)				SPEECHES (Quality)				SETTING Permanent elements /Transitory elements		
			Gd.	R.	H.	Ge.	Gd.	R.	H.	Ge.	Cost.	Obj.	Time
1	1	1	x_1								z_1		
		2					y_1						
		3									z_2		
		4					y_2						
		5	x_2									t_1	
		6					y_3						
		7					y_4						
		8					y_5						
		9					y_6						
		10					y_7						
		11	x_3										
		12	x_4										
		13					y_8						
		14					y_9						
		15					y_{10}						
	2	1		x_1									
		2						y_1					
		3					y_2						
		4						y_3					
		5					y_4						
		6						y_5					
		7					y_6						
		8						y_7					
		9					y_8						
		10					y_9						

1 *Characters (attitude)*: here we place all the signs marking stage movements, gestures, or facial expressions.

2 *Speeches (quality)*: under this heading is placed, not the content of the speech, but rather the quality of its intonation and tonality ('lively, 'anguished').

3 *Setting: Permanent elements*: places or accessories that remain unchanged throughout the play. *Transitory elements*: to those already indicated – costumes, objects, and time – must be added such aspects as music, sound effects, lighting, make-up, hair-styling, and so on, as required for the description.

LEGEND:
Gd, Gertrude; R, Renaud; H, Henri; Ge, Geneviève.
x: arbitrary choice of letter to designate all the signs in the 'characters' catgeory; the subscript indicates the order of appearance of the signs in this same category. This also applies for y (Speeches), z (Permanent setting), t (Costumes), and so on.

TABLE 1b
Graphs

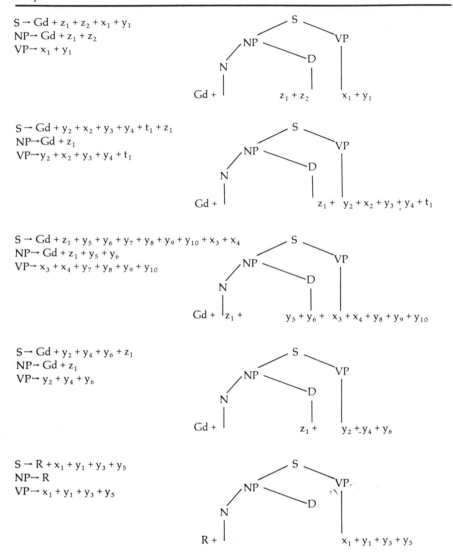

$S \rightarrow Gd + z_1 + z_2 + x_1 + y_1$
$NP \rightarrow Gd + z_1 + z_2$
$VP \rightarrow x_1 + y_1$

$S \rightarrow Gd + y_2 + x_2 + y_3 + y_4 + t_1 + z_1$
$NP \rightarrow Gd + z_1$
$VP \rightarrow y_2 + x_2 + y_3 + y_4 + t_1$

$S \rightarrow Gd + z_1 + y_5 + y_6 + y_7 + y_8 + y_9 + y_{10} + x_3 + x_4$
$NP \rightarrow Gd + z_1 + y_5 + y_6$
$VP \rightarrow x_3 + x_4 + y_7 + y_8 + y_9 + y_{10}$

$S \rightarrow Gd + y_2 + y_4 + y_6 + z_1$
$NP \rightarrow Gd + z_1$
$VP \rightarrow y_2 + y_4 + y_6$

$S \rightarrow R + x_1 + y_1 + y_3 + y_5$
$NP \rightarrow R$
$VP \rightarrow x_1 + y_1 + y_3 + y_5$

LEGEND: S, sentence; NP, noun phrase; VP, verb phrase; N, noun; D, determiner.

TABLE ɪc
Functions

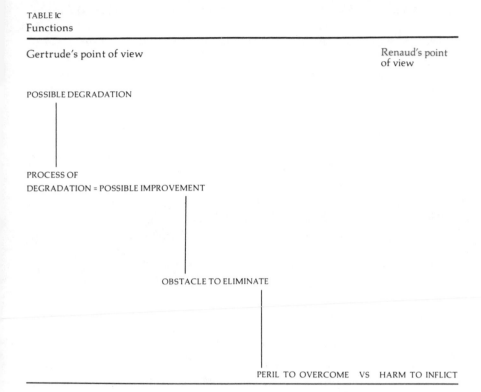

Gertrude's point of view	Renaud's point of view
POSSIBLE DEGRADATION	
PROCESS OF DEGRADATION = POSSIBLE IMPROVEMENT	
OBSTACLE TO ELIMINATE	
	PERIL TO OVERCOME VS HARM TO INFLICT

7 TREE GRAPHS

According to certain developments in modern linguistics, a language system (*langue*) should not be considered as being completely distinct from individual utterance (*parole*); in the same way, the field of dramaturgy cannot be totally separated from any particular performance or individual dramatic text. It is therefore to our advantage to analyse the process / system of a particular dramatic text in the same way that linguistics analyses the process of linguistic utterance.[16]

Using Chomsky's notions of competence and performance, we shall present as an hypothesis that the competence of a dramatic writer may be defined as the sum of knowledge that enables him, at the level of performance, to create – ultimately – limitless numbers of dramatic texts. In essence, this knowledge is the ability to use processes and to play with

rules. What laws or rules does the playwright use to turn all these heterogeneous dramatic signs into a narrative / spectacle, a performance? To reply
to this question would be to know the playwright's real competence. Or to
put the question differently, above and beyond the surface structure of the
concrete achievements of the performance, is there a deep structure of
dramatic language for each playwright to draw from while creating his
work? This would put us within the limits of a 'grammar' of the dramatic
narrative, which should include a complete set of rules capable of generating an infinite number of dramatic narratives. Thus, we propose that the
'logic of possible narratives' formulated by Claude Bremond[17] be considered this finite set of recursive rules capable of generating the 'kernel
sentences' whose predicates would become the 'functions' of the narrative
in the Proppian sense of the word.

This 'grammar' should provide each 'sentence / function' with an
unequivocal and structural description, which Chomsky has fashioned in
the form of a tree graph; called a phrase indicator, its fundamental principle
has been described by N. Ruwet as follows: 'the tree has a certain number
of labelled node points (NP, VP); we shall say that all elements that can be
connected to a particular node point are a component of the type designated by the label assigned to the node point.'[18] In this way, signs which are
contiguous but which cannot be connected to the same node point cannot
be part of the same component.[19] (See Table Ib.)

We propose to consider any and all of the signs that appear in a scene in
the order provided by the stage directions as being capable of playing a role
in the sentence / function as either a determiner, a noun, or a predicate. This
involves knowing their signified in order to be able to know to which node
point they should be connected as components. Thus we shall have a
number of sentences equal to the number of functions in the play. These
functions are in turn organized according to a logic of the kind Propp,
Bremond, and Greimas have studied in their semiological writings. In this
case, we have chosen Claude Bremond's triadic model.

8 DIAGRAM OF THE FUNCTION LOGIC

It should be sufficient for our purposes to recall only a few of the basic
concepts in Bremond's study. The narrated universe, the history or diege-
sis, is governed by laws which are expressed both in the logical restrictions
that any narrative or series of events must respect if it is to be intelligible
and in the conventions proper to any 'literary genre.' The basic unit is the
function in the Proppian sense of the word: an action or event which, when

organized into a triad, generates a narrative. The triad corresponds to the three necessary phases of any process, and can be compared analogically to the expansion of a verb form into the infinitive, the present participle, and the past participle, with one function establishing the potential of the process, one function realizing this potential, and one concluding the process in the form of the obtained result. Also, these triads are linked to one another in a normative narrative cycle to form what since Benveniste's study[20] has generally been called the historical level. (See Table Ic.)

9 SEMIOLOGY OF THE CHARACTER

Understanding the functions of the narrative brings us to the next step in our description of the dramatic work, which is to examine the actors/characters who assume these functions. The study of actors/characters is all the more necessary in that the entire drama/narrative can be said to depend on them and that, for all practical purposes, they are the only area in which the 'content of the utterance' is reached, as Lévi-Strauss points out in his article 'La structure et la forme.'[21] In order to clarify this part of the study, we shall make reference to recent works by François Rastier, Sorin Alexandrescu, Lévi-Strauss, A.-J. Greimas, and more particularly to Philippe Hamon's article on the semiological status of the character.[22] We shall use as our example Marcel Dubé's play *Au retour des oies blanches.**

It would take too long in the context of this article to provide a detailed rationale for the analogy between the dramatic character and the sign. The most we can do is to enumerate a certain number of the characteristics proper to natural languages which seem to us also to be evident, *mutatis mutandis*, in dramatic language and in its signs/characters: theatre is an intended communication process, a sign system with enough linearity to allow the identification of sign sequences proffered in time and perceived in time, which are also discrete and often arbitrary in nature.

Hamon suggests a classification into referential, deictic, and anaphoric characters, modelled on the three subdivisions that have been recognized by many semiologists: semantics, syntax, and pragmatics. This allows us, first of all, to identify the father, Achille, as being both a referential and an anaphoric character. He is referential in the sense that he belongs to a well-defined social category, the dishonest politician, and his first name is

*Translated by Jean Remple as *The White Geese* (Toronto: New Press 1972); all quotations from this play are taken from this translation. (ed.)

also referential. The reference to mythology is made explicit by the words of his son, Robert, who has entitled his recently finished novel *Achille's Heel*; he summarizes it as follows: 'I tell the story of a man who was dedicated to greatness by his mother and who realizes at fifty that he has in fact inherited all the family faults and weaknesses.' Achille is also an anaphoric character because of the role he plays as a 'memory,' recalling certain facts about his own past and also about his wife, Elizabeth, and his half-brother, Tom. He is also anaphoric in that he leaves a trail of false clues intended to mislead his associates and particularly his daughter Geneviève. And finally he is anaphoric because of the phoney projects he advocates for his own personal future and that of his family. Of all the characters in the play, Achille is shown in the classification as being the one who sustains the greatest number of features.

As an analogon of the sign, the character must be described as both signifier and signified.

· The signifier of the character of the father in *Au retour des oies blanches* is designated by forty-seven different components; these form a grammatically heterogeneous paradigm, since we find the pronouns I – me (*je – me – moi*) and you – he (*tu – vous – il*) as well as the phrase 'my dear little deflated Papa.' They also form a semiologically heterogeneous paradigm that includes his two costumes, his gestures, and his words. The order in which the components of the father's signifier appear, as well as their distribution and recurrence throughout the play, reveals that the signified undergoes a profound transformation at the same time. The very proper, traditional suit worn during most of the play is replaced in the final scene by a 'clown costume,' while such neutral terms as 'your father' or 'papa' are replaced by expression such as 'the worst kind of dirty little cheat.' In this respect, we can affirm that the 'grammar' of the signifier is already quite indicative of the process of inversion of the content, which a study of the signified reveals to us.

Our description of the signified of the sign / character is designed to help us understand the characters; in this case the personality of the father, Achille, is revealed not so much by characterial indicators as by his relationships with other characters. Clearly, a character is defined less by his essence than by his existence, that is, by the complex network of similarities and differences revealed with the help of a relatively large number of pertinent and recurrent semantic axes. In this way, the character is considered as a sememe, a semantic unit composed of a bundle of semantic features called semes which are analogous to the semantic axes. Thus, in *Au retour des oies blanches*, we have retained the semantic axes of psychological motivation, love, sexuality, morals, and of overrated and underrated family relationships, all of which are functional axes. We shall not deal with the qualifying semantic axes because they seem less important in the workings of our drama / narrative. In other circumstances, however, they might be relevant. (See Table II.)

The semantic axes we have retained indicate that the father, Achille, is a character with deep psychological motivations since he has been marked both by his childhood and by an important event in his adult life. In this, however, he is no different from his wife, Elizabeth, and his children Geneviève and Robert, who belong to the same class as he does. The love axis, conversely, makes us aware of an important difference between Achille and his wife on the one hand, and between Achille and his daughter on the other hand. Although he is not marked by it in any way, Geneviève is – she is often described as a loving person, and she engages in several functional acts of love. Elizabeth, for her part, is once described as a loving person, and she has also engaged in one functional act of love. Although the father in the play is excluded from the semantic axis of love, he nevertheless joins his wife and daughter in the semantic axis of sexuality, in which he appears to be one of the most sexual characters. One thinks here of his relationship with Laura, whom he has practically raped. The moral axis is even more revealing of Achille's antagonistic relationship with his wife and children. Unloving but sexual, he describes himself several times in terms of conventional morality, while at the same time he performs and has performed various acts that run counter to this morality. Meanwhile his daughter, Geneviève, is contrasted with him because of the coherence of her self-descriptions and of her actions, both of which go against unconventional morality (for example, her affair with her uncle, Tom). Finally, Achille's relationship with his mother is overrated and his relationship with his wife, children, and his half-brother Tom are underrated. Thus Achille is an important character in the workings of the drama / narrative because he is defined by four of the five semantic axes we have dealt with. Essentially he is an antagonistic character, divided against himself and particularly opposed to the people who are close to him, excepting his mother; in him we see the continuing struggle between being and appearance.

In order to get a clearer view of the sign / character relationships, we can divide a certain number of semantic axes into distinctive, relevant, simultaneous features just as the phoneme in linguistics is considered to be a bundle of relevant, simultaneous features. Using the constitutional model proposed by Greimas in Du sens,[23] which deals with the effects of semiotic restrictions, we shall retain for the purposes of our analysis the semantic axes of sexuality, love, and morality. (See Table III.) The results obtained from this reveal a great deal about Achille's behaviour. He maintains with

TABLE II
Semantic Axes

C	Psychological motivation		Love				Sexuality				Morality				Overrated and underrated family relationships			
	a	b	a	b	c	d	a	b	c	d	a	b	c	d	a	b	c	d
Amélie	ø	ø	ø	ø	ø	ø	ø	ø	ø	ø	ø	+c	+n	ø	ø	+u	+o	ø
Achille	+	+	+	ø	ø	ø	ø	ø	+	ø	ø	+c	ø	+n	ø	+u	+o	ø
Elizabeth	+	+	+	ø	+	ø	ø	ø	+	ø	ø	+c +n	+c +n	ø	ø	+u +o	+u +o	ø
Robert	+	+	ø	ø	ø	ø	+	ø	ø	ø	ø	+n	+n	ø	ø	+u +o	ø	ø
Geneviève	+	+	ø	+	ø	+	ø	ø	+	ø	ø	+n	ø	+n	ø	+u +o	+u +o	ø
Laura	ø	+	ø	ø	ø	ø	ø	+	ø	ø	ø	+n	ø	ø	ø	ø	ø	ø
Richard	ø	ø	ø	+	ø	ø	+	ø	ø	ø	ø	+n	ø	ø	ø	ø	ø	ø
Manon	ø	ø	ø	ø	ø	ø	+	ø	ø	ø	ø	ø	ø	ø	ø	ø	ø	ø

LEGEND: F, functional semantic axis; C, characters; +, presence of one or more functions
Psychological motivation: a = childhood event; b = important event in adult life.
Love, Sexuality, Morality, Family Relationships: a = single attribute; b = several attributes; c = single act; d = several acts.
Morality: +c = respect for conventional morality; +n = disregard for conventional morality.
Family Relationships: +u = overrated family relationship; +o = underrated family relationship.

TABLE III
Hexagonal Model

SYSTEM OF SEXUALITY

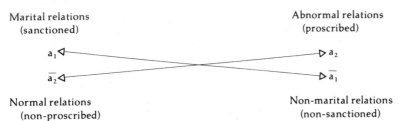

Marital relations
    (sanctioned)

Abnormal relations
    (proscribed)

a_1 ◁   ▷ a_2

$\overline{a_2}$ ◁   ▷ $\overline{a_1}$

Normal relations
    (non-proscribed)

Non-marital relations
    (non-sanctioned)

Profitable sex. rel.   Harmful sex. rel.   Desired sex. rel.   Feared sex. rel.

b_1 ◁   ▷ b_2 c_1 ◁   ▷ c_2

$\overline{b_2}$ ◁   ▷ $\overline{b_1}$ $\overline{c_2}$ ◁   ▷ $\overline{c_1}$

Non-harmful   Non-profitable   Non-feared   Non-desired
sex. rel.   sex. rel.   sex. rel.   sex. rel.

Achille ——▷ Elizabeth: $a_1 - b_1 + \overline{c_1}$ = antagonistic sexual relationship, whose shortcomings
             are compensated for by
Achille ——▷ Laura: $c_1 + \overline{b_2} - \overline{a_2}$ = compatible sexual relationship

---

SYSTEM OF MORALITY   SYSTEM OF LOVE

Moral rel.   Amoral rel.   Love rel.   Fear rel.

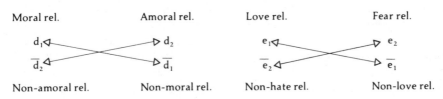

d_1 ◁   ▷ d_2 e_1 ◁   ▷ e_2

$\overline{d_2}$ ◁   ▷ $\overline{d_1}$ $\overline{e_2}$ ◁   ▷ $\overline{e_1}$

Non-amoral rel.   Non-moral rel.   Non-hate rel.   Non-love rel.

Achille ——▷ Elizabeth: $d_1 + \overline{e_1}$ = antagonistic relationship between morality and love

---

his wife, for example, an antagonistic social and sexual relationship whose deficiencies are compensated for by his relationship with Laura. To take another example, in his relationship with his daughter, Geneviève, the inadequacies of his strong, antagonistic love are compensated for by his relationship with his own mother, Amélie.

As a distinctive and significant unit in the network of relationships revealed in the constitutional model, Achille is increasingly defined in terms of an obedient son, an unfaithful husband, and an unworthy father. He can be further and more precisely defined by 'the nature of his relationship to a much larger glossary of characters / types – the actants.'[24] Whether in a functional form, as with Propp, or in the form of astrological signs, as with Souriau, or according to the nomenclature proposed by Greimas, we find that in all these cases we are dealing with a paradigm at a higher level of abstraction; this will enable us to know which character holds which actantial position in a given sequence of the drama / narrative. I have opted here for the actantial model proposed by Greimas in his *Séman-tique structurale*.[25] 'The narrative text being a prescribed system of combinations of complementary logical classes,' we must begin by dividing the drama / narrative into sequences, if this has not been done already. We may use either the division provided by the preliminary study of function logic, or we may adopt the one proposed by Greimas and influenced by Lévi-Strauss. What matters, in the end, is whether we can see, by dividing the utterance into sequences, the major functions performed by the characters in the narrative. For the purposes of this analysis, and in order to provide a more varied demonstration, we shall make use of the semantic criteria suggested by Greimas, who maintains that at a discursive level there may be three kinds of syntagms: performative, contractual, and disjunctional narrative syntagms.[26] When *Au retour des oies blanches* is divided in this way, we find the father, Achille, involved in a disjunctional syntagm when he first arrives on stage as the apparent hero; later he is involved in two performative syntagms, the first when he is fighting with his wife, the second when he has to confront his daughter, Geneviève, who with the help of her friend Laura is identified as the real hero. By the end of the first scene, the father has changed from an apparent hero to a non-hero. The second scene (see Table IV) again shows Achile involved in a performative syntagm as the fight with his daughter continues. However, his admission of political failure confirms his condition as a non-hero. In the third scene, again involving performative syntagms of trial, the father's defeat at the hands of his daughter is completed. He changes from a non-hero to a villain. Finally, after the death of his daughter, the true hero, in the fourth scene, the villain / father is involved in a contractual syntagm in which he proposes a settlement with his mother, Amélie, which is accepted. Life will go on, and the villain will again become an apparent hero.

This division into narrative syntagms reveal a number of the functions of the actors/characters: return, mandate, combat, victory, or defeat. These are the functions that will now enable us to identify the actants in each sequence, because the sequences are both 'creators of actants'[27] and at the same time dominated by them, since the actants represent a hierarchically superior model of organization. Present in seven out of twelve sequences, Achille appears basically as the opponent (T) in the actants' table, since he is there five times. However, he also appears as the giver or sender (G), although even in this latter role he is still an opponent since he suggests to Elizabeth that she forget about Geneviève and to his mother that he return to see the prime minister in order to obtain the favours he is seeking. In the entire course of the play he is never a subject (S) nor a helper (H), two roles which are eminently active.

In summary, the character of the father in *Au retour des oies blanches* may be defined as referential and anaphoric, with his signifier distributed in such a way as to indicate a profound transformation of the signified. In turn, the signified shows a total absence of love but considerable sexuality, a moral conduct that does not conform to the moral principles he himself proclaims, an overrated relationship with his mother, and an underrated relationship with his wife and children. Defined in this way by his relationships, this father/character finally appears as an antagonistic person who submits to events rather than governing them. An apparent hero, the inversion of the contents of the drama/narrative through the influence of the real hero, his daughter, shows him up as a definite anti-hero.

These partial conclusions might well be enlarged when we have completed our analysis of the information obtained during a recent seminar on the subject of the father/characters in the plays of Marcel Dubé. At least this is what our preliminary survey would seem to suggest.[28]

By integrating the semiological study of the character with the theoretical descriptive model of a dramatic work, our theoretical goal has been to formalize the project of Philippe Hamon and at the same time to complete a detailed analysis of Dubé's father characters, which reveals the importance of the sign/character in dramatic polysemia.

10 ESTABLISHING THE COHERENCE OF THE DRAMATIC WORK

The next step in the description of the dramatic *œuvre* consists in establishing its coherence, which is essentially based on the existing relationship between the sequences and the presence or absence of functions in them.

TABLE IV
Narrative Syntagms in *Au retour des oies blanches* by Marcel Dubé

SYNTAGMS:	DISJUNCTIONAL ...	PERFORMATIVE ...	CONTRACTUAL
Conjunction	Disjunction	Trial	Contract

SCENE ONE: DESIGNATION OF THE SUBJECT/HERO

Tom's return			
		Geneviève's struggle with and victory over Elizabeth	
Robert's arrival			Elizabeth's request for help from Robert
			Acceptance
	Robert's departure		Denial
Amélie's arrival			
		Elizabeth's struggle with and defeat of Amélie	Double denial of help
	Amélie's departure		
Arrival of Achille APPARENT HERO			
		Struggle between Achille and Elizabeth	
Geneviève's return with Laura and Richard			
		Geneviève's struggle with Achille. Victory. Designation of Geneviève = TRUE HERO Achille = NON-HERO Laura = Helper	

SCENE TWO: PRINCIPAL CONFRONTATION OR TRIAL

	Geneviève's departure to go change		
			Mandate: Laura Acceptance: Robert
		Laura's struggle and failure	

Geneviève's return to the living room Achille's return		Mandate: Geneviève Denial: Robert
	Struggle between Geneviève and Achille Geneviève's half-victory Achille confirmed as NON-HERO	

SCENE THREE: VICTORY OF HERO — FAILINGS OVERCOME

		Geneviève determines to avenge Tom Acceptance
	Geneviève's struggle against Achille, Amélie, Elizabeth. Qualifying ordeal: receiving of Laura's help: designation of the SUBJECT HERO Geneviève's struggle with and victory over Achille Struggle: Geneviève vs Amélie Struggle: Geneviève vs Elizabeth	
		Mandate: Elizabeth Acceptance: Geneviève Mandate: Laura Denial: Geneviève
	Geneviève's struggle with and victory over Elizabeth	
		Mandates: Laura, Richard, Robert, Elizabeth
DEATH of the HERO: Geneviève		Denial: Geneviève

SCENE FOUR: FINAL SEQUENCE

	Elizabeth's madness	Mandate: Achille Acceptance: Amélie Achille once again becomes the APPARENT HERO

Our approach here is the same as the one proposed by Steen Jansen, although we are not dealing with the same elements as he does. Actually, it seems to us more appropriate to retain the functions as our criteria of coherence, since in the final analysis they are what the narrative is made from.

From the beginning of this article, we have defined the dramatic work as both a process and a system, and it is in terms of these two aspects that the coherence of the work can be established. As a process, a theatrical work presents a series of sequences that are related to their immediate neighbours either by juxtaposition or anteposition. In order to determine what relationship we are dealing with, we must test it for change. If sequence B, because of the function or functions it contains, cannot be placed before sequence A, we shall say that it has a dependent relationship or is in anteposition with sequence A. In the opposite case we shall call it independence or juxtaposition. As a system, the dramatic work presents a set of sequences which among themselves have relationships that are independent (combination), dependent (selection), or interdependent (solidarity). In order to identify the relationships between these sequences, we must test them for omission. If sequence B, because of the function or functions it contains, cannot be omitted without modifying the function or functions of sequence A or C or both, we shall say that its relationship is one of dependence or interdependence. In the opposite case, we shall call it an independent relationship.

Based on these criteria, then, the analysis of the coherence in Dubé's play, *Un matin comme les autres*, reveals a perfectly coherent process and system, while a similar analysis of *Pauvre amour* reveals a process and system in which the independent sequences are very numerous, particularly because of the absence of functions. In these latter cases, we are sometimes dealing with empty sequences and sometimes with sequences that are indicative rather than functional and which, consequently, play a complementary role in the economy of the drama / narrative.

11 STUDYING THE STATUS OF THE EXTRADIEGETIC RECEIVER

A final step is the one in which the status of the extradiegetic Receiver must be studied. Everyone will agree that dramatic texts, except for rare exceptions that should be re-examined, exist only in order to be staged. This must be remembered in our examination of the actual dramatic text. For example, the deictic characters in *Au retour des oies blanches*, acting as spokesmen for the extradiegetical Receiver (or R extra), clearly reveal the presence of this fictitious spectator. Thus Richard says, 'I still don't know what kind of a *show* I've been invited to,' or 'There's starting to be some suspense! I have to admit I'm even developing a taste for it.' Robert provides another example: 'Are we in a Greek tragedy or vaudeville? I really don't know." And Richard provides us with a final example, stating, 'Perhaps we're going to witness new revelations. Let's stay alert.' In *Pauvre amour*, the Louis, Luigi, Ludovic character is the ultimate deictic character, since he speaks directly to the R extra. Louis, before leaving, says to the audience, 'What will they celebrate? The young people leaving or new discoveries? They are alone. They alone shall decide. My business now is to keep quiet.' (Second scene.)

The R extra cannot be compared to the real spectators for, with some exceptions, the real spectators can tell whether they are in a Greek tragedy or vaudeville. Thus the R extra is fictitious. However, he is not the potential spectator imagined by Dubé either, since after one or two generations the potential spectators have changed and even their children are no longer the same kind of spectators as their parents. Would it occur to them, for example, to contrast Greek tragedy with vaudeville? And finally, the R extra must not be confused with the ideal spectator, since a comment like the one in which Richard states 'I still don't know what kind of a show I've been invited to' reveals a spectator who is ignorant or absent-minded and thus far from being the ideal spectator that all playwrights dream of.

The R extra is a fictitious rational being who is part of the intended communication process that is theatre; like the characters themselves, who are also fictitious, he serves as a sort of intermediary between the playwright and the audience. Just as Genette[29] and Prince[30] have recognized and described the important role of the receiver of the narration (*le narrataire*) in the narrative system, so we must recognize the role of the R extra in the system of dramatic signs; with the aid of the theoretical model, we can also describe his functions. This analogy between the *narrataire* and the R extra will be instructive as well, since Prince's study of the *narrataire*, on which he has already done serious work, can serve as an indication of how to proceed in order to define the R extra and to classify and identify his functions in the dramatic writing.

As an example, and in order to limit our study, *Les belles-sœurs** by Michel Tremblay has an R extra who is not the real, potential, or ideal spectator from Montreal, Sainte-Justine-de-Dorchester, or Paris. he is invisible, yet

---

*Translated by Bill Glassco and John Van Burek as *Les Belles-Sœurs* (Vancouver: Talonbooks 1974); all quotations are taken from this translation. (ed.)

his situation in the drama, for which the Sender provides numerous and revealing explanations, makes his presence felt continually; thus we have Germaine Lauzon's telephone monologue at the beginning of the play, or the frequent comparisons or metaphors that depend on the R extra knowing about them: 'If I don't stop thinking about it,' says Marie-Ange Brouillette, 'I'm gonna go nuts.' We also have various staging procedures that use choruses of women, black-outs, or spotlights focused on individual characters as they explain their own feelings. Such dramatic techniques, which are also signs in the system, make it possible in *Les belles-sœurs* to convey the message reserved for the R extra, whose primary function is to act as an intermediary.

Relaying the message, however, is not the only function of the R extra in the play. Like Prince's *narrataire*, for example, he may be used to convey a particular characterization. Pierrette Guérin, the bar girl, is thus defined as much in terms of her relationship with the R extra in her monologue as she is by her contacts with the other characters: 'A girl who's been at it for ten years is all washed up. Finished. So just *try* explaining that to my sisters.' Or to take another example: 'Ten years! Ten years for nothing. *D'you not think* that's enough to make you want to pack it in?'

The R extra can also contribute to the verisimilitude of the drama in spite of the improbable aspects of the stage technique. Thus in Angéline Sauvé's monologue the R extra allows her to make the confession that makes her behaviour believable: 'I suppose clubs aren't for everyone, but me, I like them. And of course it's not true that I only have a coke. Of course I drink liquor!'

Finally, our study of the R extra reveals another of his functions, which is to show agreement or disagreement with the message of the play, and to act as a sort of spokesman for its moral attitudes. Thus in *Les belles-sœurs*, the understated tone of the monologues, the simplicity of the sentences which are often just interjections of despair or deep misfortune, the isolation on the stage which clearly shows the sad isolation of the Senders / characters – all show an R extra who is less inclined to condemn than to be compassionate and even supportive.

If the observations of Gérald Prince[31] concerning the *narrataire* and the narration are transposed to theatre, we can affirm that the R extra is one of the necessary elements in any dramatic system. A thorough study of what he represents as a decoder of the signs that are addressed to him in the intended communication process will enable us to make a more precise and more clearly defined interpretation of the work in question.

To conclude briefly, semiological research into theatre is still making its first steps, as is the semiology of language on which it is based. Several notions must still be defined more accurately, various methodological errors may need correcting, and various intuitive insights must be verified. It seems to us, however, that by comparing dramaturgy to polysemia, or to a sign system that is also an intended communication process and not simply a method of significance or stimulation, we are making it possible to undertake a methodical study of this still mysterious 'infernal machine' whose make-up and workings we are finally beginning to understand

NOTES

1 Eric Buyssens *La communication et l'articulation linguistique* (Brussels: Brussels University Press 1970) 11
2 Ferdinand de Saussure *Cours de linguistique générale* (Paris: Payot 1969) 33 [tr. Wade Buskin *Course in General Linguistics* (New York: McGraw-Hill 1959) 16]
3 Roman Jakobson *Essais de linguistique générale* 1 (Paris: Minuit 1963) 209
4 George Mounin *Introduction à la sémiologie* (Paris: Minuit 1970) 92
5 Jakobson 213
6 de Saussure 103
7 Mounin 73
8 Mounin 71
9 Mounin 71
10 Roland Barthes 'Eléments de sémiologie' *Communications* No. 4 (1964) 91–144
11 An alternative definition: 'The simplified representation of a process or a system.'
12 Louis Marin *Etudes sémiologiques* (Paris: Klincksieck 1971) 250
13 Emile Benveniste 'Sémiologie de la langue' *Semiotica* 1, No. 1 (The Hague: Mouton 1969) 1–12; No. 2, 127–35.
14 Steen Jansen 'Esquisse d'une théorie de la forme dramatique' *Langages* No. 15 (December 1968)
15 I.I. Revzin 'Les principes de la théorie des modèles en linguistique' *Langages* No. 15 (September 1969)
16 See J. Peytard and E. Genouvrier *Linguistique et enseignement du français* (Paris: Larousse 1970) 122
17 Claude Bremond 'La logique des possibles narratifs' *Communications* No. 8 (1966) 60–76
18 Nicolas Ruwet *Introduction à la grammaire générative* (Paris: Plon 1968)

19 Noam Chomsky *Structures syntaxiques* (Paris: Seuil 1969) 29–55. [Originally published in English as *Syntactic Structures* (The Hague: Mouton 1969)]

20 Emile Benveniste *Problèmes de linguistique générale* 1 (Paris: Gallimard 1966) 238 [tr. Mary Elizabeth Meek *Problems in General Linguistics* (Miami: University of Miami Press 1971)]

21 Claude Lévi-Strauss 'La structure et la forme' *Cahiers de l'Institut de science économique appliquée* No. 9 (March 1960); Ser. M No. 7 pp. 3–36

22 Philippe Hamon 'Pour un statut sémiologique du personnage' *Littérature* No. 6 (May 1972)

23 A.-J. Greimas *Du sens* (Paris: Seuil 1971) 135

24 Hamon 104

25 A.-J. Greimas *Sémantique structurale* (Paris: Larousse 1966)

26 Greimas *Sémantique* 190

27 Greimas *Sémantique* 129

28 This seminar, given at Laval University in the winter semester, 1974, included the following participants: Marie Grenier-Francœur, Alison Baxter-Walker, Raymond Fleury, Réjean Boutin, Gilbert Tremblay, Jean-Guy Hudon, and Jean Vermette. I wish here to thank them for their invaluable contributions.

29 Gérard Genette *Figures III* (Paris: Seuil) 265

30 Gérald Prince 'Introduction à l'étude du narrataire' *Poétique* No. 14 (1973) 178–96

31 Prince 196

JACQUES BRAULT

Notes on a False Dilemma

Poet, playwright, translator, philosopher, medievalist – Jacques Brault is also a literary critic whose range of knowledge seems almost encyclopaedic. His writings draw their support from a familiarity with such varied fields as anthropology, literary theory, linguistics, political science, history, and philosophy. Abreast of the latest currents of thought in Europe and America, the author is equally attuned to intellectual developments in Quebec; and, rare among the Quebec intelligentsia, he is also informed as to the cultural production of English Canada.

Nor is his awareness restricted to intellectual spheres. His criticism of such poets as Nelligan, Miron, and Juan Garcia is anchored in intensely personal and emotional responses to their works. These responses are intuitive, empathetic, patently sincere, and fully complemented by the critic's mastery of the traditional scholarly apparatus – as evidenced in his book-length study of Alain Grandbois and his critical edition of the works of Saint-Denys-Garneau.

It is difficult to place a critic of such scope within the confines of any particular movement. An ardent Quebec nationalist, he is determinedly open to the rest of the world. A philosopher, he tackles abstract questions by musings and meditations rather than by expository analyses. An intellectual, he nevertheless rejects any form of intellectual élitism, taking his values – and often his examples – from the lives and concerns of the ordinary citizen.

Like his method, Brault's style is paradoxical and idiosyncratic. The poet in him is reflected in the extreme economy and condensation of his writing; his use of ellipsis, neologism, and puns increases the intensity of his prose, and this effect is further heightened by his alternation of levels of language that range from common street expressions to the latest Marxist terminology.

In the following article, Brault explores the relationship between literature and politics by adopting one of his most characteristic approaches: the question is posed and then fretted towards resolution. This technique allows great flexibility in the discussion, enabling the author to explore a number of questions which might not at first seem relevant, until the entire problem is brought to what Brault might well call a 'non-solution.' The article, originally appearing in a 1964 edition of *Parti pris*, was included in revised form in his collection of essays entitled *Chemin faisant*; this was published in 1975, at which time the marginal notes were added.

NOTES ON A FALSE DILEMMA

Myth is the name for everything that exists and persists only in words. (Valéry). Eloquence relies a great deal on the armaments of myth: slogans, catch-words, political mot-toes, advertisements, religious and ritualized orations – all of which work together to depict relatively inauthentic things as being radically authentic. To believe in the causality of language is to make mystification the norm: any partial truth, provided it can gain enough power (credibility), becomes the whole truth. In this respect, the literary (and annoying) paradox described by Paulhan in *Les fleurs de Tarbes* is still quite relevant.

Eloquence is what I call any mythical language. Eloquence perverts action into self-relief, exudes passion like an infected wound, and feeds on absolutes and faith alone. Paradoxically, it is the language both of extremes and of the 'golden mean,' of both magic and digestion, of the starveling and the glutton.

Poetry is what I call value-language; its verbal totality is meant to be both object and objective, external and inalienable. Poetry tends to *be* meaning.

Prose is what I call implement-language; it is operative and designed to free the meaning it *has*.

The trouble is that pure prose and poetry do not exist, both being eloquent. This causes the problem – more practical than theoretical – of the relationship between the political (prose) and the literary (poetry), which are in constant danger of being absorbed into one other, of becoming fixed, quintessential, embalmed, or in a word, of becoming *mystified*. When the words *national-socialist* are paired, each of them remains steeped in infamy for as long as they are kept together. Because it is continually veiled in mystery, mythical language foists upon us the illusion of possessing meaning, whereas it is meaning that possesses us.

Every person is a conglomerate of diverse levels of existence; this is the risk, and the freedom. For each of us, the fact of being multifarious poses a problem of coherence and unity – in short, an identity problem. The endless task of choosing oneself, and thus of living a life in which one's self is always intermingled with its opposites, weighs heavily upon many of us. And this is where political ideologies exert their power of attraction, for they offer to deliver us from the problem of choice by solving it once and for all. From then on, there is no need to worry about one's goals or one's future; a body of doctrine takes care of everything. Moreover, such ideological comfort costs hardly anything – just the uncertainty of freedom.

Perhaps the ideologization of revolution remains an inevitable stage in its development; when successful, however, total revolution has precisely the effect of completely overturning the very situation and structures in which the revolutionary ideology was required, conceived, and set into motion. Thus it is also necessary for committed writers, among others, to avoid projecting the literary into the political. What we expect from them is for our language to precede us, as it were, so that it can link what we are with what we shall be.

All this, the expressible and inexpressible, muddled and barely reflected in what I say and do not say – all this results only in a cry. But it is a cry I wanted to *write*, and to write before it relapses into a murmer, silence.

It must be admitted that we have never been lacking in cries about and against ourselves. The story of our literature is one of hard times and high talking. Even today the public opinion sections in the newspapers are constantly filled with cries: bravos, insults, declarations. Anyone here who lets his sentence run on for more than five lines is running a risk

The worst ideological pitfall is the ignorance of ignorance. This is why we adhere so readily to a cult of 'revelations'; in order that the powers that be can be left in peace, a corps of psycho-political dieticians is busily maintaining us in a state of stupor which is fostered, curiously enough, by the very 'news' bulletins that should in fact jolt us out of it. *There are a great many unbelievable systems, but their architecture is agreeable and they do tend to be sensational. The metaphysicians of Tlon are not seeking truth or even verisimilitude: they are seeking amazement.* (J.L. Borges)

Brute emotion is neither patient nor courageous; it cries out, and the echoes of its cry drown the sound of its fear. Emotion imagines itself as having a taste for transgression, for forbidden fruits; actually it tends toward repetition, devoting its energies to reduplication

198 Jacques Brault

and settling into stereotypes (look at where language has been officially instituted – in schools, sport, advertising, songs, information). And the dangling sentence, still so common with the Québécois, is as much a strength as a weakness. Theory (Chomsky) holds that the sentence is justifiably infinite. The 'right' people – the educated, the sophisticates, the culture-vultures – – always complete their sentences or bust their asses trying to. Those who do not finish their sentences, according to the best rules of grammar and society, allow themselves the possibility (only the possibility ...) of leaving language and social behaviour open to counter-ideological activity.

of syntactical error, or, at the very least, of getting into difficulty and not being able to finish: go on to the next sentence, which will preferably be short – very.

It is not that we are particularly inept at speaking correct language (which is a form of social existence); nor do we suffer from some congenital speech impediment. Not at all. The explanation, I think, is political.

Words and the relationships among words do not express us. We speak and write, as is indicated by the common expression *'de manière empruntée,'* – in a borrowed manner. Our language does not come from us; it was not created by us, for us, or among us; it is not us. It is but indirect and intransitive, coming to us ready-made, packaged, and wrapped – from somewhere else. It knows everything, has seen the world, is loquacious and well fed; it has ancestors, and children who are the future; it tells of justice, the economy, life in the streets, love. French: the mirror of our shame.

It is inevitable, under the circumstances, that our literature should only be poetry – and, above all, eloquence. This poetry, a language of confines and exorcism, in so far as it succumbs to eloquence, is a mark of political impotence, of servitude, of a dull inability to live in the everyday world. If by chance this language, with its poverty concealed beneath cheap finery, should take hold of us and lead us down into the street, it then resorts to extreme eloquence, to *excess*, to the safety of absolutes. It dances when it should walk, and instead of action produces only tumult.

These remarks are futile, however, in that they remain simply statements. The freedom of speech, since this is what is at stake, can be reached only with total political freedom. Quebec is still reaching, and for the time being, this language of French and 'joual' remains a long litany of complaints, a confused chorus of cries.

In the writings of Roland Barthes (*Le degré zéro de l'écriture, Mythologies,* etc.) we find a moral philosophy of signs that attempts to make a connection between the literary and the political.

A language becomes ambiguous when the sign is presented as being both a product and at the same time random. This combination gives rise to myth, and myth is the polished, assimilative, literary form of political violence against indigenous people. It is a mixture that we know well – I dare say we live on it. Police violence, for instance, because it supposedly occurs *in the policeman's line of duty,* is considered as something quite natural. In spite of protests and rather doubtful inquiries, this particular form of violence has a legitimate basis in the assumption that policemen will be punished if they lack a *sense of proportion.* For the equality of social inequality must be maintained at all costs; otherwise the *rights* of the small farmer, *respect for the individual* oppressor, *concern for the common good,* in short all the values that transcend any particular situation would then go down the drain.

The only way to clear up the ambiguity of this language in which the political intrudes into world literature is to destroy the myth, to contrast the produced sign with the random sign, prose with poetry. On the one side, algebra and artifice; on the other, invention and naïve truth.

This is a task of liberation. But can revolution, the success of which has to be incontestable, invent a language which separates the literary and the political? Can revolution do without eloquence?

A determination to make the whole language responsible implies the freedom of the whole language; such is the basis of the political character of language. Indeed, the principal function of bourgeois language is to perpetuate its meaning, in the guise of a certain relativism. Poetry has the same function, although its goals are different: the imposture of

Our consciences should not be eased too soon or too swiftly with the pretence that we are taking on the role of the protester. The revolutionary myth also has room for impostors; this is how it resembles the bourgeois myth. *In the revolutionary history of the Andean Republics, there is no more widespread misconception than the distinction between an 'official country' made up of a blind, self-centred, oligarchical clique and a 'real country' in a state of latent rebellion. This stereotype has so much power in people's minds that a great number of intellectuals carelessly interpret any minor incidence of peasant violence as a warning sign of inevitable revolution in one country or another.* (François Bournicaud). Well-founded expressions often become birdcages (or rat-traps). We continually define literary commitment exclusively in terms of content (*signifiés*) and the degree to which the non-literary subordinates the literary. Sartre, in *Qu'est-ce que la littérature?,* does not choose to commit poetry, preferring to leave it aside, in a class with painting and music. This is one way of avoiding the confrontation of opposites and of perpetuating a false dilemma between politicism and aestheticism. But what if beauty, which is now considered reactionary, were only sister and sweetener to liberty, her visible face touching and touchable, with no chance of again becoming a goddess, a maternal refuge, the royal road to regression?

poetry begins when it pretends that it encompasses all the language of the situation and that it makes all existing signs in some way dependent upon it.

Prose is the only real language of political combat, the only literature that is truly committed. For prose is the only conditional language, the only one not averse to pointing out its own artifice and, if need be, opposing it with another artifice. Prose has no rest until it has objectivized and unveiled the things that are hidden in the subjective night and that pretend to the innocence of Human Nature. And much more importantly, prose is made for exploration and for reconnaissance in open ground. Not only is it committed, it commits. Whether it is outside literature or still half-literary is of little importance, for prose is totally caught up in its own work, which is to give itself over to speech as one gives oneself over to sun and air.

Still, there are limits. History is not only historical, man is not completely aware of his own behaviour, and language cannot be compared to a currency or an instrument. Besides, freedom is not just something one takes. The literary does not reach completion in the political. The ultimate limit is that writing and speaking are only indirect means of acting. Moreover, prose is literary only to the extent that it is poetic. Thus the ambiguity remains, even for the literature of commitment. Writers do not make revolutions, whatever their role in them. They are necessary in their place, like those poets who steal back from heaven the fires that men need to set their prisons ablaze.

If a writer writes badly because he has been doing too many 'good deeds,' he immediately recoups his losses – not in literature, admittedly, but in the bosom

However revolutionary he may wish to be, the writer can never be classed as one of the exploited. If he has courage and lucidity, he will guard himself against an often frantic desire to share a condition which those who have to endure it wish only to escape. Especially if he is a philosopher or a poet, the

writer lives in part elsewhere; his is a defined existence, and even if he dies quietly or violently from it,
he will have been able to *name* what is wrong and thus
not be completely at its mercy. From the moment he
feels and knows, *in the order of language*, what alienation
means in terms of inexistence, he has already begun
to lose the innocence of the victim. His death will not
have that infinitely irreparable quality of barren loss
that the death of a little Indian has in the hell of the
Amazonian jungle, or (in this area, there is no lack of
examples to choose from) the long continuing death
of all our own people who never find any escape,
even in dreams, for they never learn what causes the
unnameable fear that lives like some kind of tapeworm in the pit of their stomachs. Nothing, absolutely nothing can redeem these absolute failures
that once, in the cries of a newborn baby, had an
identity, a solid meaning in flesh; but this name
passed in a breath over their heads, for, in truth, they
never heard it. This is not sad – it is *meaningless*. The
writer, on the other hand, is condemned to signs. I
am not saying his life is better but, quite simply, that
he is already saved.

Since he has the impression of not deserving this
salvation, this kind of native grace, (or rather of
deserving it to the detriment of lower mortals), he
therefore wants to expiate it, to pay a price for his
superior language – since the abundance, the flexibility, the love of words make him rich. There is
nothing for it, however, unless he leaves literature
forever and even then he would still be 'on the right
side.' A rich man who throws away his property does
not become poor; on the contrary, he becomes rich in
a new way, assuming he does not take to wearing a
halo.

Brecht's famous concept of detachment aims at sub-
stituting prose for eloquence and even for poetry,
inasmuch as the latter allows itself to be drawn
towards eloquence. Rather than the hero, Brecht

of suffering, militant
history. He who has
never conceded any-
thing, who has never
given up even a single
line, will regard failure
as an indelible blemish.
He falls, from the
heights (sometimes),
into insignificance.
And this is only just.
Because writing never
ends in intrinsic suc-
cess (other successes
are only misunder-
standings), it is easy to
see which side to
choose, which way to
approach the still-
knotted knot of the
famous question of
commitment. I shall
not carry this any
further; a sentence
from Gabrielle Roy
causes me to backtrack:
*Any living thing that dies
from not being expressed,
seemed to him to be the only
death.*

Here, elsewhere, and
for all time, poetry,
however prosaic it may
seem, neither denies

nor affirms anything other than poetry. Of all the acts of language, the poetic act is carried out with a freedom that cannot be reduced even to social values. *Athenians, I love you; but I shall obey the god rather than you*, declared Socrates during his trial. Socrates cuts to the quick of the debate: he invokes the *daimon*, the baseless basis of freedom in which are rooted the distance and the difference essential to everyone so that together with others they can form an *us* which does not degenerate into any form of *-ism*. Why poetry? So that prose can exist. And conversely.

sings the common man, for he sees the epic as being incapable of revealing the transformable nature of society.

This revulsion of the hero stems from a refusal to give symbolic identification to power that is based on charisma (Hitler). It is thus a question of declaring a break with indifferentiation and a rejection of compromise so that in times of great crisis, when the oppressor seeks to *pervert* the least revolt, a dialectic of patience and explosive action can be established.

This concerns literature. For this distancing effect causes signs to lose their density; myth begins to rear its ugly head, and meaning becomes double, triple, manifold, reversible, and unforeseeable. Language oscillates like the needle on a crazy compass, and the times are ripe for prose to take over from poetry.

I think any poetry, if it pretends to be *committed* and if its success is only the opposite of the failure of prose, is deceptive and mythical. Quebec literature has definitely too many *poetizers* and not enough prosetizers. This is a symptom of its still being a tribal and ritualistic literature in which the writing moves from the sacred to the profaned, from eloquence to eloquence.

In my view, poetry, which I seem to be holding in contempt here, is something quite different from a 'literary genre' that is more difficult to grasp than the others. Poetry is all the language of advent and return, of origin and junction. However, since poetry exists only in the present, it can be written only in mixture with prose; it can be *risked* only in prose, and its task is to build up this prose, to open it up to the world. This is a banal observation, but one we are in the process of forgetting, we who once more feel tempted by literature that is *nationalistic*, which is to say parochial.

In the course of a lecture he once gave in Montreal (in 1946, I believe), Sartre remarked that the occupation in France had forced the Resistance writers into verbal economy: a single superfluous word could mean a few seconds' more work for the typesetter and thus enough time for the Gestapo to come breaking through the door of the clandestine printing press.

In such a radical situation, anything that is written must be important. The commitment is then clear, unequivocal, and total. It is rather exceptional, however, for a writer in his actual work of writing to be driven to such purity, such explicit efficiency, such a perfect coincidence of writing and action. Risking the life of one or more comrades with every line that one writes is a stylistic regimen that makes short work of any inclination to complacency, but it is as frightening as it is reassuring.

In such dire situations we gain the innocence of direct action, thanks to which we can set ourselves goals that are equal to the situation; at the same time we lift ourselves to the level of our writing. Compromises, give and take, tactical ploys and tangents, all the contradictions of the literary process and all the lies are justified and absolved *a priori*. Man is reconciled with the writer and saves him; error, which is always possible, absolutely takes the place of fault. Writing is thus *a good deed*.

Such clarity and such dirty-handed cleanliness, however, can be claimed by the writer only on the grounds of a covenant he knows cannot last. One day the war will end or the revolution will triumph and it will no longer be necessary to write, as before, under the pressure of facts and in protection of the historic moment. Once again there will be a long and tortuous distance between writing and political action. The risk connected with each word will have to be faced from within the language itself. It is not difficult to see how peace often brings an end to a certain kind of committed literature.

This is also because a radical situation has the effect of *radicalizing* those who are caught up in it. From then on there is no possible existence; one is only what history wants one to be.

To speak ill of Ezra Pound presents no difficulty. Even in his *Cantos* (XXX-LII), he manages to drag poetry into reactionary politics and politics into irresponsible poetry. Here is a writer who writes from both sides of a crevasse, sometimes choosing formalism and sometimes humanism, letting the immanence of language overlap into its transcendence, and vice versa. He knows neither shame nor guilt, nor critical vigilance. He keeps intact the famous dilemma (prose *or* poetry? politics *or* literature?), which is a source of aberrations, poisoning relations among words and thus among men. Language is double and symbolic, social and cultural; it chooses us as choose it. A responsible writer places his writing at the centre of the crevasse, suspended, above the depths of the chasm, between linguistic integration and semantic disintegration. He can only say, both loudly and softly, that social and personal misery is also made from an imagination that has each day been misled, forbidden, condemned, and tortured by the direct brutality of new forms of Fascism, by the syrupy violence of the 'Colgate smile.'

The myth of the national hero ends with a death that is ingeniously magnified into a form of super-life. With all his enemies dead or dispersed, the hero (whether he wields a gun or a pen) feels alone, unused to this strange peace, dispossessed of his holy hatred for the Other. Against whom can he enlist now? There is no one left on the appointed battle-ground. And so the hero must die – anything is better than being sentenced to *life*, than reverting to the human condition and – the ultimate disgrace – 'entering politics,' accomplishing tasks that are rather circumscribed and almost always devoid of immediate significance.

This example teaches us an invaluable lesson: the writer who becomes committed can do so only for political reasons. Any other reasons, avowed or otherwise, are suspect: nothing else, whether it be a bad literary conscience, bourgeois guilt feelings, or the desire to be done with God or daddy – nothing else can establish an order or political conduct in his writing. Too many writers become committed as if they were trying to guarantee themselves a kind of moral security; this is to consider political action as a kind of medicine for liberation and adaptation, or even as an expedient for cleansing the writing of any stain or aestheticism. What is ultimately important for them is *to be part of their age* at all costs, even if the price is to fall into step with the age, to take up political writing as if it were a contact sport, a sort of total, intoxicating risk that automatically and generously compensates for any possible literary failings.

What a long and tiresome 'piece of road' this is! With each step you grow older, and the least little curve a bit difficult to get around gives you a feeling of being left behind, remaindered.

Does a novel weigh much in comparison to a billion undernourished people? A nice big question, good for getting to the bottom of things. A 'no' answer is a decision to put away your paper and typewriter (or, more modestly, your ball-point pen) and become *committed*. Period. A 'yes' answer means going through the worst rationalizations, and no matter how much you try to delude yourself, it means facing up to the fact that you have aligned yourself with the well-fed. Faced with this dilemma, certain writers opt for a simple solution: they commit their writing. Others make a division, separating their writing from their actions. But the question remains, not so much involving the man who writes but rather the man's writings. The answer must be either yes or no. And thus it is not a question, for the way it is formulated heedlessly forces one to adopt an extreme position, as much in a political as in a literary sense. It is not a question but an ultimatum.

A billion people are dying a slow death because they have reached a point beyond even the threshold of despair. A refusal to see things manicheistically should not blind us, however; some people are guilty, belonging to the same breed as our own exploiters. As long as they keep growing fat on the established order, hunger will keep gnawing its way through country after country. And that is something that you and I cannot now be held accountable for.

Otherwise, adopting one form of radicalism after another, political action itself would be impossible, at least for the great majority of us. The man who addresses pamphlets in the party headquarters, the man who organizes the workers in the village factory, all those who have no political rank, including the woman who cleans the ashtrays of the leaders of the revolutionary party – all this shadowy army of people will find their *practical* justification only in an Other; this, in a real sense, is to exist only vicariously or by proxy. Yet people here, and elsewhere, continue to die of hunger and shame. And pamphlets can do nothing more about it than can novels.

When he is not in a situation like those previously described as cases of the extreme, the writer can only write, creating what he alone can create and what must be created: poems, novels, essays, and so on.

I firmly believe that this is necessary, that it is necessary to have this language of freedom in a world where men are not free, that it is necessary to

The same old story? Yes and no. Tomorrow doesn't begin of itself, all at once. *You young people are right to be presumptuous! Now we are old, and ready to be discarded. The world belongs to you already and you intend to dispose of it as you wish, which you are perfectly right to do. You return home from our interment with tremendous appetites, full of plans and vitality. Going to bed that evening, you feel a tiny pain to the right of your stomach – nothing to worry about, for the moment.* (Dino Buzzatti.) Writers who imagine themselves converting literature into something operational are deluding themselves, seeking shelter in something that will swallow them up. To reveal the world by shrouding it with thingified concepts, to remain without any direct contact with events, always to be ahead of or behind in the exigencies of politics: this is one of the fates of literature. There do remain, however, a few small things to say and say again: *During that period, RATHER THAN PUNISHING THE GUILTY ONES, they mistreated the girls. They even went as far as cropping their hair.* (Eluard) have this committed *gratuitousness* between men and societies, this expenditure and *luxury*. We need these things, just as poor human creatures need useless songs, songs in the evenings to fill up the space that has not been filled with food, that has never been filled by women and children. These things are necessary so that hunger will not fill all the space, so that there still remains a chance for humanity. They are necessary so that the son, who will perhaps be saved, will associate the memory of his father (who will no doubt die in the most total neglect) at least with a gleam of true tenderness, something like a possibility that has remained on the edge of the crevasse after all else has toppled over into anonymity. It is necessary that the death of the Other, including the death of a sworn enemy, possess a minimum of meaning; it has to be *someone* who dies, so that we can be reconciled through our homicidal actions. Otherwise a moment's hate makes the necessary evil and endless necessity, and he who is tortured today will tomorrow be the torturer. When the political looks to its pressing concerns and makes decisions in the heat of the moment, the literary must let our common voice be heard. And even if it says that we are not all on the same side, this is in no way a betrayal. But it is one way – perhaps the last – to be together, as human beings.

Eluard's poem *Comprendra qui voudra* should be reread. Here 'burning reason' opposes 'cold ideology,' setting into action again the old dialectic of the pleasure principle and the reality principle. Heroism is rather facile, often incidental, sometimes accidental, and always subject to scorn and manipulation (as

Writers who are ashamed to write without immediate political security would be better off to give up writing. Those who want the situation to do the work for them are dreaming dangerous dreams. As for the others, whose writing is done completely in opposition to the situation, they give no cause for concern at all: their disgrace will always be only that they do not write, do not write enough, and do not write well enough – that is, in the time and place of their choice.

Certainly, as far as I know, no one is pre-ordained to be a writer. But from the moment one has chosen to speak or write, even occasionally, his commitment is from then on centred *on language*. The responsibility has to be here, or else one falls into a church-like moralism, judging the action / writing according to the good it *causes* the faithful and the bad it *causes* the unfaithful. An entire literature, falsely represented as revolutionary, has also played the mollifying role of the heartthrob press. The toughest of the tough all outdid each other to ease the suffering of a poor hero who had to go through hell in order to reach the Good. Here we recognize the famous *crisis of conscience* of the bourgeois writer who has decided to join the proletariat. He has seen the light and converted. And he writes books about it, telling his story of self-accusation, crying out his sincere regret and his firm intentions – asking, in short, for absolution.

From all these scattered remarks, this much can be grasped: that a phenomenon like the literature of commitment can be harmful both to politics and to literature. Also, actual revolutionary literature hardly exists, in the political sense of the word *revolutionary*, which as far as I am concerned is the only sense that is not deceptive. Literature is pre-revolutionary and post-revolutionary. For the historical moment of revolution is a point in time; it cannot bear the in-betweens of existential freedom, it demands the unconditional, and it causes poetry and philosophy to be defeated (or, at best, to be put in brackets). Revolution, until now, has only used eloquence – yes indeed! – that is, a pedagogical programme of action and one that dangerously consents to the myth of idologism. Such language is initiatory and alienating, and therefore, from a literary point of view, it must be transitory.

shown by the people we have statues of). Both poetry and history contest each other; because poetry is not only historical, because it is the reverse side of history, poetry proclaims (or murmurs) that life dreams as much as it is awake, that it is as much a question of having the courage to *go on* with one's daily life as it is of performing brilliant exploits – – as much the quiet, calm melody of the morning as the superb blue darkening of the nights when, as if by magic, the sacred fear delivers us from the sordid fears. To write without wages – intransitively.

Appendix

SOURCES AND ORIGINAL TITLES OF TRANSLATED MATERIALS

ETHIER-BLAIS, JEAN 'Our Pioneers in Criticism,' 'Les pionniers de la critique,' *Signets* Vol III. Montreal: Le Cercle du Livre de France 1973, pp 97-117

HAYNE, DAVID M. 'The Major Options of French-Canadian Literature,' 'Les grandes options de la littérature canadienne-française' (1964), *Conférences J.A. de Sève*. Montreal: Les Presses de l'Université de Montreal 1969, pp 27-52

AQUIN, HUBERT 'The Cultural Fatigue of French Canada,' 'La fatigue culturelle du Canada français,' *Liberté* 23 (1962) 299-325; copyright Les Editions Quinze

LALONDE, MICHÈLE 'The Mitre and the Tuque,' 'Entre le goupillon et la tuque,' *Maintenant*, Nos. 137-8 (1974) 62-64; copyright Editions Seghers/ Laffont, Paris 1979

FALARDEAU, JEAN-CHARLES 'The Evolution of the Hero in the Quebec Novel,' 'L'évolution du héros dans le roman québécois' (1968), *Conférences J.A. de Sève*. Montreal: Les Presses de l'Université de Montréal 1969, pp 237-66

MARCOTTE, GILLES 'The Poetry of Exile,' 'Une poésie d'exil' (1958), *Une littérature qui se fait*. Montreal: HMH 1962, pp 65-70

CHAMBERLAND, PAUL 'Founding the Territory,' 'La fondation du territoire,' *Parti pris* 4, Nos. 9-12 (1967) 11-42

BESSETTE, GÉRARD 'Psychoanalytic Criticism,' 'La psychocritique,' *Voix et images* 1, No. 1 (1975) 72-9

210 Appendix

FRANCŒUR, LOUIS 'Quebec Theatre: Stimulation or Communication?',
'Le théâtre québécois: stimulation ou communication?' (1974), *Voix et
images* 1, No. 2 (1975) 220–40
BRAULT, JACQUES 'Notes on a False Dilemma,' 'Notes sur un faux dilemme'
(1964), *Chemin faisant*. Montreal: Editions La Presse 1976, pp 61–72

Bibliography

The following are considered useful sources for those interested in learning more about Quebec criticism.

BIBLIOGRAPHIES

COTNAM, JACQUES Contemporary Quebec: an analytical bibliography
    Toronto: McClelland and Stewart 1973
STRATFORD, PHILIP Bibliography of Canadian Books in Translation: French to English
    and English to French 2nd ed. Ottawa: HRCC/CCRH 1977
WYCZYNSKI, PAUL 'Histoire et critique littéraire au Canada français' Littérature
    et société canadiennes-françaises Quebec: Les Presses de l'Université Laval 1964

LITERARY HISTORIES

GRANDPRÉ, PIERRE DE Histoire de la littérature française du Québec 4 vols. Montreal:
    Beauchemin 1967
MAILHOT, LAURENT La littérature québécoise Paris: Presses Universitaires de
    France 1974
TOUGAS, GÉRARD Histoire de la littérature canadienne-française. Paris: Presses
    Universitaires de France 1960
WYCZYNSKI, PAUL, ed. Archives des lettres canadiennes 5 vols. Mouvement littéraire
    de Québec 1860 Vol. 1. Ottawa: Editions Université d'Ottawa 1961
– L'école littéraire de Montréal Vol. 2. Montreal: Fides 1963
– Le roman canadien-français Vol. 3. Montreal: Fides 1964
– La poésie canadienne-française Vol. 4 Montreal: Fides 1969
– Le théâtre québécois Vol. 5. Montreal: Fides 1977

CRITICAL ANTHOLOGIES

Conférences J.A. de Sève 1–10: Littérature canadienne-française Montreal: Les Presses de l'Université de Montreal 1969
MARCOTTE, GILLES *Présence de la critique; critique et littérature contemporaine au Canada français* Montreal: HMH 1966

INDIVIDUAL VOLUMES OF CRITICISM

BRAULT, JACQUES *Chemin faisant: essais* Montreal: Editions La Presse 1975
BROCHU, ANDRÉ *L'instance critique 1961–1973* Montreal: Leméac 1974
ETHIER-BLAIS, JEAN *Signets* 3 vols. Montreal: Le Cercle du livre de France 1967–73
FALARDEAU, JEAN-CHARLES *Notre société et son roman* Montreal: HMH 1967
MARCOTTE, GILLES *Une littérature qui se fait, essais critiques sur la littérature canadienne-française* Montreal: Editions HMH 1962
– *Le temps des poètes: description critique de la poésie actuelle au Canada français* Montreal: HMH 1969
– *Le roman à l'imparfait: essais sur le roman québecois d'aujourd'hui* Montreal: La Presse 1976
ROBIDOUX, RÉJEAN, and A. RENAUD *Le roman canadien-français du vingtième siècle* Ottawa: Editions de l'Université d'Ottawa 1966
WARWICK, JACK *The Long Journey: Literary Themes of French Canada.* Toronto: University of Toronto Press 1968

BACKGROUND

Dictionnaire des oeuvres littéraires du Québec: des origines à 1900 Montreal: Fides 1978
Dictionnaire pratique des auteurs québécois Montreal: Fides 1976
STORY, NORAH *The Oxford Companion to Canadian History and Literature* Toronto: Oxford University Press 1967

COMPARATIVE CANADIAN CRITICISM

HAYNE, DAVID M., and ANTOINE SIROIS 'Preliminary Bibliography of Comparative Canadian Literature (English-Canadian and French-Canadian).' *Canadian Review of Comparative Literature* 3, No. 2 (1976) 124–36; 'First Supplement, 1975-6' 4, No. 2 (1977) 205–9; 'Second Supplement, 1976-7' 5, No. 1 (1978) 114–9

MOISAN, CLÉMENT *L'âge de la littérature canadienne: essai.* Montreal: HMH 1969
SUTHERLAND, RONALD *Second Image: comparative studies in Quebec/Canadian literature* Toronto: New Press 1971
- *The New Hero: essays in comparative Quebec/Canadian Literature* Toronto: Macmillan 1977

Index